WORLD FILM LOCATIONS SINGAPORE

Edited by Lorenzo Codelli

First Published in the UK in 2014 by Intellect Books, The Mill, Parnall Road, Fishponds, Bristol, BS16 3JG, UK

First Published in the USA in 2014 by Intellect Books, The University of Chicago Press, 1427 E. 60th Street, Chicago, IL 60637, USA

Cover photo by han: *Ilo Ilo* (2013) ©Fisheye Pictures

Copy Editor: Emma Rhys

A Catalogue record for this book is available from the British Library

World Film Locations Series
ISSN: 2045-9009
eISSN: 2045-9017

World Film Locations Singapore
ISBN: 9-781-78320-361-1
ePDF ISBN: 978-1-78320-346-8

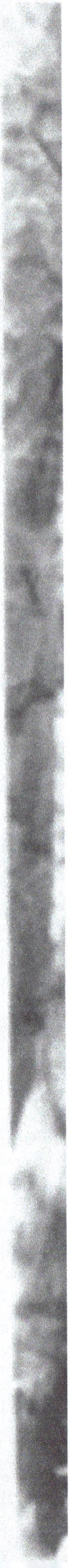

WORLD FILM LOCATIONS SINGAPORE

EDITOR
Lorenzo Codelli

SERIES EDITOR & DESIGN
Gabriel Solomons

CONTRIBUTORS
Philip Cheah
Adrien Gombeaud
Wahyuni A. Hadi
Daniel Hui
Low Zu Boon
Carlo Montanaro
Hubert Niogret
Warren Sin
Ben Slater
Stephen Teo
Toh Hun Ping
Jan Uhde
Yvonne Ng Uhde
Silvia Wong

LOCATION PHOTOGRAPHY
Toh Hun Ping
(unless otherwise credited)

LOCATION MAPS
Greg Orrom Swan

PUBLISHED BY
Intellect
The Mill, Parnall Road,
Fishponds, Bristol, BS16 3JG, UK
T: +44 (0) 117 9589910
F: +44 (0) 117 9589911
E: *info@intellectbooks.com*

Bookends: chensiyuan (wikimedia commons)
This page: *Saint Jack* (Kobal)
Overleaf: *Forever Fever* aka
That's the Way I Like It (Kobal)

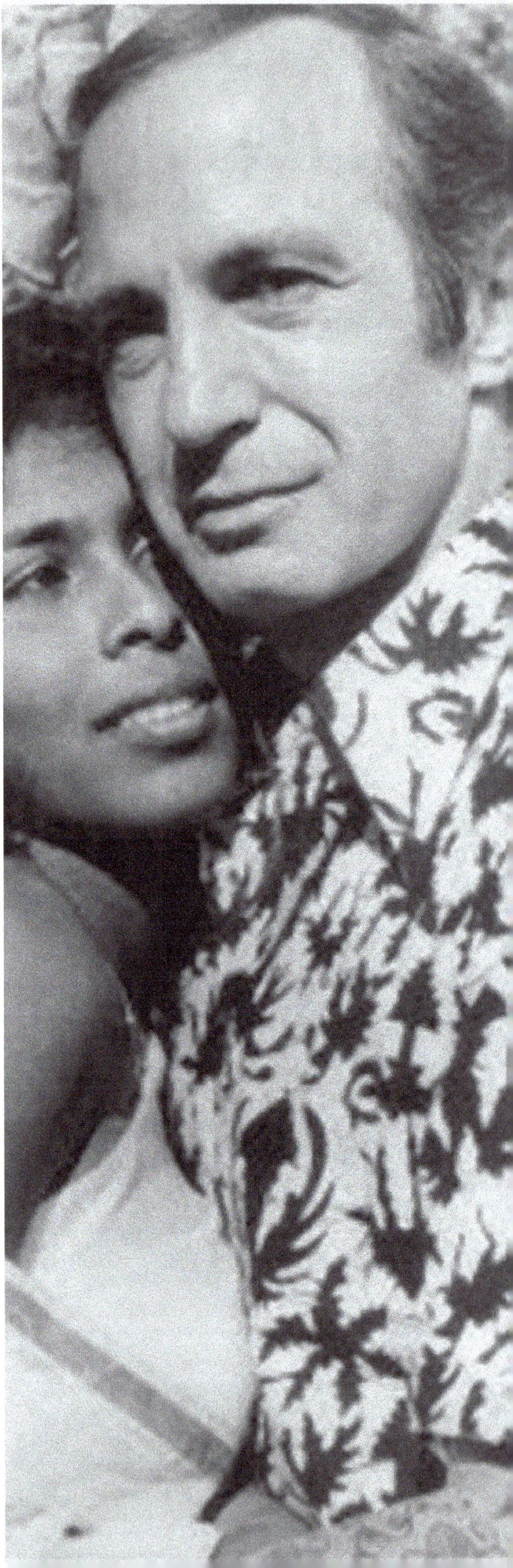

CONTENTS

Maps/Scenes

10 **Scenes 1-7**
1910 - 1958

28 **Scenes 8-14**
1961 - 1966

46 **Scenes 15-21**
1967 - 1990

64 **Scenes 22-28**
1995 - 2002

82 **Scenes 29-35**
2004 - 2009

100 **Scenes 36-42**
2009 - 2013

Essays

6 **Singapore: City of the Imagination**
Toh Hun Ping

8 **Malay Screen in a Predominantly Chinese Singapore**
Jan Uhde and Yvonne Ng Uhde

26 **The Outsider's Singapore: A Brief History of 'Western' Film-makers' Expeditions in Singapore**
Ben Slater

44 **A History of Saying No: Singapore International Film Festival and Censorship**
Daniel Hui

62 **Eric Khoo**
Silvia Wong

80 **The Cultural Materialism of Singapore in Jack Neo's Cinema**
Stephen Teo

98 **A View of Public Housing in Singapore Cinema**
Warren Sin

Backpages

116 *Go Further*
118 *Contributor Bios*
122 *Filmography*

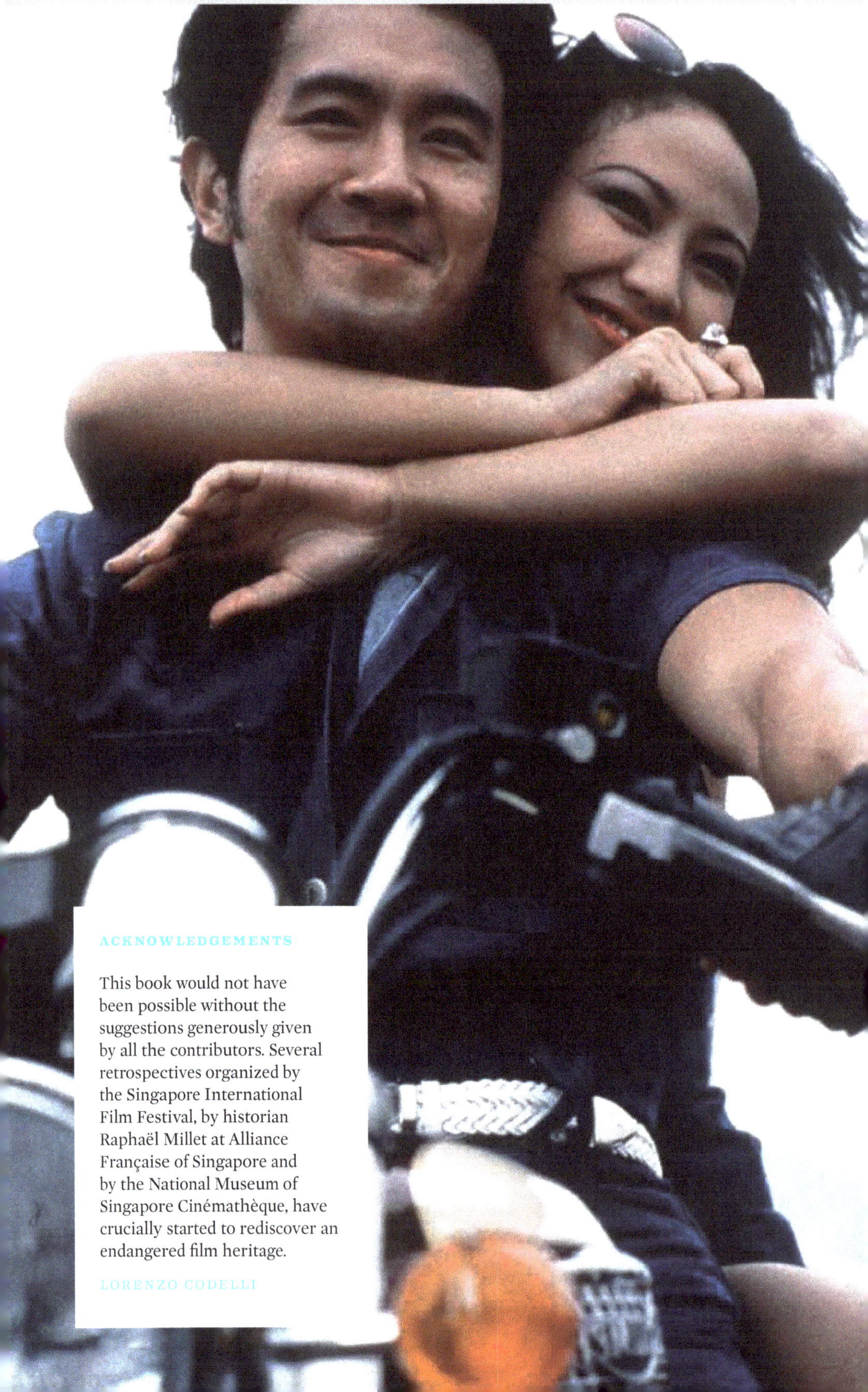

ACKNOWLEDGEMENTS

This book would not have been possible without the suggestions generously given by all the contributors. Several retrospectives organized by the Singapore International Film Festival, by historian Raphaël Millet at Alliance Française of Singapore and by the National Museum of Singapore Cinémathèque, have crucially started to rediscover an endangered film heritage.

LORENZO CODELLI

INTRODUCTION

World Film Locations *Singapore*

WHILE JOYFULLY PREPARING for celebrations of her 50th anniversary of independence in 2015, fast and furious Singapore never stops changing both her external looks as well as her heartbeat 24/7. Myriad of her ancient streams of consciousness, of her obsolete 'kampong' villages, of her multicultural yearnings, of her lost traditions, are luckily recorded by the 35mm, 16mm and video cameras of Malay, Chinese, Indian and international film-makers.

Still it is hard to enjoy those images in proper conditions and on a big screen due to a lack of preservation and restoration. These reels currently dispersed all over the world represent priceless time capsules, and frequently works of art too. Let me call them 'Ministructures', handcrafted by pioneers aiming to tell entertaining stories to the crowds and not to record anything historical – as compared to National Geographic's TV series *Megastructures* that enshrined the breathtaking mushrooming of *Singapore's Vegas* (2012) or *Gardens by the Bay* (2013). This series' time-lapse technique seems the only one able to express today's geophysical metamorphosis.

On an opposite front, contemporary auteurs Eric Khoo, Glen Goei, Royston Tan, Kelvin Tong, Ho Tzu Nyen, Wee Li Lin, and their colleagues, prefer to express themselves on a much less frantic pace, through *soul-lapse* approaches catching the slightest, deepest nuances of their city-state. These Zeitgeist snatchers seem quite conscious of descending from an illustrious line of movie-dwellers who had built a booming empire all over the former British colony: Run Run Shaw, Loke Wan Tho, wonder boy P. Ramlee, Lakshamanan Krishnan, to name just a few. Except for comedian Jack Neo's broad farces, the home-brewed productions are mostly snubbed by local audiences, whose top amusement by far remains multiplex-going. Singapore film-makers patiently persist to 'do their job', shooting in real streets and buildings, and rather rarely using studio facilities. 'All of those places I shot in, are gone!' exclaims Eric Khoo.

Both the in-depth researches by the writers contributing to this book, and the low-budget experiments by the Singapore film-makers, capture vanishing slices of life inside an 'Invisible City'. In *To Singapore, with Love* (2014) Tan Pin Pin pierces the souls of old political exiles contemplating their homeland from Johor Bahru, the Malaysian end of the Causeway. Their moving illusions are permeating *in absentia* the ever-developing island.

Each one of the hundreds and hundreds of graduates from top film and art schools is finishing a short, many hoping one day to shoot a hit feature, Hollywood or bust-lah! Endless mazes of Singapore's heroic and sometimes controversial past are waiting to be explored by them. Every building, every neighbourhood, every hawker centre, every temple, every void deck, every bar, hides legends or myths. Look for instance how scrupulously Anthony Chen in his multi award-winning *Ilo Ilo* (2013) has chiselled 1997's HDB (Housing and Development Board) flats and roofs, public schools, airport alleys. His extraordinary fresco of Singapore's spirit of resistance and fraternity might inspire a whole new wave of talents.

For over a century a phenomenal army of 'invaders' has fortified the national conscience. Gaston Méliès, Yasujiro Ozu, Gualtiero Jacopetti, Peter Bogdanovich, Roger Corman, Bruce Beresford, Shohei Imamura, Johnnie To, Rakesh Roshan, George Lucas, and several other less acclaimed film-makers, have offered their own capricious visions. A paradise lost, as chronicled by doctor Ivan Polunin's innocent lens, or a futuristic spaceship as fantasized by 'Lucky Star' Zhang Ziyi? ⁜

Lorenzo Codelli, Editor

SINGAPORE

City of the Imagination

Text by
TOH HUN PING

IN JANUARY 2014, the new 'Sandcrawler' building, regional headquarters of Lucasfilm, was unleashed to much fanfare in Fusionopolis (a 'business park' on the outskirts west of downtown Singapore). Expectations are high. This world-class production complex is anticipated to 'tap Asian talent to support future Star Wars movies' and assist in manufacturing other special-effects-heavy, big-name international blockbusters.

Imagining Singapore for the movies started over 88 years ago. In July 1926, a humble film production studio, the first ever in Singapore, was established by an entrepreneur from Muar. Named after himself, the Low Pui-kim Nanyang Independent Film Production Company was located in a bungalow at 58 Meyer Road in Katong, a suburban district in the east, and was to produce Chinese films with a 'Nanyang' (literally 'South Seas'; broadly refers to South East Asia) flavour using homegrown talents. It made a silent feature *The New Immigrant* (Guo Chao-wen, 1927) which told the story of a fresh Chinese immigrant's experiences in Singapore. The studio subsequently moved to 333 Pasir Panjang Road, on the western outskirts, and did not manage to complete a planned second feature.

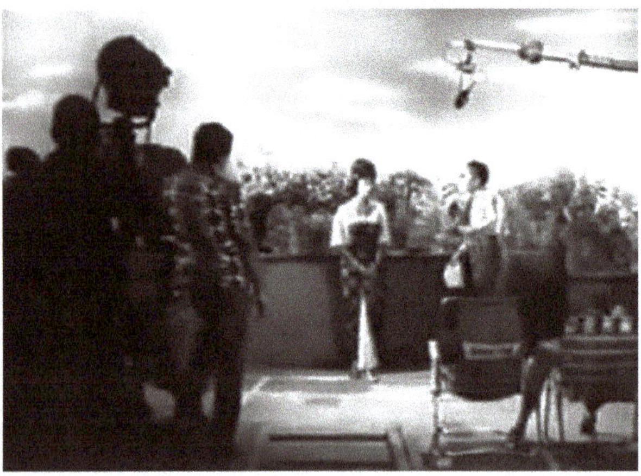

In May 1933, Motilal Chamria, a film producer from Calcutta, set up Indo-Malay Talkies Co. along the same road where Low Pui-kim left off, at Lions' Gate, Pasir Panjang Road. With B.S. Rajhans – an Indian film director who would make a greater impact in Singapore's post-World War II film industry – at the helm, the studio by the seafront aimed to produce films with 'a local atmosphere and featuring Malay artistes'. Eventually, the only film Motilal Chamria produced was 1934's *Leila Majnun*, a Malay talkie adaptation of 'a world famous Arabian love tragedy' (*The Straits Times*, 27 March 1934, p.6).

The Shaw Brothers Ltd – a well-established film distributor/cinema operator in Malaya run by brothers Runme and Run Run – also began producing films locally in 1940. They imported Chinese directors and second-hand equipment from Hong Kong, while recruiting local Malay (*bangsawan*) artistes to act for a handful of Malay films with titles such as *Mutiara/Pearl*, *Bermadu/Polygamy* and *Toping Saitan/Devil's Mask* (all directed by Hou Yao and Wan Hoi-ling, 1940-41). To facilitate the expansion of their film business, the Shaws converted a warehouse into a studio at 8 Jalan Ampas, in a suburb not too far from town. There were ambitious proposals to produce Malay and Cantonese talkies and establish a newsreel service. However, the Japanese occupation (1942–45) put paid to their plans.

After the Japanese surrendered, there was a flurry of interest in making movies about the war experience. A group of Chinese artistes active in local performance troupes joined Zhonghua Film Production Studio, which had its studio in a mansion along Geylang Lorong 24, in the heart of what is today a famous red-light district. The studio produced a trilogy of films about the tribulations of overseas Chinese during the

Opposite *The Young Ones* (1965) / Below *The Nitwit Movie Stars* (1961)

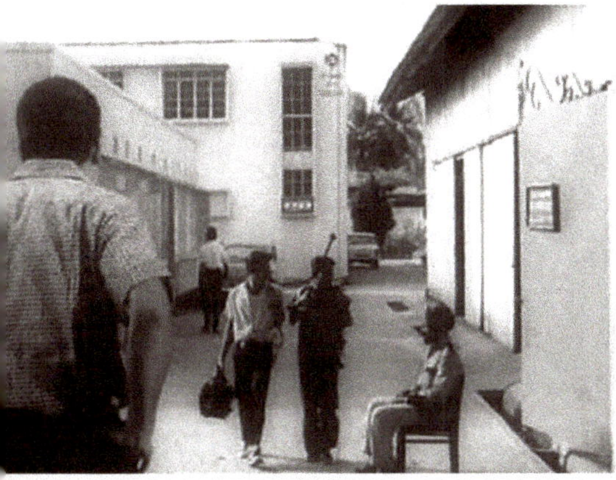

Above © 1961 Malay Film Productions Ltd.
Opposite © 1965 Cathay-Keris Films

Japanese occupation.

The Shaw Brothers joined in the fray by reopening its Jalan Ampas studio to produce its trilogy of post-war Chinese films. They also revived their Malay film venture by employing seasoned director B.S. Rajhans to oversee production, and beefed up studio facilities with American imports. They founded Malay Film Productions Ltd (MFP) to churn out huge outputs of popular Malay films to feed their expanding film exhibition circuit. At its peak in the 1950s, MFP was producing more than ten films a year. The Jalan Ampas studio was even prominently featured in several MFP films, e.g. as a factory with picketing workers in *Mogok/Strike* (K.M. Basker, 1957) and as itself, a 'dream factory', in *Seniman Bujang Lapok/The Nitwit Movie Stars* (P. Ramlee, 1961). By then, Shaw Brothers had acquired the studio's neighbouring land plots to build new soundstages, rebuilt the old studio complex and housed their employees in quarters at nearby Boon Teck Road. (The abandoned buildings at 8 Jalan Ampas are still standing today.)

Competition to MFP's monopoly on local Malay film production came from two studios established in the 1950s – Nusantara and Cathay-Keris. Nusantara Film Productions Ltd ('Nusantara' refers to the Malay Archipelago) was founded in 1950 by Penang cinema entrepreneur Ong Keng Huat, and was managed by Hsu Chiao Meng, a photographer/cinematographer active in the local Chinese cultural scene. Nusantara's first studio was located in the South Winds Hotel at Tanjung Balai (a remote location in the western part of Singapore; now the Jurong Fishery Port). Then, it moved to a factory at Bukit Timah Road 8th milestone (219J De Souza Avenue). The studio was noted for being the first to use Malay directors like Naz Achnaz and A.R. Tompel, in contrast to MFP which had employed non-Malay directors from overseas. Nusantara finally folded in 1954 due to a lack of access to local exhibition venues and after Indonesia imposed restrictions on Malay films made in Malaya/Singapore. The premises at Bukit Timah evolved into an independent film factory named Nanfang (literally 'Southern') Film Studio, and was used in the shooting of a number of Hokkien dialect and Mandarin films up to the 1960s.

In July 1926, a humble film production studio, the first ever in Singapore, was established by an entrepreneur from Muar.

Cathay-Keris had its roots in Rimau Film Productions, founded in 1951 by Ho Ah Loke. Ho built a film studio, essentially two makeshift tin sheds, at Tampines Road 9th milestone in the far north-eastern reaches of Singapore. After two unprofitable films, the irrepressible Ho renamed his company Keris Film Productions and persisted with making movies that were characteristically Malay/Malayan, often adapting from local folklore and novels. Later, Ho collaborated with Cathay Organisation's head Loke Wan Tho to form Cathay-Keris Films in 1953, with a new studio at 532D East Coast Road, including two new soundstages and existing buildings that were former barracks used by the Japanese. In *Muda Mudi/The Young Ones* (M. Amin, 1965), a story about an aging and out-of-favour actress, one would be able to see depictions of studio life in Cathay-Keris.

Adopting a similar strategy as the Shaw Brothers – vertical integration of production, distribution and exhibition within a single organization, Cathay-Keris would release a total of 125 feature films (mostly Malay) in its twenty years of existence (1953–73). Add to that MFP's output of more than 150 Malay films (1947–67), the total *oeuvre* by the two major studios was considered astounding, in an era now often lauded as the 'Golden Age of Malay cinema'. A mix of political factors, labour issues and competition from television led to financial losses and the ultimate decision to close the studios for good by 1972, thus marking the end of a boom period for local movie production and the start of a lull until the next 'revivals' in the 1990s and beyond.

SPOTLIGHT

MALAY SCREEN IN A PREDOMINANTLY CHINESE SINGAPORE

Text by JAN UHDE AND YVONNE NG UHDE

ONE OF SINGAPORE'S conspicuous characteristics is its multi-ethnic and multicultural character. In 2013, the city-state was home to 74.2% Chinese, 13.3% Malays, 9.1% Indians and 3.3% Eurasians and other ethnic groups. Reflecting the island's history, it is the Malays and the Malay language who enjoy indigenous status in Singapore while the Chinese have grown to become the city's most numerous and politically influential ethnic group, with the exception of the years between 1963 and 1965 when Singapore was a part of Malaysia.

Singapore feature film production, born in 1926, saw a remarkable creative surge in the 1950s and 1960s. In 1965, Singapore left Malaysia and became an independent republic. It also marked the beginning of the decline of the film industry there. In its heyday (roughly between 1950 and 1965), some 250 features were made, averaging sixteen annually. A number of accomplished film artists such as B.S. Rajhans, P. Ramlee, Hussain Haniff and Maria Menado, left a significant cinematic heritage – the 'Golden Age' of Singapore (Malay) cinema. In comparison, only a handful of Chinese-language films were made in Singapore during this time.

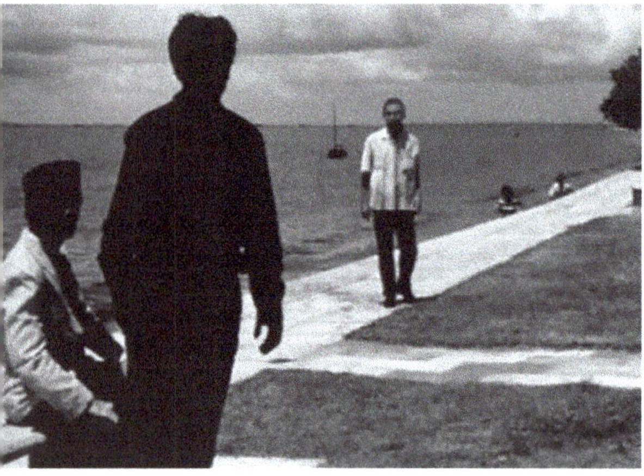

The film-making activities in this fecund period involved all major ethnic groups of the city. The Chinese, led by two major corporations, Shaw Brothers (Malay Film Productions) and Cathay Organisation (Cathay-Keris), acted as producers and distributors. A number of trained film professionals – directors, cameramen and film editors – came from India bringing with them their technical know-how and experience, as well as dramatic and moviemaking traditions and styles. The Malays, frequently employed as actors, were the most visible element in these movies. Probably the most popular among them was P. Ramlee, an extraordinarily gifted composer, singer, performer and director. Most of the Malay feature productions between 1950 and 1965 exploited popular genres such as contemporary dramas and melodramas, accenting family, romantic and social issues; comedies usually in present-day settings; historical or costume dramas exploring local and regional Malay history; and horror films, centring on the local *pontianak* and 'oily man' folklore.

A noticeable characteristic of the Singapore-Malay movies were songs, integrated with the action or separated from it. Such scenes were mostly lyrical, lending the films a poetic flavour. This stylistic feature, familiar in Bollywood movies, was introduced by the Indian professionals involved in the Malay film production. This import fell on fertile soil in the Malay performance

Opposite *Victim of Slander* (1959) / **Below** *Three Wives* (1964)

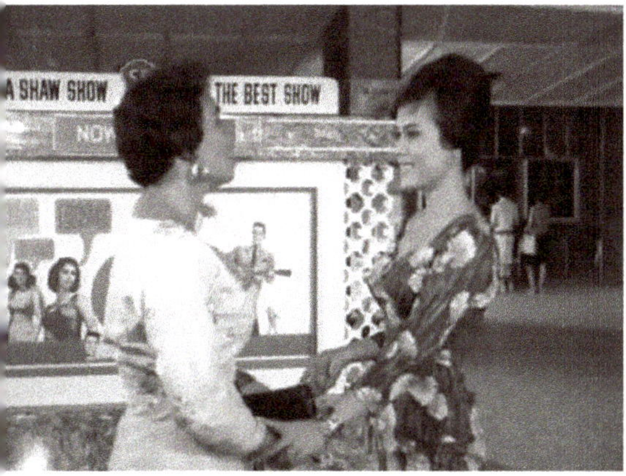

culture where it easily blended with the tradition of *bangsawan* (Malay opera).

Despite the involvement of Singapore's entire ethnic spectrum in the city's feature production, the great majority of these films focused exclusively on the Malay culture, which could also be appreciated by the Malays in the region. These movies put forward Malay life, values and identity. Other ethnic groups were filtered away, which is most apparent in films set in contemporary Singapore. Watching almost any Singapore-set Malay movie of the 1950s and 1960s period, an audience unfamiliar with the city's actual ethnic composition and visual appearance, would hardly believe that more than three quarters of Singapore's population were not Malays. Here are a few examples illustrating the screen image of Singapore as a Malay city:

In his popular *Penarik Beca/Trishaw Puller* (1955), director P. Ramlee moved away from the Indian model that characterized the Malay movies until then. He turned to a contemporary, socially conscious subject and rendered it in a realistic style. The film's melodramatic plot centres on a poor trishaw puller (P. Ramlee) and a girl from a rich family (Saadiah). The girl's father is against her marriage to a poor man but an incident involving a callous criminal opens the father's eyes. As in a number of the Malay Film Productions movies, *Trishaw Puller*'s introductory shots feature the iconic clock tower between what was then the Victoria Theatre and Victoria Memorial Hall, followed by shots of busy boulevards and streets and a Cold Storage grocery outlet. They confirm Singapore as the film's location. In the following scenes however, virtually every character, even minor ones, including the police, hospital and restaurant staff and guests, is Malay. The Chinese and Indian segments of the population are practically invisible.

Today, Singapore is a much more cosmopolitan city, and its film-makers are more sensitive to the ethnic balance on the movie screen.

Korban Fitnah/Victim of Slander (1959), directed by P.L. Kapur (pseudonym of the acclaimed Indonesian director Usmar Ismail), produced by and starring Maria Menado, includes a number of visual Singapore references: the protagonist's transfer from the Outram Prison to the District Court, the Wyman's Haven restaurant, the C.K. Tang store and the Tanjong Pagar Railway Station. On the whole, however, the viewer sees mostly the city's Malay visage, as only a handful of non-Malay characters appear in the role of extras: a turban-wearing young man among the merry group of cyclists, two Caucasian females and a couple of Chinese guests being entertained by the singers in Wyman's Haven, a Hokkien-speaking servant Ah Peck and the Caucasian ophthalmologist are among the few who represent the other side of Singapore.

Madu Tiga/Three Wives (1964), directed by the versatile P. Ramlee, was awarded Best Comedy Film at the Asian Film Festival in Taipei, 1964. Its 1960s Singapore setting is anchored through a number of easily recognizable locations throughout the film, including the Shaw House/Lido complex built in 1958–59, the Fitzpatrick's supermarket, Hotel Ambassador and several tracking shots along busy streets. The film's plot, however, which focuses on the Malay community, reduces the visual presence of other ethnic groups to a couple of salespersons in a Chinese goldsmith shop and a secretary in the workplace of the main character. The film's impression of multi-ethnic Singapore is again that of a Malay city.

In an interesting reversal, post-2000 Singapore projects onto the movie screen an opposite image. Malay feature production in the city is sadly negligible at present. Most of the local feature production is now focused on the Chinese majority of the city, reflecting its political and economic influence in the city-state. The disparity in ethnic representation on-screen, however, is less radical than it was half a century ago. Today, Singapore is a much more cosmopolitan city, and its film-makers are more sensitive to the ethnic balance on the movie screen. ✣

N

LOCATIONS MAP

SINGAPORE

maps are only to be taken as approximates

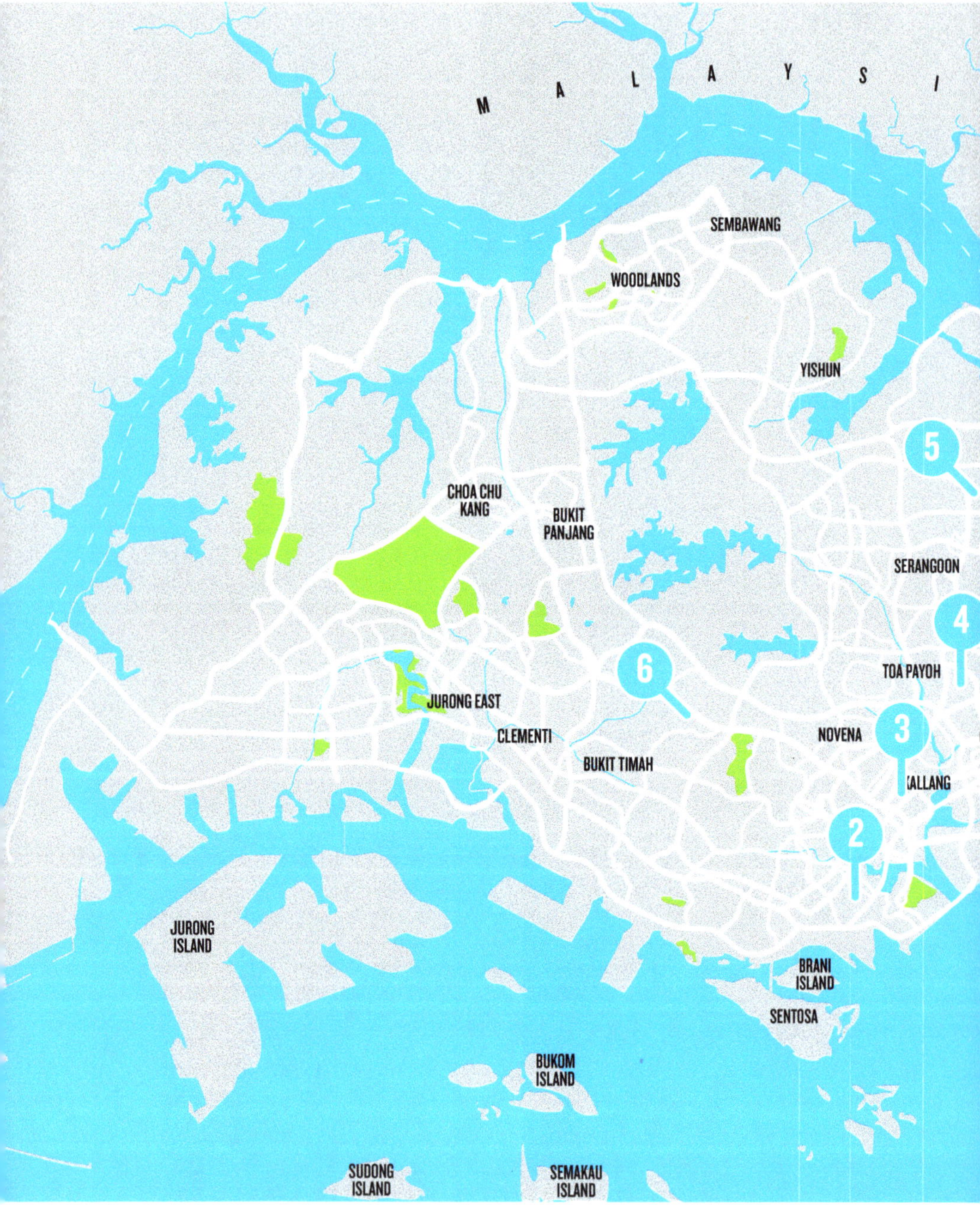

SINGAPORE LOCATIONS
SCENES 1-7

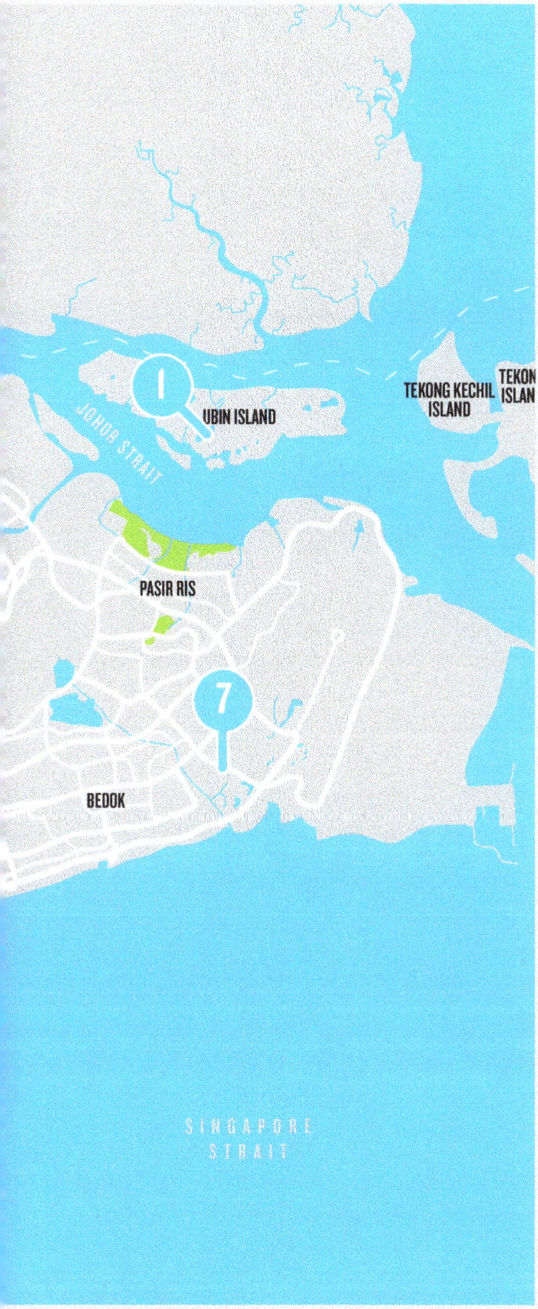

1.
COCONUT PLANTATION/
À TRAVERS UNE PLANTATION DE COCOTIERS À SINGAPOUR (1910)
Unidentified palm grove [photo taken at Pulau Ubin's coconut plantation]
page 12

2.
MALAYA WAR RECORD: A RECORD OF THE MARCH ONWARD/
MARE SENKI: SHINGEKI NO KIROKU (1942)
City centre – Anson Road and Padang
page 14

3.
SINGAPORE (1947)
Rochor Canal
page 16

4.
BROKEN HEART/PATAH HATI (1952)
Former Alkaff Gardens, off Upper Serangoon Road (now Cedar Girls' Secondary School)
page 18

5.
THE MOULDY BACHELORS/
BUJANG LAPOK (1957)
'The Kampong' [photo taken at Kampong Lorong Buangkok]
page 20

6.
MOON OVER MALAYA (1957)
Hwa Chong Institution (formerly The Chinese High School), 661 Bukit Timah Road
page 22

7.
CURSE OF PONTIANAK/
SUMPAH PONTIANAK (1958)
Former kampongs on the east coast (now golf courses, condominiums and 'business parks')
page 24

COCONUT PLANTATION/À TRAVERS UNE PLANTATION DE COCOTIERS À SINGAPOUR (1910)

LOCATION

Unidentified palm grove [photo taken at Pulau Ubin's coconut plantation]

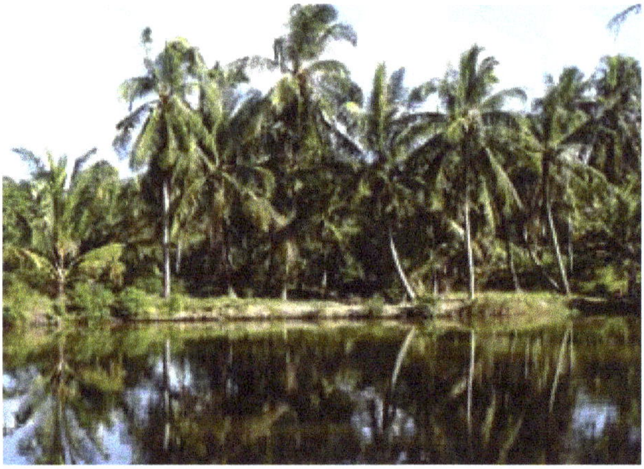

PATHÉ WAS ONE OF the forerunners of colour cinema. The *pochoir* technique was developed in 1906, transformed into Pathécolor, and exploited until the early 1930s. Pathé travel and exotic films had without any doubt a very significant impact on the diffusion of cinema. The precise description of the handling of coconuts in *Coconut Plantation/ À travers une plantation de cocotiers à Singapour* is countered by the spectacular depiction of large palm groves using a smooth cameracar. Five intertitles divide the reel. 'CLIMBING THE TREES TO OBTAIN THE SAP OF COCOANUT.': a brief panning shot over a coconut grove. A man climbs on top of a tree and begins to cut the fruits and throw them down. On the ground a wagon is pulled by an ox. Other natives are carrying coconuts. The first climber descends from the tree. 'PLACED IN JARS AND LOADED IN WAGONS.': bringing coconuts on their head and shoulders the natives put them on the wagons. Wagons are beginning to move. 'CATERING THE COCOANUTS.': another man climbs up the palm tree. From the top the fruits are cut and made to fall to the ground where natives are collecting them. 'REMOVING THE HUSKS WHICH ARE USED BY THE NATIVES FOR MANY PURPOSES AMONG OTHERS FOR MAKING TOOTH BRUSHES.': a man standing takes a knife from the ground covered with coconuts, he cleans it up then opens it – looking straight into the camera – and offers it to another man who begins to drink from it. At his side a child is waiting. A close-up of the man cleaning up his teeth with pieces of the coconut bark. 'THE ROAD HOME.': a square with some houses among the palm groves. A man protecting himself from the sun with an umbrella. Other natives move towards the camera, some of them carried by rickshaws. From 1910 till 1915, Pathé produced five short reels in Singapore and Malaysia. ➾ ***Carlo Montanaro***

Directed by Unidentified Pathé cameraman

Scene description: The gathering of coconuts in a palm grove

Timecode for scene: 0:00:15 – 0:03:01

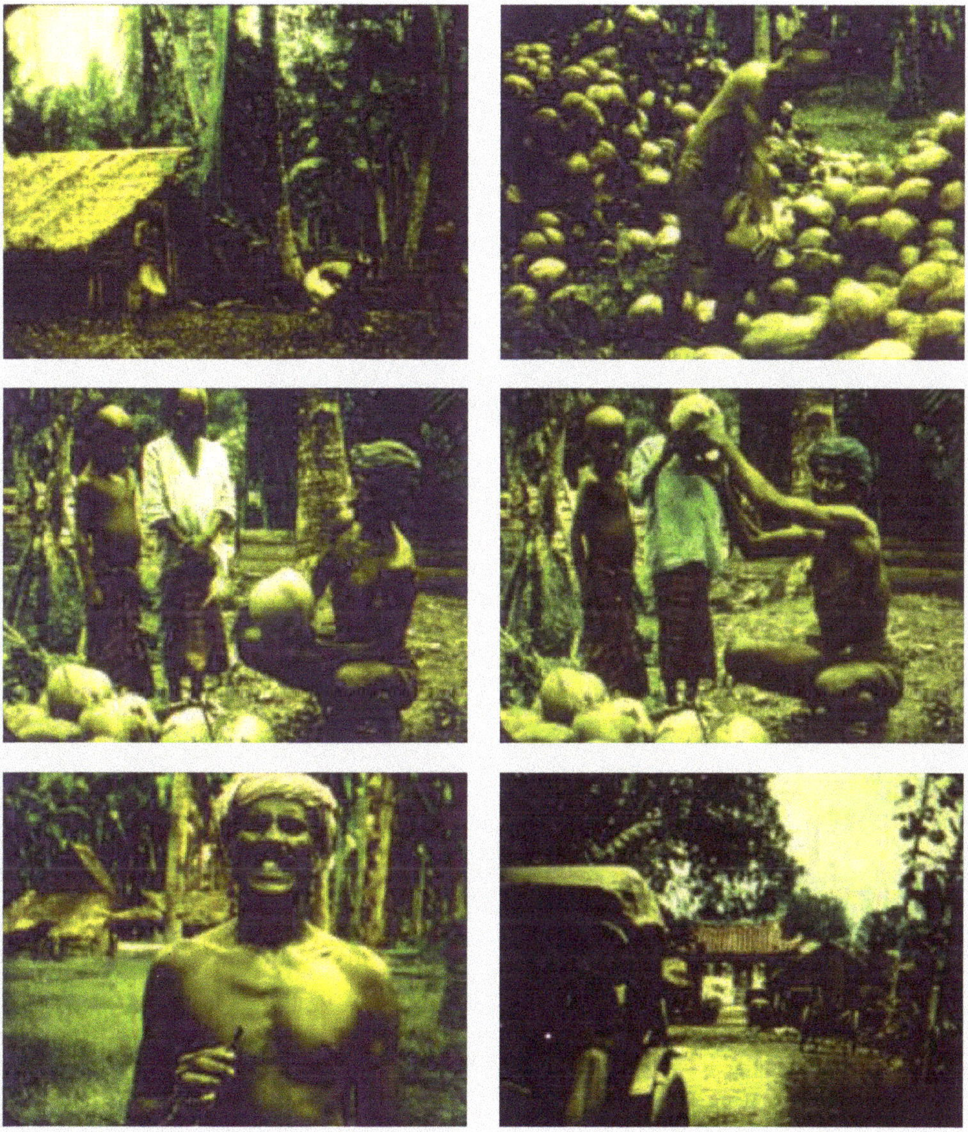

Images © 1910 / Archivio Carlo Montanaro, Venice

MALAYA WAR RECORD: A RECORD OF THE MARCH ONWARD/MARE SENKI: SHINGEKI NO KIROKU (1942)

LOCATION *City centre – Anson Road and Padang*

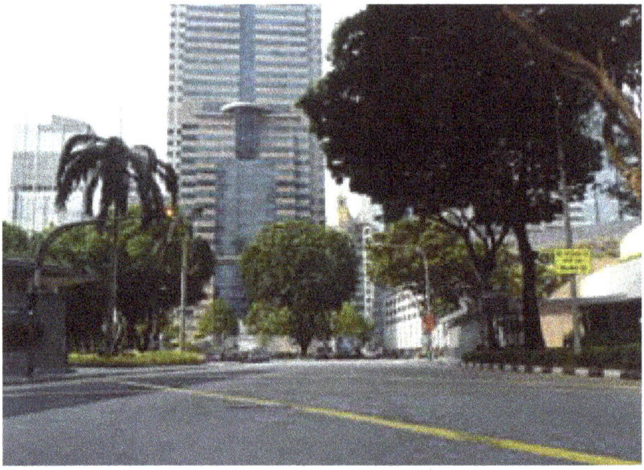

ASSEMBLED FROM JAPANESE war news footage and confiscated British newsreels, *Malaya War Record: A Record of the March Onward* was a feature-length combat documentary that recorded Japanese military operations against the British in the Malayan Peninsula and Singapore from December 1941 through to the surrender of Singapore on 15 February 1942. Told from the perspective of the victors, this was to be a propagandistic filmic document created for the consumption of the Japanese home population. One of the most striking segments of the film was the portrayal of events immediately after the surrender, that which spoke of the psyche of General Yamashita's army after the conquest of Singapore. A day after the surrender, the Japanese army organized a procession of tanks into the Singapore city centre. The documentary depicted tank soldiers in dignified poses, bearing the urns containing the ashes of their dead comrades. It was not a portrayal of a triumphal parade, but a sombre commemoration for the dead as the tanks executed a symbolic takeover of the city centre, which had a concentration of architectural icons and monuments built during the reign of the former masters. The Japanese flag was shown mounted on one such icon – the Cathay Building – where, incidentally, Yasujiro Ozu was drafted to work in Singapore from June 1943. He had proposed a shot of the Union Jack flag atop the same building (to depict the era of British colonization) for the film *On tsu Delhi/On to Delhi*. Some footage was shot for this film but was reportedly destroyed before the eventual Japanese surrender in August 1945.
Toh Hun Ping

Directed by Iida Shimbi and Miki Shigeru (editors)
Scene description: Tank procession in the city to commemorate dead comrades
Timecode for scene: 0:57:24 – 0:59:00

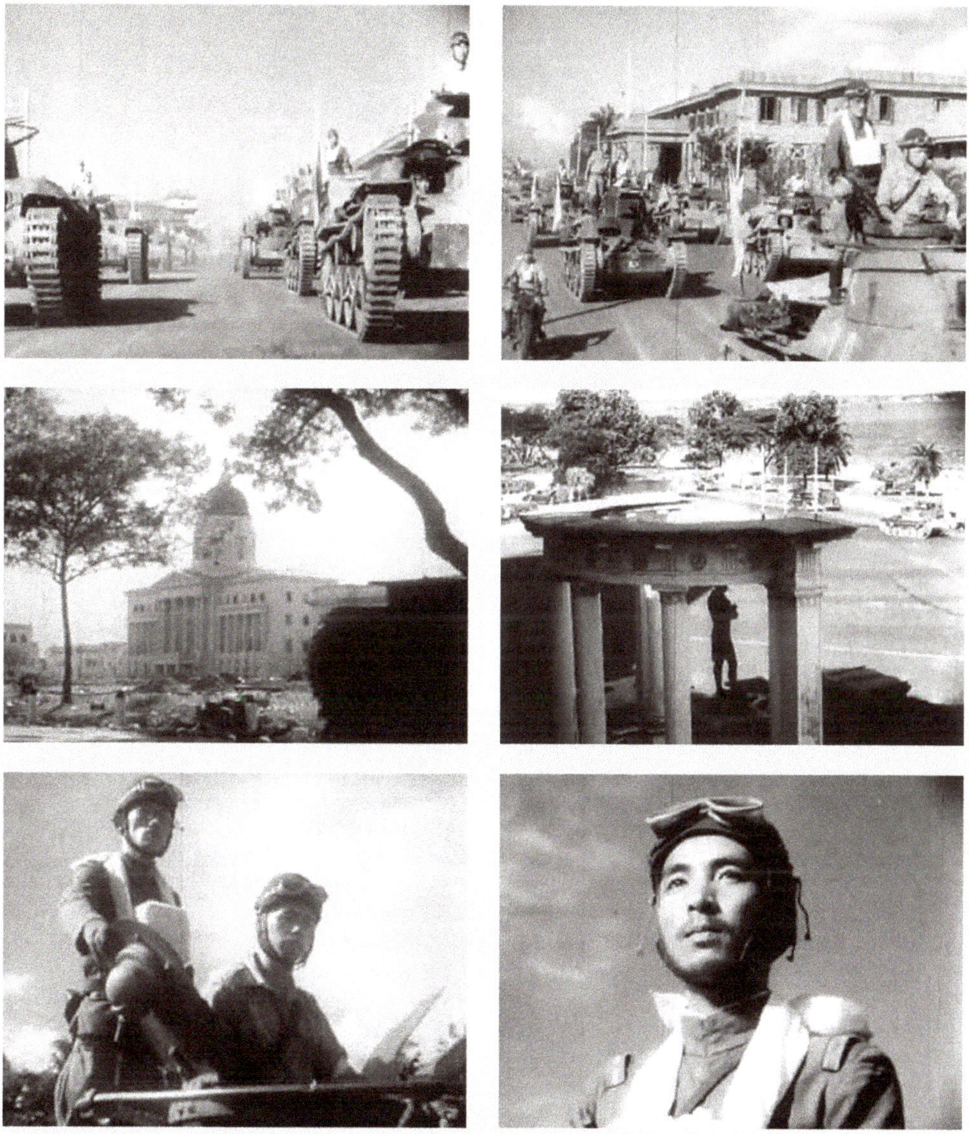

Images © 1942 Nihon Eigasha (Nichiei)

SINGAPORE (1947)

LOCATION *Rochor Canal*

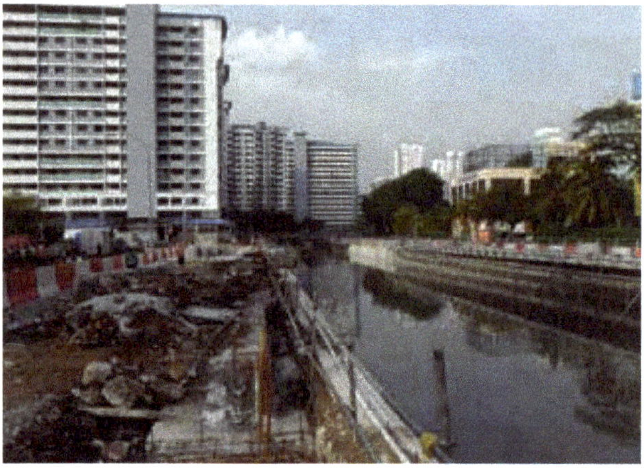

A LOOSE REWORKING of *Casablanca* (Michael Curtiz, 1942), John Brahm's deeply contrived, melodrama-adventure, is set immediately after World War II. Cynical pearl smuggler Fred MacMurray returns to the place where he lost his love *and* his fortune – Singapore! Ava Gardner is the woman he pines for, and believes dead in an air raid on the eve of Japanese occupation, but in fact she's lost her memory and is happily married to an upstanding plantation owner. MacMurray is determined to win her (and his pearls) back. Without travelling beyond Burbank, an imaginary Singapore is recreated through sparing use of stock footage alongside lavish recreations of a colonial Raffles-like hotel, Chinatown backstreets and a seedy waterfront bar. The only place that's actually named is Rochor Canal in one fascinating sequence. Gardner's amnesia is partly cured by the memory of Ming Ling, her faithful servant girl, and with an address in hand she goes searching in a *kampong* (village), complete with wooden stilt houses and various 'oriental' extras, including washerwomen doing laundry along the canal, which in reality runs from Serangoon to Kallang Road. Remarkably, Gardner makes her enquiries in Malay, the primary local language of Singapore at that time (and its cinema), and would continue to be Singapore's National Language even after independence. It's easy to dismiss the film's studio-fabricated Singapore as merely a backdrop for the rekindled romance of the American lovers (Ming Ling is the only notable 'Singaporean' character), but the film-makers got one important detail right. ➾***Ben Slater***

Photo © Toh Hun Ping

Directed by John Brahm
Scene description: Searching for Ming Ling
Timecode for scene: 0:42:00 – 0:43:23

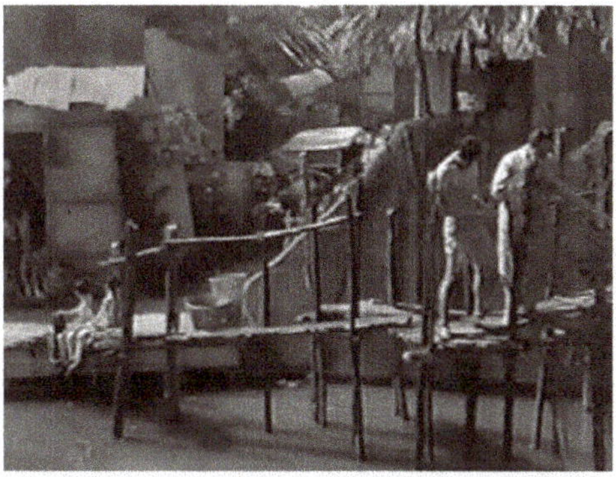

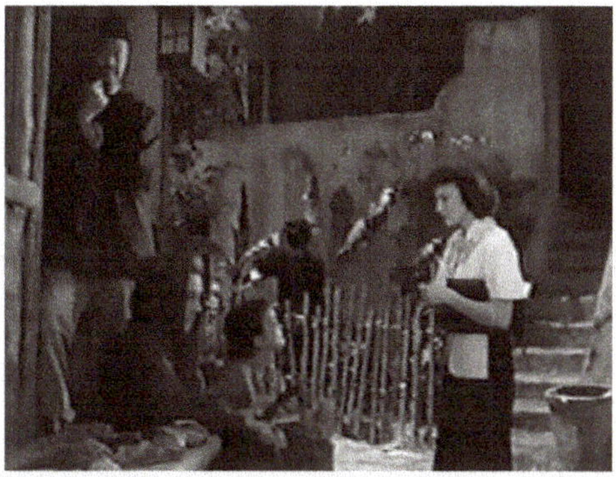

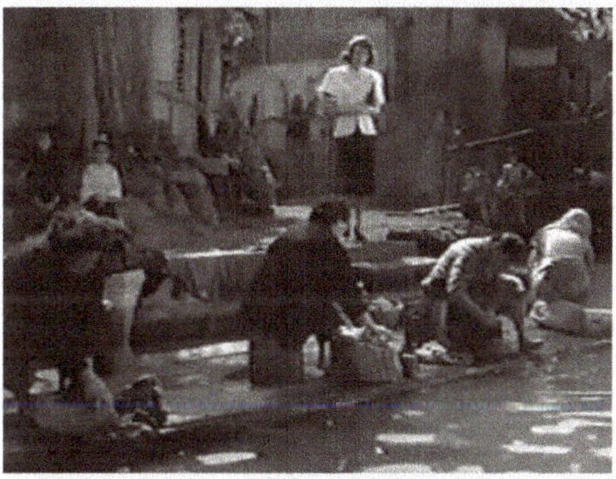

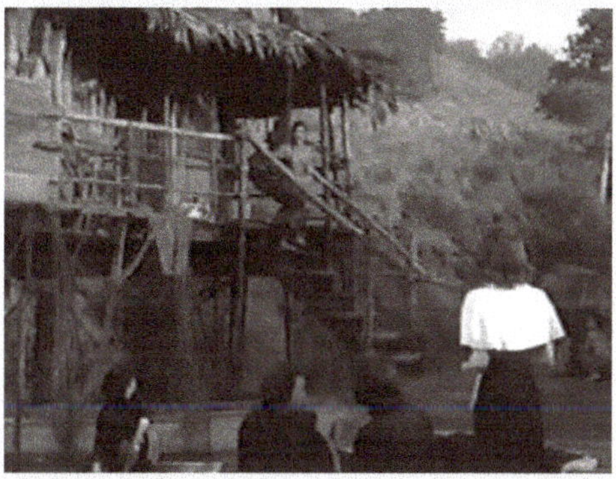

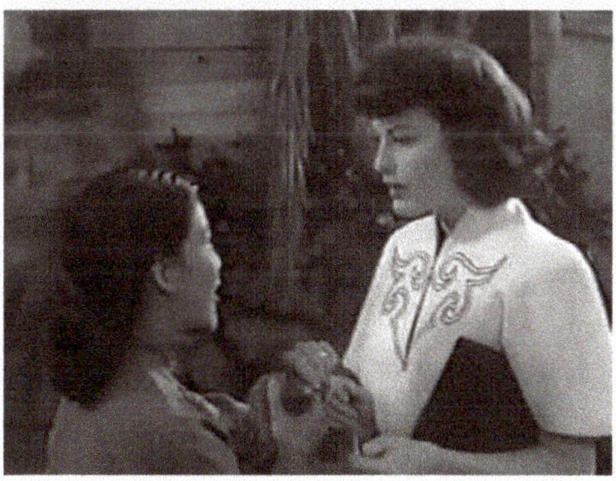

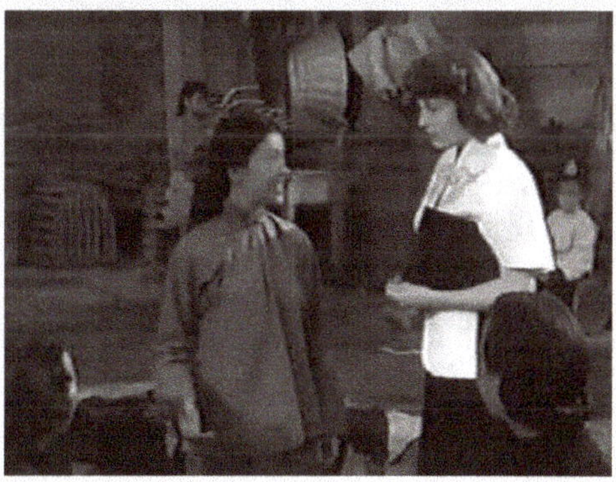

BROKEN HEART/PATAH HATI (1952)

LOCATION

Former Alkaff Gardens, off Upper Serangoon Road (now Cedar Girls' Secondary School)

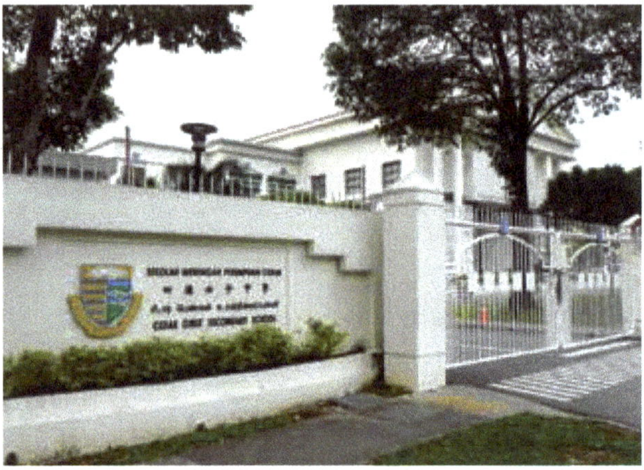

A WAVE OF INDIAN film directors including Balden Singh Rajhans, Lakshamanan Krishnan and K.M. Basker, had a strong influence on Malay cinema. As historian Raphaël Millet explains, 'Indian film conventions influenced mannerisms and dialogue. Acting was overstylised, songs expressed emotions, dance scenes suddenly broke up the narration.' *Broken Heart* was one of the five vehicles conceived for rising star P. Ramlee in 1952. Still skinny and slightly introverted, he plays a young guy educated abroad who is forced to leave a florist, his true love, in order to marry a wealthier girl. '*Patah Hati* is a melancholy portrait of regret and bitterness', according to film-maker Amir Muhammad. Thanks to the engaging nuances of P. Ramlee's acting, and to his subdued ways of singing, dancing and suffering, the melodramatic peaks never look too contrived. A wordless romantic interlude set in an untouched Arcadia immortalizes Alkaff Gardens, one of the lost wild areas of central Singapore. Several Malay films used to be shot over its green fields, which should not be confused with Alkaff Mansion, located within a still enjoyable park at Telok Blangah Hill. ➾***Lorenzo Codelli***

Photo © Toh Hun Ping

Directed by K.M. Basker
Scene description: Lovers P. Ramlee and Neng Yatimah dance around the gardens
Timecode for scene: 0:26:37 – 0:27:48

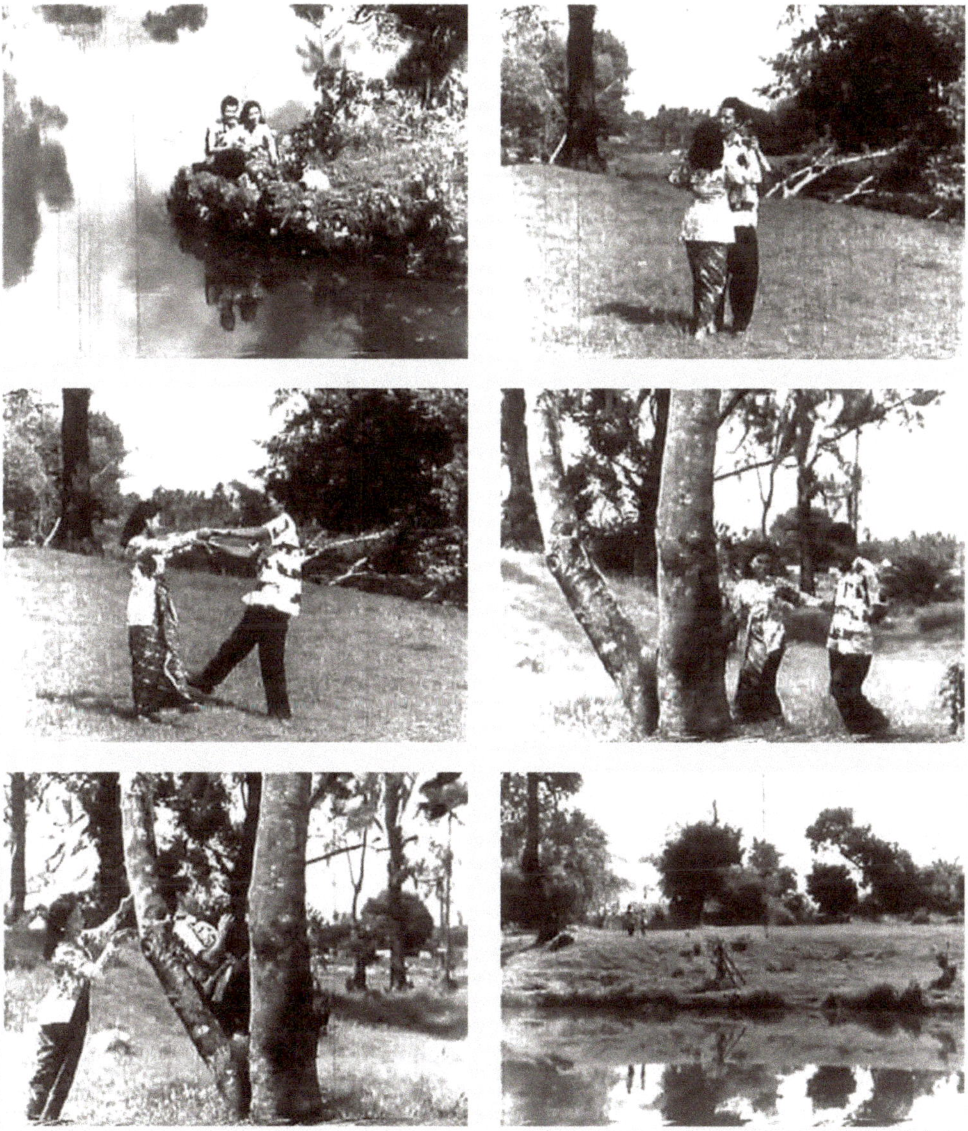

Images © 1952 Malay Film Productions (Shaw Brothers)

THE MOULDY BACHELORS/BUJANG LAPOK (1957)

LOCATION

'The Kampong' [photo taken at Kampong Lorong Buangkok]

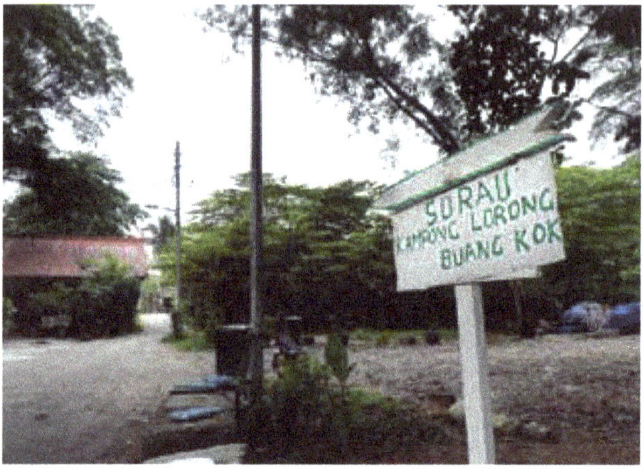

AN UNDISPUTED CLASSIC of the 'Golden Age' of Malay film-making in Singapore, *The Mouldy Bachelors* was written and directed by P. Ramlee (and he stars and wrote the music!), who'd gone from being a Shaw Brothers Studio supporting-player to their one-man cinematic powerhouse in less than a decade. It's a deceptively charming tale of three past-their-prime single guys trying to find romantic love, loaded with pointed observations about modernization, relationships and tradition. As with many films of the era, the traditional *kampong* (village) is depicted as a vibrant community in stark contrast to the alienating modernity of central Singapore, and yet the village is not entirely idealized. The painted artifice of the village where the bachelors reside (shot inside the Shaws' Jalan Ampas studio) contrasts harshly with glimpses of real locations, including an impoverished village where Ramlee follows a girl who steals cash from men in a western-style cafe. She tries to give some of her ill-gotten gains to her despairing mother, whose rejection inspires an impassioned soliloquy about the need to lie and cheat in order to survive; Ramlee responds philosophically, and leaves her alone. We then shift from this 'real' poverty, to the studio-created village, where another bachelor, Aziz, cheerfully goes to bestow a gift on the girl he loves, who's been traumatized by her debt-ridden stepfather. When he passes her money she's horrified, associating it with sexual submission. It's a devastating pairing, both scenes show rural life poisoned by poverty and affluence. Of course, *The Mouldy Bachelors* is a comedy, and all differences and problems will be happily resolved in the heart of the *kampong*. After independence, villages were replaced by high-rise housing estates, although there are traces of this old life left in Buangkok and on Pulau Ubin. ➾ ***Ben Slater***

Photo © Toh Hun Ping

Directed by P. Ramlee
Scene description: Money corrupts the kampong
Timecode for scene: 1:10:17 – 1:13:03

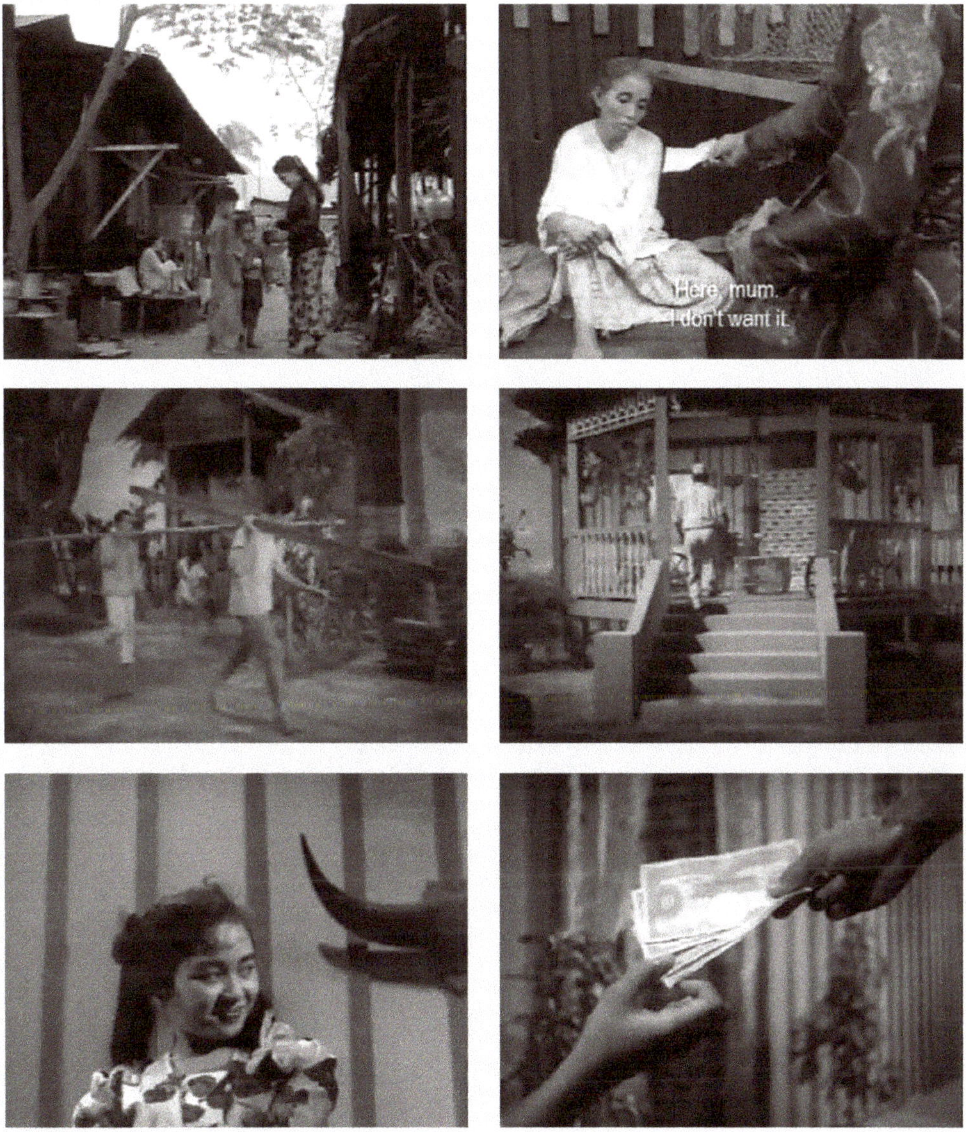

Images © 1957 Malay Film Productions (Shaw Brothers)

MOON OVER MALAYA (1957)

LOCATION

Hwa Chong Institution (formerly The Chinese High School), 661 Bukit Timah Road

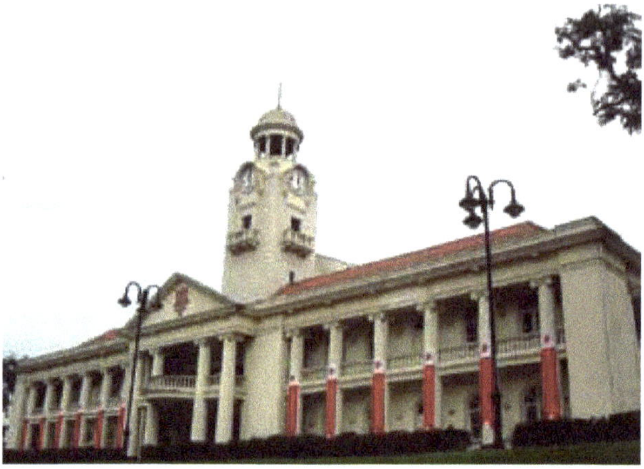

ON THE MORNING of 26 October 1956, the police unleashed tear gas into The Chinese High School compounds, to forcibly disperse a large group of Chinese middle school students who were staging a sit-in protest. They were objecting to the government's arrest of student leaders alleged to be involved in political subversion. Violence erupted as mobs outside the school grew into an island-wide riot. The clash was also over the status of Chinese vernacular education, which was facing marginalization by the incumbent government and colonial machinations. About a month later, a film crew from Hong Kong was in the school to shoot *Moon over Malaya,* a Cantonese movie about the tribulations of a young graduate who advocates education for the Chinese masses in Singapore and Malaya. (It is the final installment of Kong Ngee Film Company's famed *Nanyang Trilogy,* 1957) The film begins with Ngok Ming (Patrick Tse) returning from self-imposed exile to the school that he had co-founded. After a welcome ceremony at the school's entrance (which was shot at Nan Hua Girls' School), he retreats to the school's rear gardens (actually the front lawn of The Chinese High School). Here, he recalls a poignant and melodramatic past: his fervour for Chinese education had encountered resistance from a domineering and antipathetic father-in-law. If one takes into account the historical context in which the film was made, the fictional Ngok Ming's recollection of past events at The Chinese High School can potentially be construed as an indirect and muted remembrance of the Chinese school students' struggle and activism against suppression in the real world. ➾***Toh Hun Ping***

Photo © Teo Di Kai (wikimedia commons)

Directed by Chun Kim and Chor Yuen

Scene description: Ngok Ming recalls a painful and poignant past

Timecodes for scene: 0:06:34 – 0:07:02; 0:16:02 – 0:16:27; 1:16:32 – 1:17:35

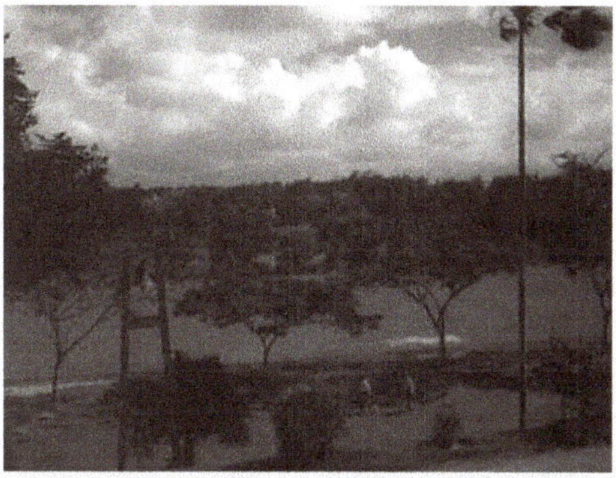

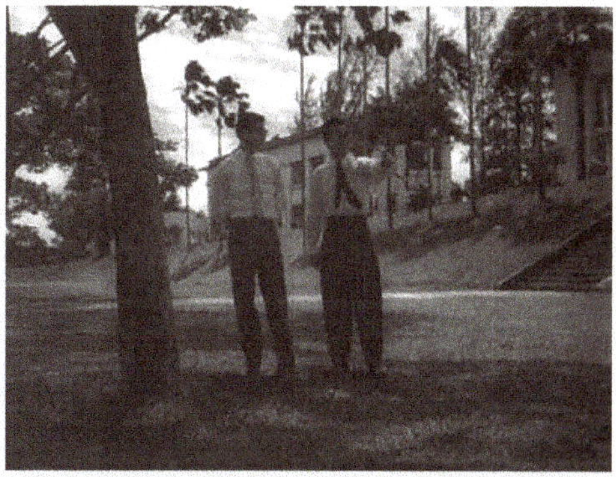

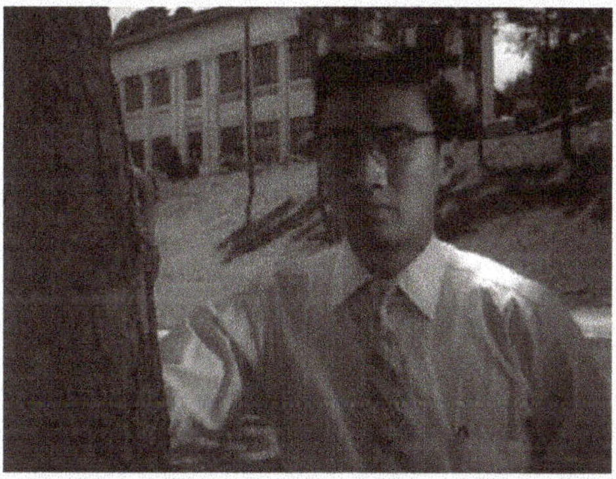

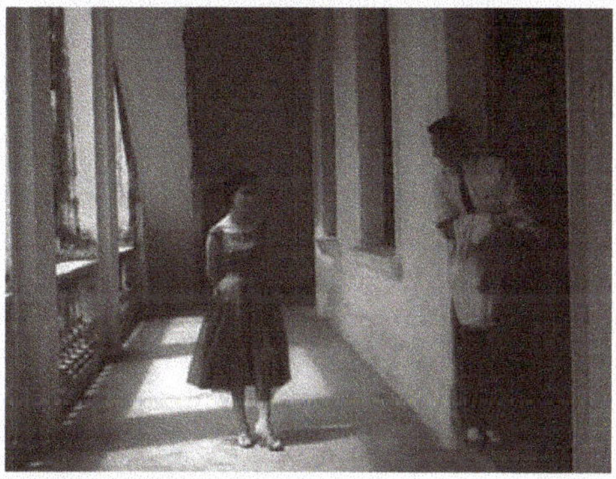

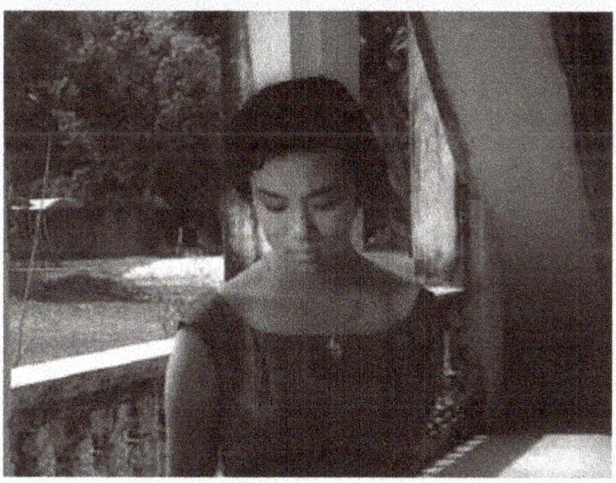

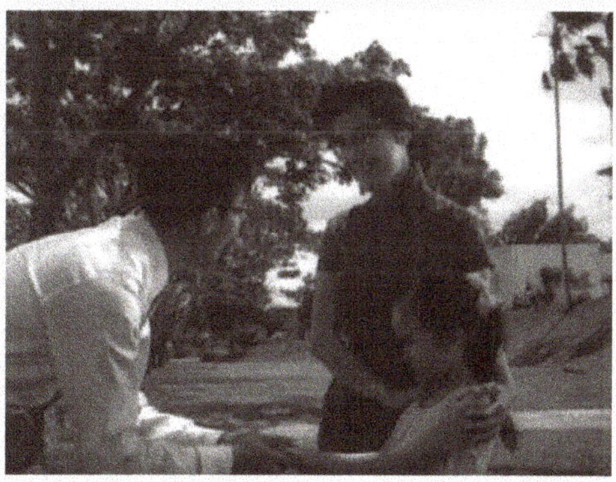

CURSE OF PONTIANAK/ SUMPAH PONTIANAK (1958)

LOCATION

Former kampongs on the east coast (now golf courses, condominiums and 'business parks')

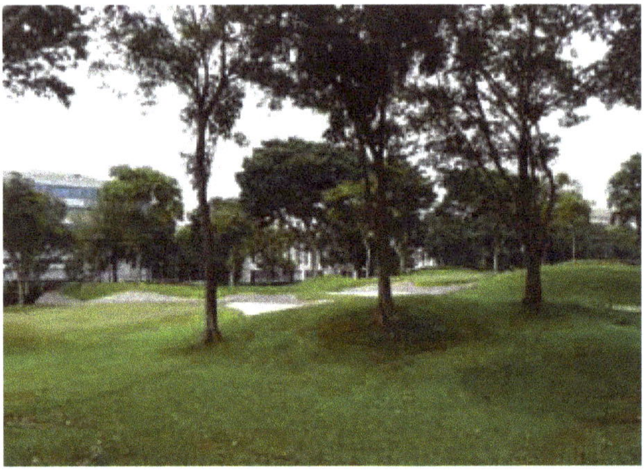

'PONTIANAK' IS ONE AMONG the numerous vampire-ghosts that thrive in Malay folklore and is commonly described as the ghost of a female who died in childbirth, often taking on the guise of a scented, seductive woman. *Curse of Pontianak* is the third in a trilogy of *pontianak*-themed Malay horror movies that capitalized on the local population's fear for this most treacherous of vampires. (The first two films – *Pontianak* and *Dendam Pontianak/Pontianak's Revenge*, both directed by B.N. Rao and released by Cathay-Keris Studio in 1957 – are believed to be lost after Ho Ah Loke, the films' producer, reportedly threw the original prints down a mining pool in a fit of rage.) The *pontianak* in the third installment, though, is a benevolent one who rescues her daughter and *kampong* (village) dwellers from the threats of other devilish creatures. Actor Wahid Satay, who provided comic relief in the trilogy as a singing satay-seller, once revealed that the movies' exterior scenes were filmed in the *kampongs* of Siglap, Padang Terbakar and Tanah Merah, all situated along Singapore's eastern coast. They served as excellent rural settings for the films' supernatural antagonists to perform their homicidal feats and induce panic in the fictional neighbourhoods. In the real world, little did the *kampong* residents expect that they would be confronting something more haunting than *pontianaks*: the bulldozers summoned by government authorities to demolish their houses, beginning from the 1970s. These last surviving fishing *kampongs* and their well-established communities were destined to make way for urban redevelopment – a comprehensive reinvention of the landscape to suit the needs of a modernizing, forward-looking industrial society. ➾ ***Toh Hun Ping***

Photo © Toh Hun Ping

Directed by B.N. Rao

Scene description: A satay-seller sings a tune for the kampong folks

Timecode for scene: 0:19:35 – 0:22:30

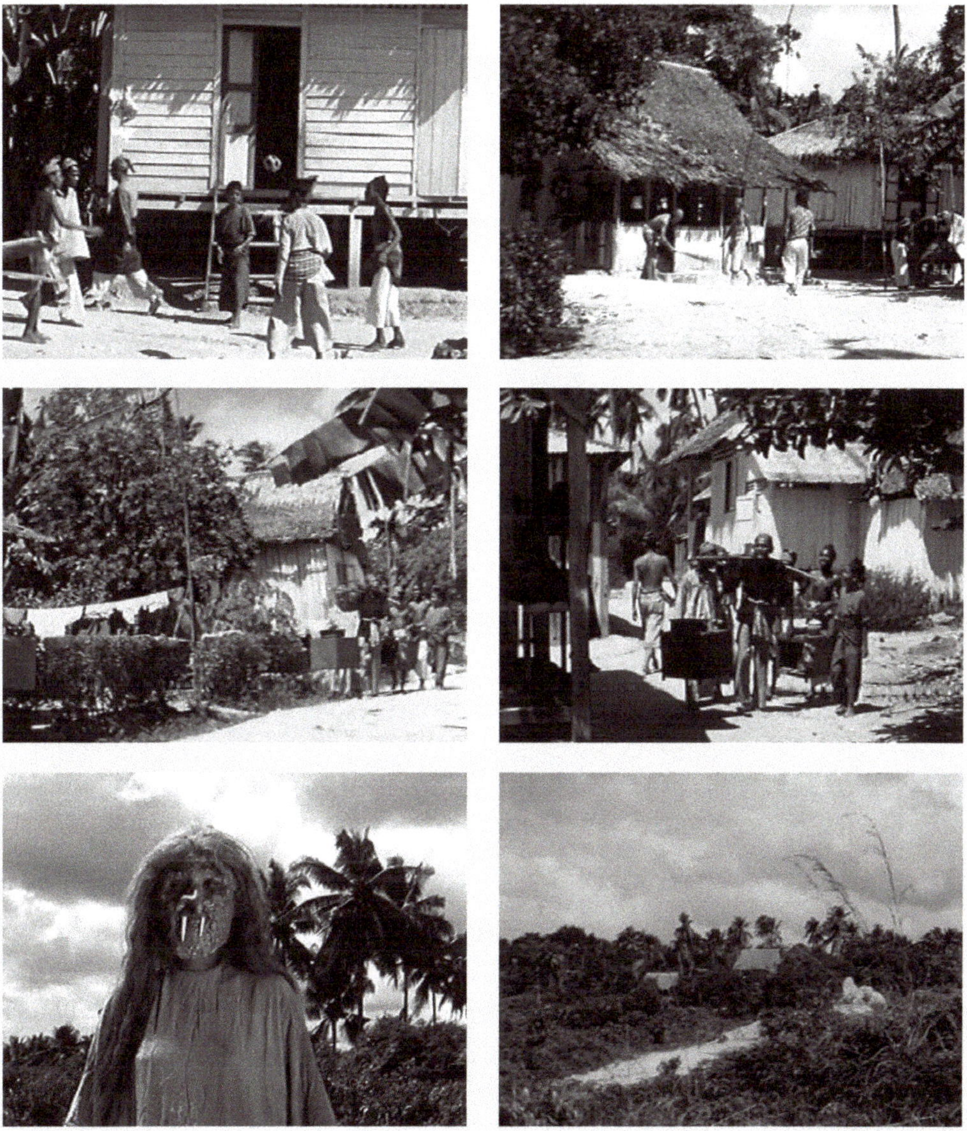

Images © 1958 Cathay-Keris

THE OUTSIDER'S SINGAPORE

SPOTLIGHT

A Brief History of 'Western' Film-makers' Expeditions in Singapore

Text by BEN SLATER

IN THE EARLY 1930S, Ward Wing, a bit-part American actor turned film director, arrived in Singapore. Fascinated by Malay culture, he made *Samarang* (aka *Shark Woman*), a 'jungle adventure' for American consumption, shot on a shoestring, starring two Caucasian expatriates (an English policeman and an Armenian beauty queen!), pruriently depicting tribesfolk as semi-naked cannibals. Wing was probably the first 'western' film-maker to shoot a narrative film in the southern tip of then-Malaya (working at the same time as animal impressario Frank Buck, shooting *Bring 'Em Back Alive*). His initial impulse was to exoticize and misrepresent Singapore, and yet we can now see *Samarang* as a sublime documentary – the faces and behaviour of the extras, as well as the landscapes, are indelibly captured.

In travelling to Asia, Wing and Buck were pioneers. During this period 'Singapore' was usually conjured up from a distance with stock footage and studio recreations of dark alleys, sleazy bars and jungle roads. Singapore was an archetypal setting for Hollywood melodramas concerning desperate souls adrift in foreign climes. The lovers in Alfred Hitchcock's *Rich and Strange* (1931) wind up there, as do the heroes and *femme fatales* of *Night Cargo* (1936), *The Blonde from Singapore* (1941) and *Singapore* (1947).

From the 1960s, as Singapore gained independence and modernized rapidly, foreign film crews became more commonplace, their arrival coinciding with the steep decline of the local film industry. Several European B-movies were shot partially in Singapore, including the pirate hokum of *Sandokan, Pirate of Malaysia* (1964) based on pulp fiction by Emilio Salgari, two 'superspy' flicks in 1966, *So Darling So Deadly* and *Goldsnake: Anonima Killers*, and the French guys-on-a-secret-mission picture *Five Ashore in Singapore* (1967). All presented the island as a visually arresting, tropical 'backdrop' for exotic adventures, with mostly brutal indifference to the actual place they were passing through and the people who lived there.

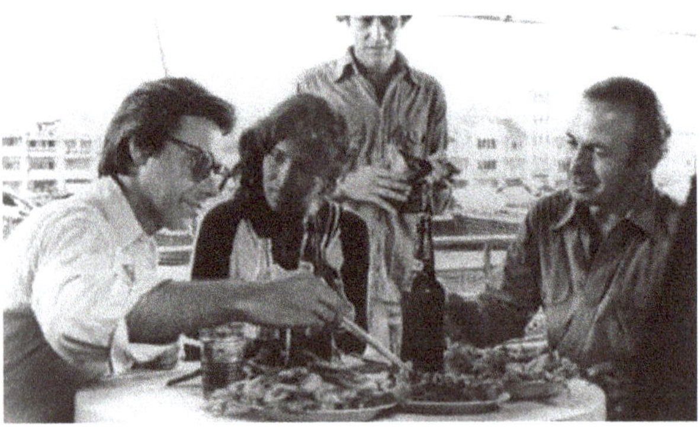

Hollywood came calling in the late 1960s, initially via two British (but American studio-backed) productions, both adapted from literary sources. *Pretty Polly* (1967) was a big-budget romantic drama from a Noel Coward short story, and despite the presence of Hayley Mills and Sashi Kapoor proved a critical and box office flop. Its tale of a young visitor gaining a worldly education from a 'native', recurs in *The Virgin Soldiers* (1969) a faithful adaptation of Leslie Thomas's poignant autobiographical novel about his experiences as a bored recruit stationed in Singapore during the post-war 'Malayan Emergency' (when the British fought communist guerrillas). Young soldier Brigg (Hywel Bennett) loses his virginity to and falls for Chinatown girl 'Juicy' Lucy (Tsai Chin), but the tedium of Singapore eventually erupts into tragic violence. Both films deal with the aftermath of the colonial era, the sun setting on empire, and the growing tension between locals and their former masters turned interlopers.

The biggest Hollywood film to be made in Singapore was never even filmed. Director Fred Zinnemann spent years preparing an adaptation of André Malraux's novel *Man's Fate* to be shot with Singapore standing in for Shanghai. Millions of dollars were spent on pre-production, locations

Opposite *Saint Jack* (1979) / **Below** *Mister John* (2013)

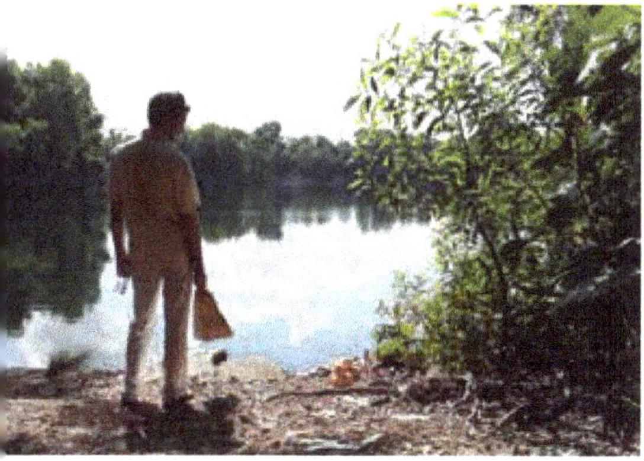

were selected, actors cast and crew hired, but at the last minute in 1969, MGM pulled the plug. It was a disaster and an embarrassment, and although in no way Singapore's fault (the film was just too expensive for the studio), for years it appeared to cool Hollywood towards the Lion City and vice versa.

In 1978, Singaporeans were greatly excited by the arrival in town of *Hawaii 5-O*, one of the biggest TV shows in the world at that time, to film two episodes. Simultaneously, newspapers reported that Hollywood *wunderkind* Peter Bogdanovich was also in Singapore scouting locations for a film called 'Jack of Hearts'. In fact he was already shooting what would turn out to be *Saint Jack* (1979), and the story of how, according to the press, Bogdanovich 'cheated' Singapore in order to make his less-than-flattering portrayal of the republic, overshadowed the merits of the film (which would be banned in Singapore for nearly thirty years). Although *Saint Jack* was another story about an American abroad, it gave Singaporeans substantial roles as Jack's friends, employees and lovers, and stands up today as a rough-edged but deeply fond tribute to the Lion City and all its contradictions.

During the 1980s, Singapore's use as a location declined dramatically. The author of the belated (and inferior) sequel to *The Virgin Soldiers* (*Stand up Virgin Soldiers*) chose not to film in Singapore again, because, he said, it had changed too much. The old cinematic city, with jungles, crumbling mansions, shophouses and bustling street-life, was now dominated by brand new skyscrapers, high-rise housing blocks and cleaned-up streets. In achieving western-style modernity, Singapore had lost many of the charms that drew film companies to its shores.

From the 1960s, as Singapore gained independence and modernized rapidly, foreign film crews became more commonplace...

There was sporadic TV production, mainly from Australia (World War II miniseries *Tenko* and *Tanamera: Lion of Singapore* were partially shot on location) as well as the starry American TV movie *Passion Flower* (1986) notable for being entirely filmed in Singapore. It glossily contrasts an earthy, sensual Chinatown with the cold, hi-tech towers of Shenton Way to evoke a world of sexual and financial deceit played out between expatriate high-flyers. Amusingly, Raffles Hotel is recast as the lavish office of a cruel billionaire. The few 'locals' with speaking parts are merely pawns in the game.

There wouldn't be a major foreign film production in Singapore until James Dearden's *Rogue Trader* (1999). Ewan McGregor starred as Nick Leeson, the real-life broker who brought about the collapse of Barings Bank on the Singapore Stock Exchange in the mid-1990s. Despite being thoroughly dull, and only partly shot on location (the exchange floor was recreated in a London studio), *Rogue Trader* is significant in that there's no trace of the orientalist clichés. It depicts the modern, cosmopolitan Singapore of condominiums, bars (along Boat Quay), cafes and restaurants, where the British protagonists mingle with Singaporean friends (not just other expats).

Few foreign productions were shot in Singapore in the 2000s. Ironically, in a throwback to the old days, Hollywood created an artificial 'Singapore' for the opening sequences of *Pirates of the Carribean: At World's End* (2007).

Having been commissioned to make a short film in Singapore, *Tiong Bahru* (2012), London-based Irish directors Joe Lawlor and Christine Molloy chose it as the main location for their feature *Mister John* (2013), which plays surprising variations on the familiar tale of a western visitor to Singapore. Gerry (Aidan Gillen) arrives to attend his brother's funeral while escaping from a troubled marriage back home, and is powerfully attracted to his brother's Singaporean widow (local TV-icon Zoe Tay), while moving through a nocturnal world of girlie bars, cheap hotels and KTV lounges. On one hand Singapore is presented as sensual and mysterious (with hints of the supernatural), but it's also remarkably ordinary. It's a place where you can get lost *and* find yourself, much like anywhere else.

SINGAPORE

LOCATIONS MAP

maps are only to be taken as approximates

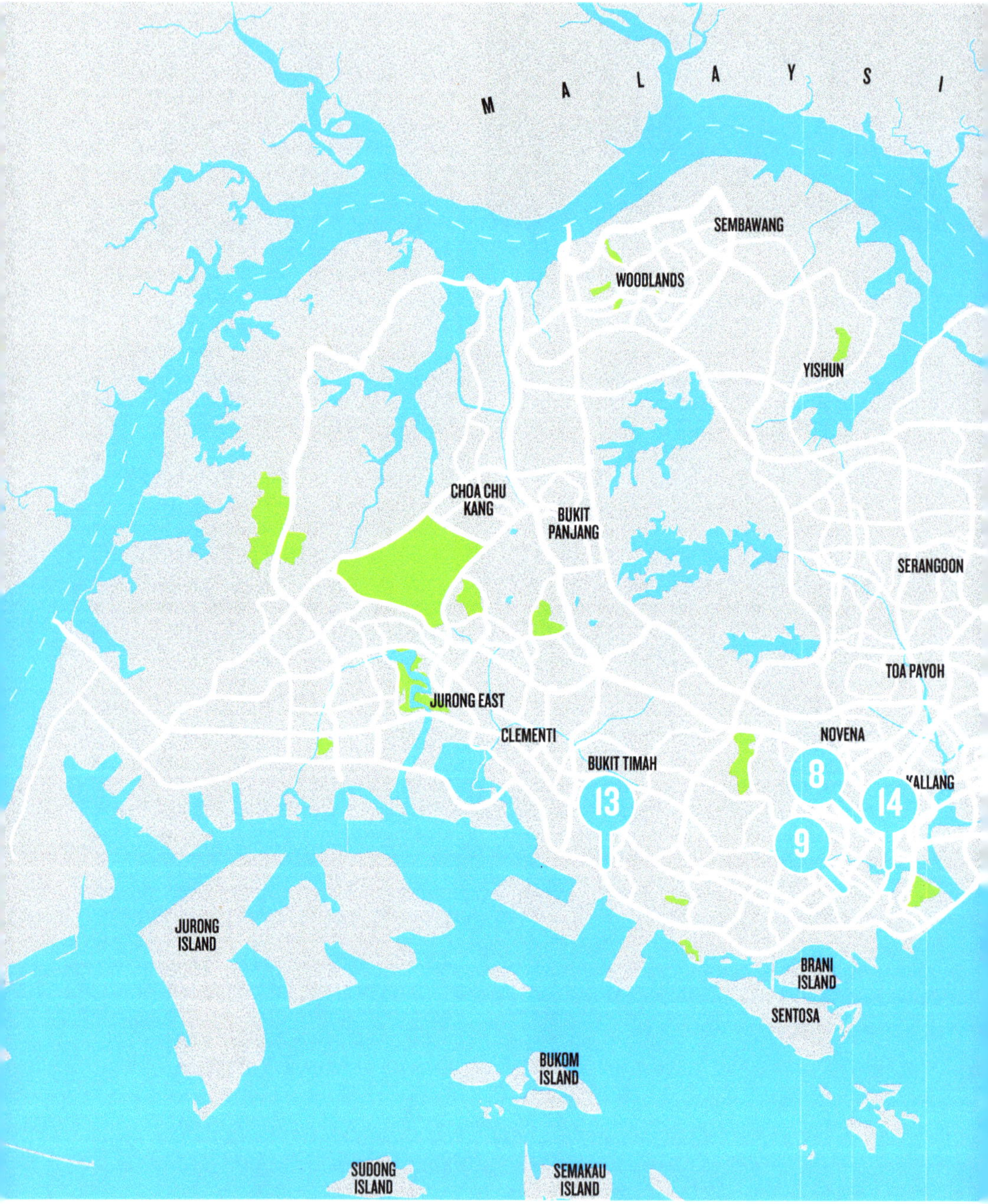

SINGAPORE LOCATIONS
SCENES 8-14

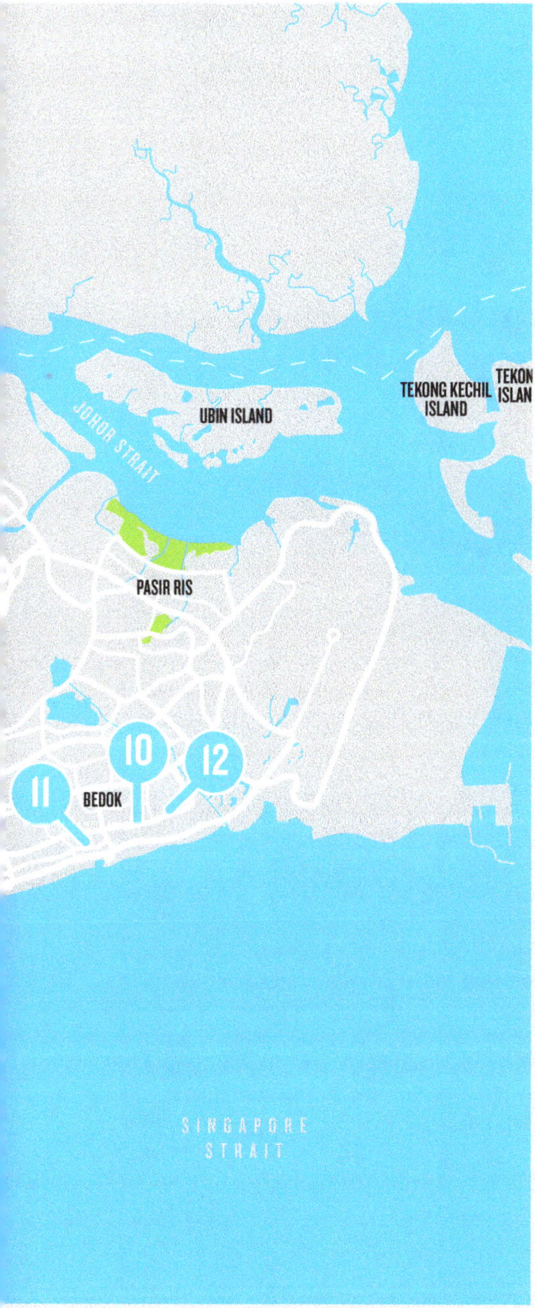

8.
POISONOUS BLOWPIPE/ SUMPITAN RACUN (1961)
Former Cathay Building at Dhoby Ghaut (now 'The Cathay'), 2 Handy Road
page 30

9.
MONDO CANE (1962)
Sago Lane's 'Kwok Mun' and 'Fook Sow' Sick Receiving Houses (demolished), Chinatown
page 32

10.
MY MOTHER-IN-LAW/IBU MERTUAKU (1962)
Former Shaw's Villa (now a childcare centre), 440A Upper East Coast Road
page 34

11.
DIVORCE MADNESS/GILA TALAK (1963)
Traditional Malay houses in former Kampong Siglap, along Upper East Coast Road
page 36

12.
MAT 3/4/MAT TIGA SUKU (1964)
Pilot Land Reclamation Project at Bedok (now the vicinity of Temasek Secondary School), along Upper East Coast Road
page 38

13.
SO DARLING SO DEADLY AKA AGENTE JOE WALKER OPERAZIONE FAR EAST AKA KOMMISSAR X: IN DEN KLAUEN DES GOLDENEN DRACHEN (1966)
Tiger Balm Garden/Haw Par Villa, 262 Pasir Panjang Road
page 40

14.
FIVE ASHORE IN SINGAPORE AKA CINQ GARS POUR SINGAPOUR AKA CINQUE MARINES PER SINGAPORE (1966)
Collyer Quay
page 42

POISONOUS BLOWPIPE/SUMPITAN RACUN (1961)

LOCATION

Former Cathay Building at Dhoby Ghaut (now 'The Cathay'), 2 Handy Road

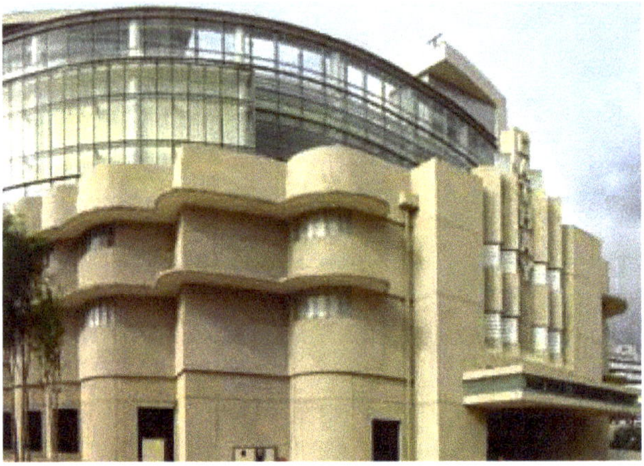

POISONOUS BLOWPIPE is a noirish detective film that follows the adventures of Assistant Superintendent of Police Latiff (S. Roomai Noor) and forensic pathologist Tan Lai Peng (Mary Lim) in a robbery-cum-murder case that involves stolen jewels, poisoned darts, villains masquerading as magicians and an alluring singer (Latiffah Omar) wanted dead for knowing too much. Besides the story/screenplay, which was written by English author and *Singapore Free Press* columnist Pelham Groom, another highlight of the film was its on-location set – the old Cathay Building at Dhoby Ghaut, a fine choice for a crime narrative based in an affluent urban milieu. Designed by architect Frank Brewer in the art deco style, the sixteen-storey Cathay was the first high-rise building in Singapore when completed in 1941 and had under its roof the Cathay Cinema, Cathay Hotel and Restaurant, and a double-storey penthouse where film magnate Loke Wan Tho had an apartment. (Loke was the head of the Cathay Organisation that owned both the flagship building and the Cathay-Keris film company that produced *Poisonous Blowpipe*.) The movie's climatic finale exploits the film location most remarkably: while being pursued by the police, the crime mastermind clambers up an aircraft warning lightpost on the Cathay Building's rooftop. In what seems to be a nod to the introductory scene in *Vertigo* (Alfred Hitchcock, 1958), this wealthy, upper-class villain loses his grip and plunges to his death; it is a suggestive fall from the peak of the very building that was a popular haunt (perhaps even synonymous) with the rich, famous and powerful of the time. ➾ ***Toh Hun Ping***

Photo © Calvin Teo (wikimedia commons)

Directed by L. Krishnan
Scene description: The criminal mastermind falls to his death from the rooftop
Timecode for scene: 1:33:10 – 1:36:49

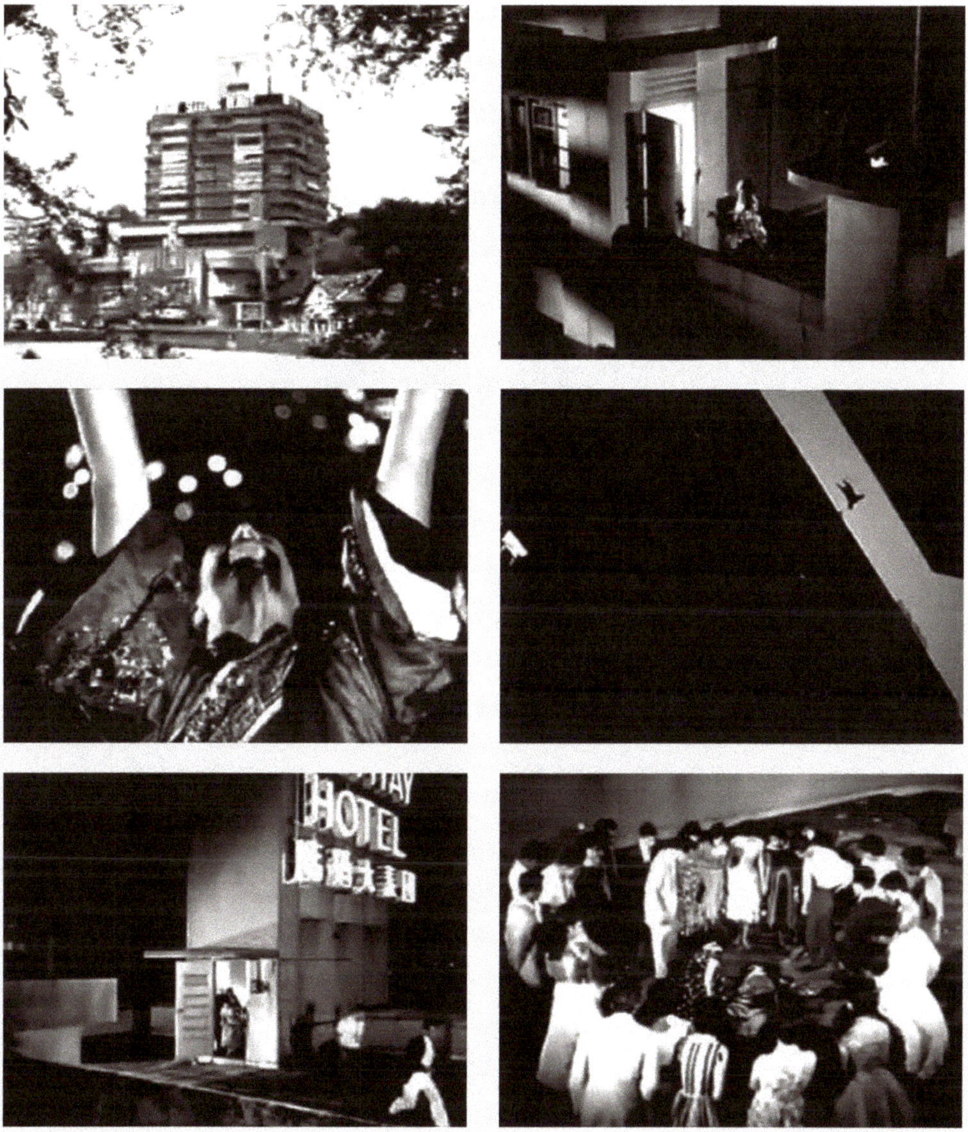

Images © 1961 Cathay-Keris

MONDO CANE (1962)

LOCATION *Sago Lane's 'Kwok Mun' and 'Fook Sow' Sick Receiving Houses (demolished), Chinatown*

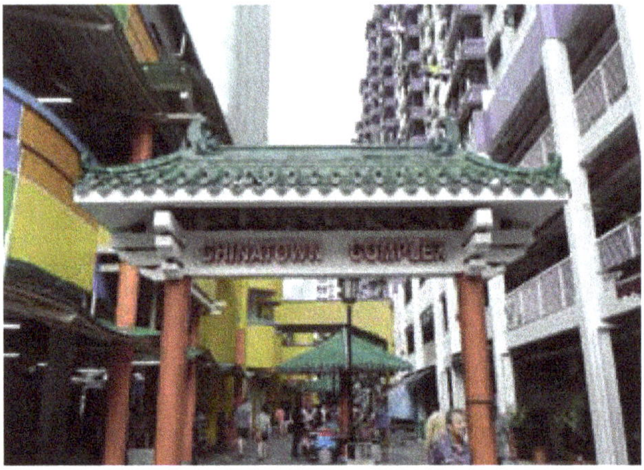

WITH *MONDO CANE* Gualtiero Jacopetti, a scandal-prone reporter who had written the commentary for Alessandro Blasetti's sexy travelogue *Europa di notte/ European Nights* (1959), created a format to be named 'shockumentary', faking or exaggerating bizarre events caught all over the world for the delight of masses of unashamed peeping toms. In Singapore, he and his brave gang defied the official prohibition of photography in the 'death houses' (or 'sick receiving houses') of Chinatown's Sago Lane. These Chinese-run establishments in colonial-era shophouses were the final abodes for the dying aged and terminally ill. (They had existed since the mid-nineteenth century and were forced to close or be converted into funeral parlours by 1962.) The dying were sent there for fear of 'spreading' the illness to the rest of the family and it was also considered inauspicious for deaths to happen at home. For Jacopetti and Prosperi, the Chinese death houses and their inhabitants were ideal subjects for exploitation. The three-minute segment on Sago Lane is a pile-up of images that serve to disturb: close-ups of the bodies, sparse living conditions and an inhabitant's contorted feet. To complete the perverse spectacle, the visuals are accompanied with a 'Voice of God' narration that imposes a distorted interpretation of the footage. Elsewhere, Jacopetti turned his cameras on the Nepalese Gurkhas then stationed in Singapore's Pulau Blakang Mati – later renamed 'Sentosa' and gentrified into a tourist-trap Disneyland. The spectacle was the ceremonial beheading of buffalos using the sacrificial kukri knife in the festival of Dussehra (Dashera). This brutal climax might have inspired Francis Ford Coppola for his bull decapitation scene in *Apocalypse Now* (1979). ➻ ***Toh Hun Ping and Lorenzo Codelli***

Photo © Toh Hun Ping

Directed by Gualtiero Jacopetti, Franco Prosperi and Paolo Cavara
Scene description: Defiance of the ban on photography in the 'Death Houses'
Timecode for scene: 1:10:48 – 1:13:50

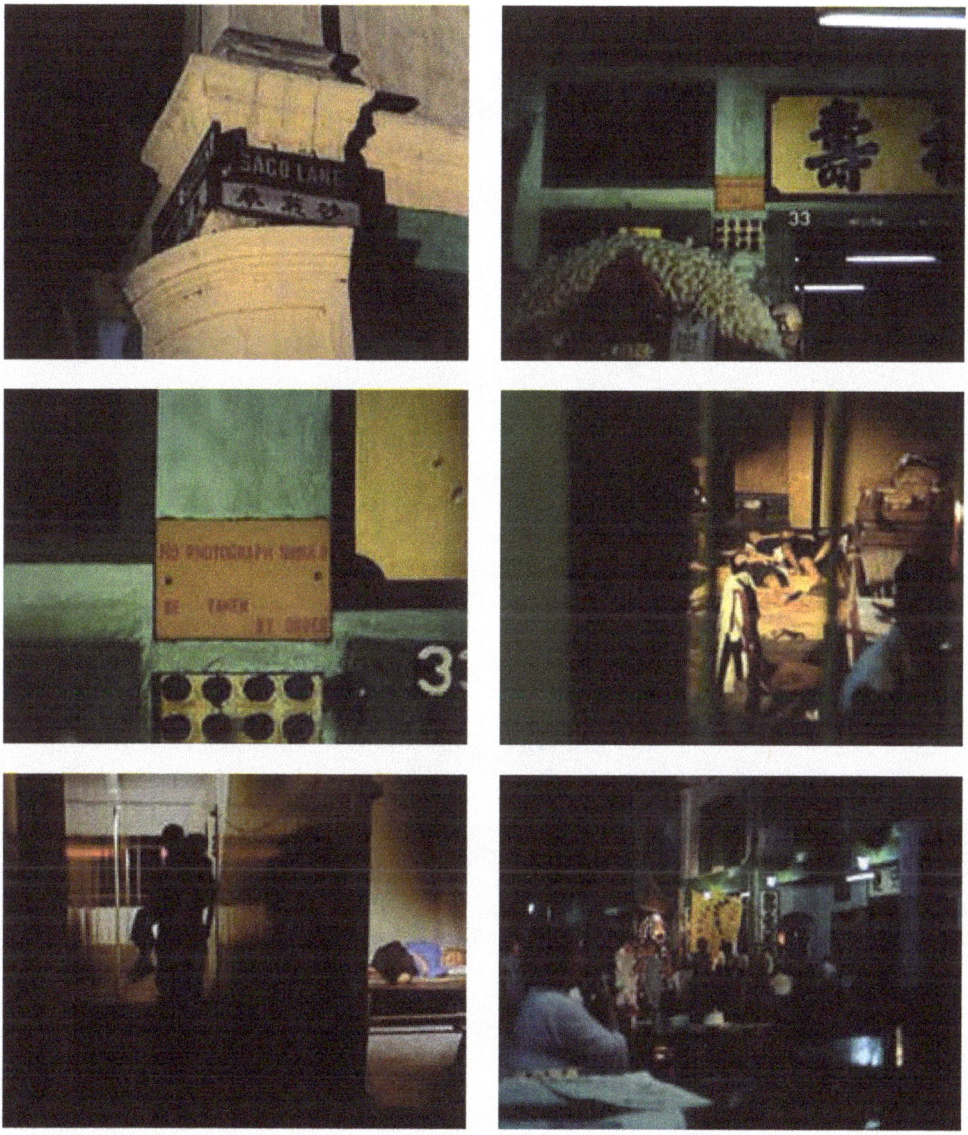

MY MOTHER-IN-LAW/IBU MERTUAKU (1962)

LOCATION *Former Shaw's Villa (now a childcare centre), 440A Upper East Coast Road*

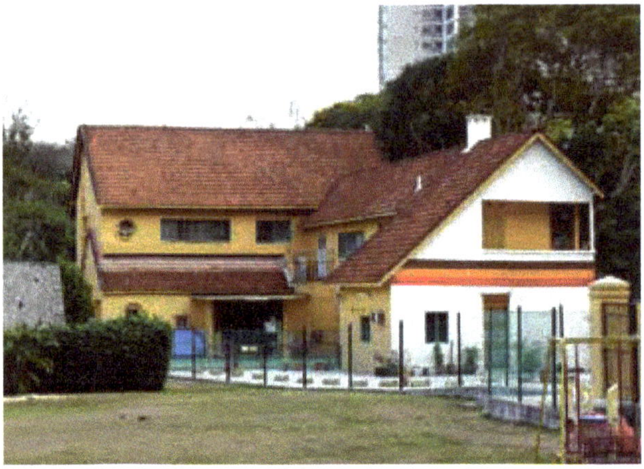

MY MOTHER-IN-LAW is a complex, cross-genre melodramatic tale about a musician's tortuous journey in search of love and acceptance. In this film that also deals with the dichotomies of rich/poor, blindness/seeing and city/hinterland, the musician Kassim Selamat (P. Ramlee) first falls in love with Sabariah Mansoor (Sarimah), the only daughter of a rich widow. Their relationship is frowned upon by her class-conscious mother, who prefers to betroth Sabariah to an eye doctor. As Sabariah is adamant with her choice of her future husband (Kassim), her mother arranges a hasty marriage ceremony and banishes them out of her home. The marriage takes place in the Mansoors' house, a two-storey seaside villa – symbolic of the wealth and status of the Mansoor family. (In reality, the villa on Singapore's eastern coast belonged to the Shaw Brothers, and was part of a stretch of upper-class bungalows which used to face the sea before land reclamation works.) The rooms in the villa are portrayed to be spacious and lonesome, where Sabariah can only find comfort in Kassim's crooning on the radio. In contrast, Kassim lives communally with his friends in crowded lodgings. When this fraternity of musicians from the *kampong* (village) accompanies Kassim to the marriage at the villa, they are nearly anticipating a 'showdown' with the Mansoors' clique of upper-class friends and relatives. The domain of the privileged emerges as a potential site of confrontation between differing social groups – an idea that director P. Ramlee had also employed in his earlier dramas about class differences, such as *Penarik Beca/The Trishaw Puller* (1955) and *Antara Dua Darjat/Between Two Classes* (1960). ➾ ***Toh Hun Ping***

Directed by P. Ramlee

Scene description: Kassim and mates attend his marriage ceremony at the villa

Timecodes for scene: 0:32:46 – 0:42:58; 0:45:27 – 0:45:53

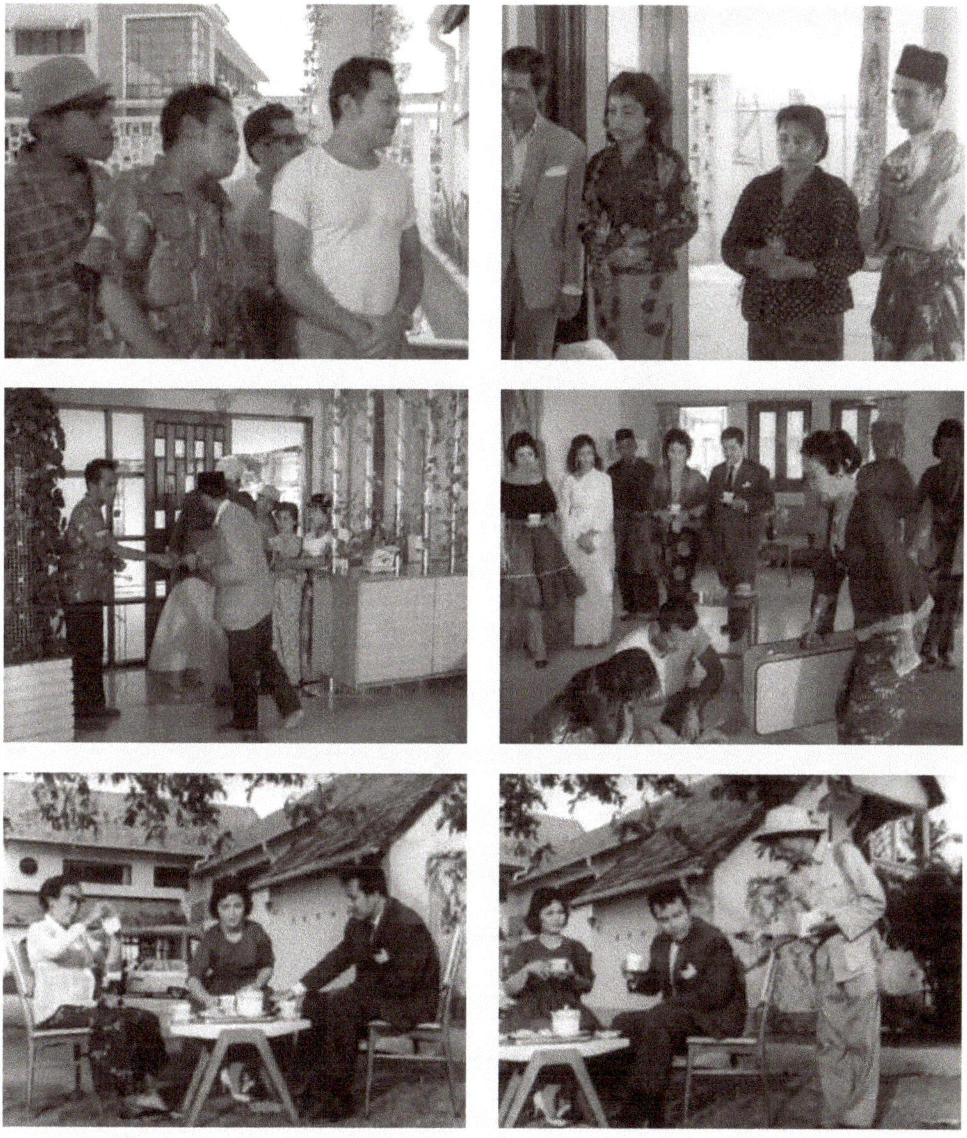

Images © Malay Film Productions (Shaw Brothers)

DIVORCE MADNESS/GILA TALAK (1963)

LOCATION

Traditional Malay houses in former Kampong Siglap, along Upper East Coast Road

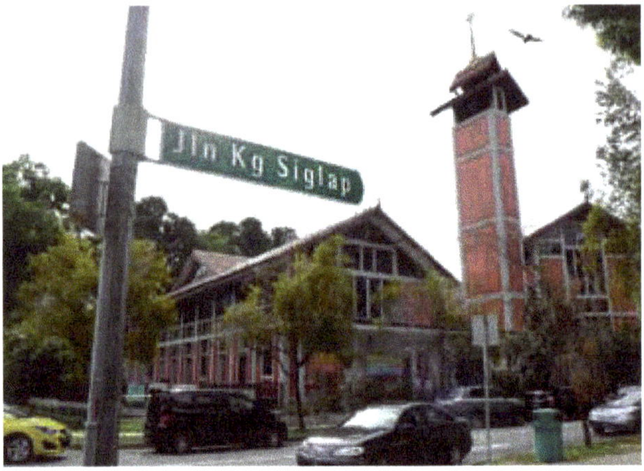

THOUGH FILM DIRECTOR Hussain Haniff was more acclaimed for his Malay period epics such as the anti-feudalistic *Hang Jebat* (1961), the handful of oft-overlooked comedies that he created were no less cinematic gems as well. Two such films, *Masok Angin Keluar Asap/Wind Enters, Smoke Exits* (1963) and its sequel *Divorce Madness*, are exuberant musical comedies set in a Malay village (or *kampong*), interweaving stories of neighbourly rivalries, family disputes, courtships, marriages, divorces and reconciliations. Being an advocate for location shooting, Hussain Haniff filmed the *kampong* scenes of both movies entirely in a real Malay *kampong* (Kampong Siglap), faithfully representing the living conditions of village-dwellers in their traditional pitched-roof timber houses on stilts, albeit with contemporary furnishings. (These scenes are of historical documentary value because *kampongs* of such nature used to spread all over Singapore. By the 1990s, most of the *kampongs* were demolished and former residents were displaced into high-rise modern apartments.) Befitting of a hilarious script written by the director himself, the protagonists in *Divorce Madness* are often captured in and around the *kampong* houses in funny or compromising situations: a tyrannical wife drags a baffled 'husband lookalike' up to the *anjung* (front porch) of her house; an elderly pair 'flirts' in the *serambi* (verandah); a love-struck *pakcik* (uncle) dances to rock 'n' roll on a table in the *rumah ibu* (main living room); and a compliant husband sulks while doing household chores in the *dapur* (kitchen) at the back of the house. One wonders if such whimsical moments still occur in that last surviving (but earmarked for demolition) *kampong* on mainland Singapore today – Kampong Lorong Buangkok.
➾ ***Toh Hun Ping***

Directed by Hussain Haniff
Scene description: Whimsical acts in and around the kampong house
Timecodes for scene: 0:02:18 – 0:25:37; 0:28:20 – 0:37:32; 0:57:13 – 1:29:07

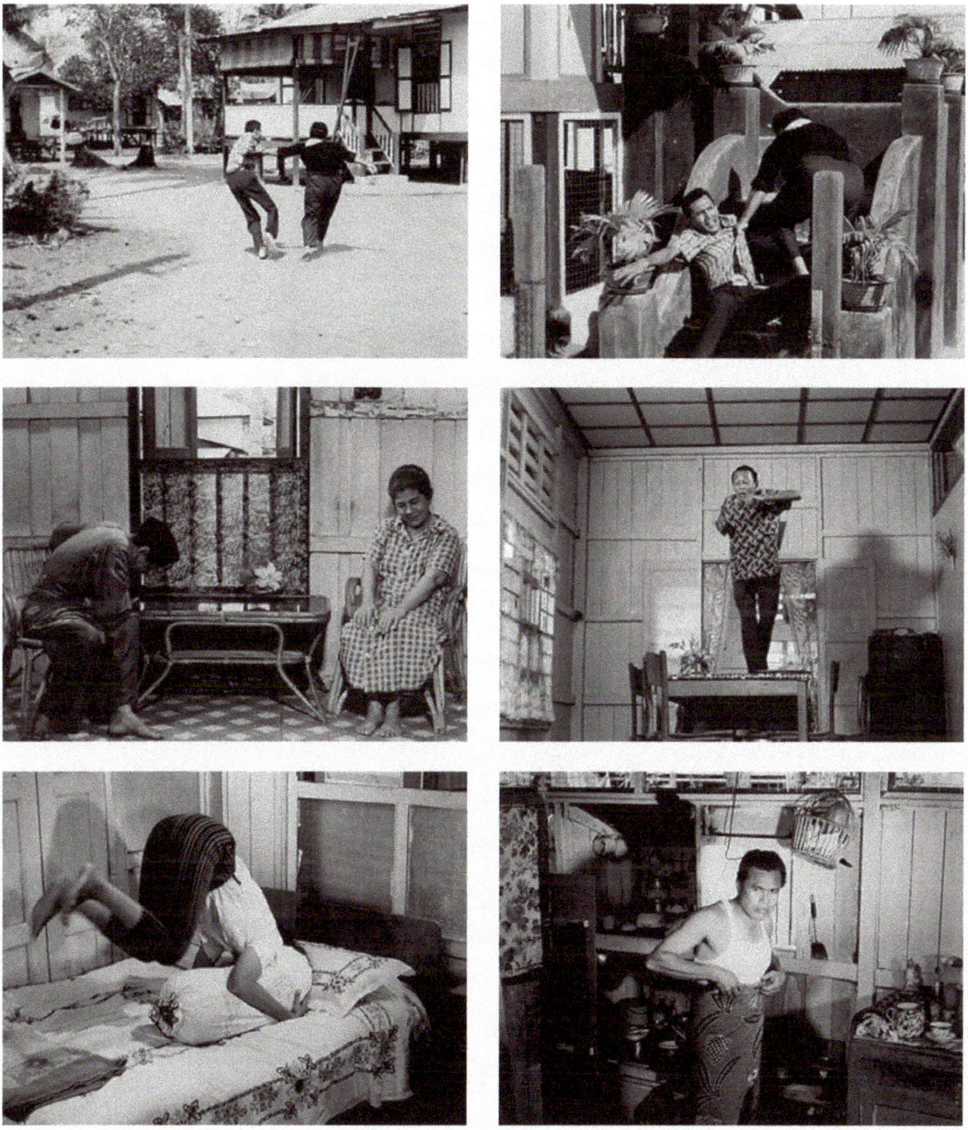

MAT 3/4/MAT TIGA SUKU (1964)

LOCATION

Pilot Land Reclamation Project at Bedok (now the vicinity of Temasek Secondary School), along Upper East Coast Road

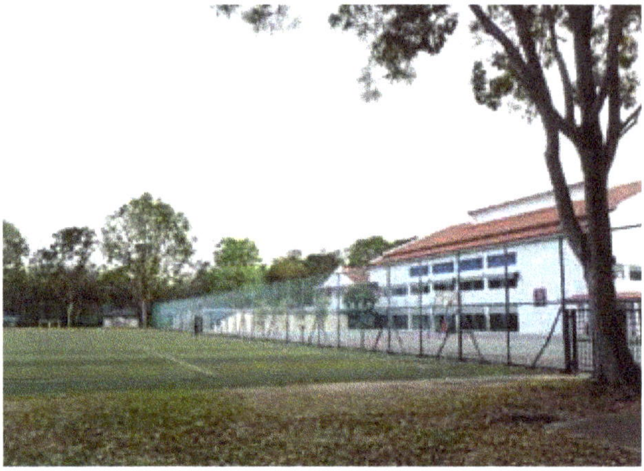

MAT *3/4* IS A COMEDY film that follows the slapstick antics of a poor and helpless oddball who, among many pranks, shifts the bus stop as he pleases, converses with his house and halts an aeroplane that does not give way. Substantial portions of *Mat 3/4* and other works in director-actor Mat Sentul's *oeuvre* were shot on location in the vicinity of the studio that produced the movies – Cathay-Keris along East Coast Road. With Mat Sentul's ingenuity, those real locations were injected with comedic feats and transformed into ridiculous, dream-like or anachronistic environments. The best example from *Mat 3/4* was his use of a plot of freshly reclaimed land from the sea – a pilot reclamation project on the east coast of Singapore – for a sequence where he runs amok moving the bus-stop post at his will, frantically pursued by a bus and its awaiting passengers. It forms a strange yet funny image of a banal act of commuting by public transport gone awry in a desert by the sea. The Pilot East Coast Reclamation Project was undertaken by the government in 1963 to increase the land area of the Singapore island by about 19 hectares. It was a test bed for an ambitious reclamation scheme that would move Singapore's entire eastern coastline several hundred metres towards the sea, thereby 'founding' massive virgin land for the rapidly developing new island-state. The mischievous Mat Sentul saw it fit to make physical jokes out on the still-to-be-developed plains, inadvertently subverting the nation-building ideals that often accompany these grand schemes for urban (re)development in land-hungry Singapore. ➾ ***Toh Hun Ping***

Directed by Mat Sentul

Scene description: Comedic subversion in Singapore's 'newfound land'

Timecode for scene: 0:05:45 – 0:06:54

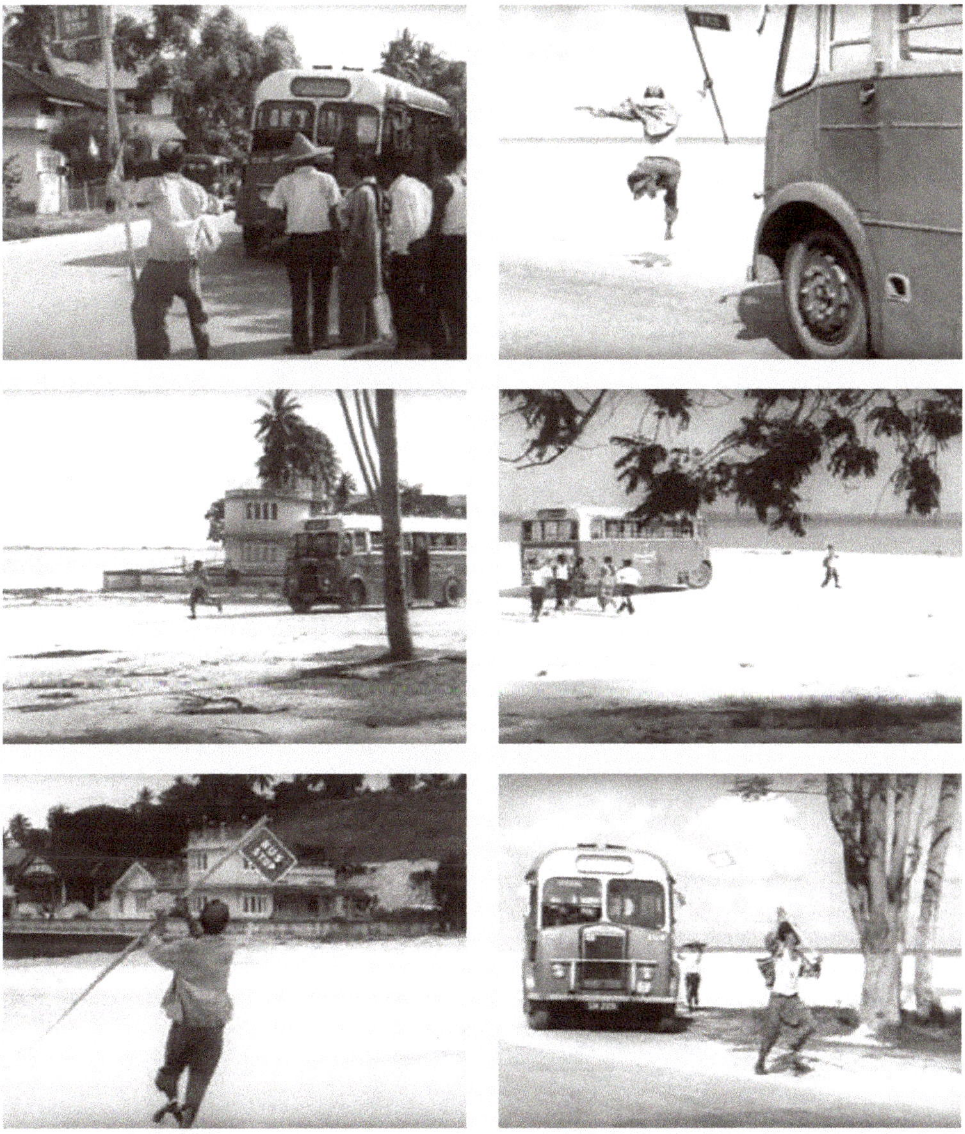

SO DARLING SO DEADLY AKA AGENTE JOE WALKER OPERAZIONE FAR EAST AKA KOMMISSAR X: IN DEN KLAUEN DES GOLDENEN DRACHEN (1966)

LOCATION

Tiger Balm Garden/Haw Par Villa, 262 Pasir Panjang Road

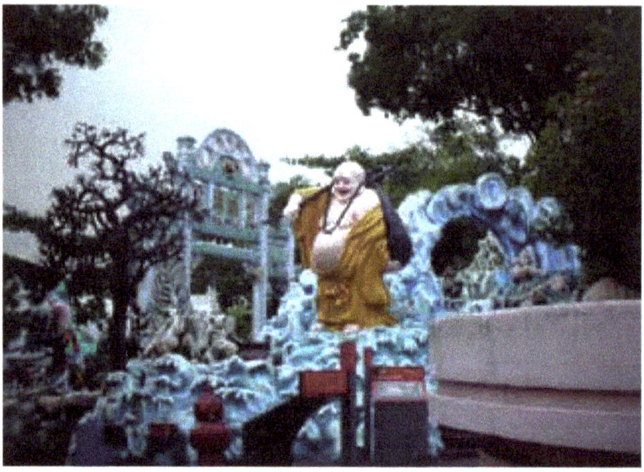

FROM THE 1960S ONWARDS, spies in movies were much like tourists. They landed in foreign, exciting countries and 'thrilling cities' (as Ian Fleming called them), and their adventures would lead them from one tourist attraction to another. After the success of Bond, thousands of 'superspy' imitators followed his jet-setting trail. While Hong Kong and Bangkok would be visited by 007 himself, Singapore had to make do with Agent Joe Walker aka Kommissar X, an American spy-cum-detective based on a popular series of German pulp fictions in a mostly Italian production starring American B-listers. Once they land at Payar Lebar Airport Walker (Tony Kendall) and his muscle-bound policeman sidekick (Brad Harris) cover a lot of ground, checking in at the Goodwood Park Hotel, getting lost in Chinatown and heading over to the then-named Tiger Balm Garden in pursuit of a double-agent, played by a Malay actor credited as 'H. Amin', presumably on loan from Cathay-Keris Studios. Opened in the late 1930s by the Aw brothers, who made their fortune from the menthol cream Tiger Balm, the site is better known as Haw Par Villa (after the brother's names). While our two heroes ineffectively run and balletically leap around the fountains above ground, below we get a glimpse of tourists among the notoriously graphic 'Hell' dioramas, which we're told by a dubbed tour guide was a 'torture chamber'. This is partly true, as the Villa scared generations of school children with its gory, grotesque scenes of sin and punishment. It's still open, although today in an era of Singapore's casinos and megahotels, no superspy would be seen dead there.
Ben Slater

Photo © Toh Hun Ping

Directed by Frank Kramer aka Gianfranco Parolini
Scene description: A chase though hell
Timecode for scene: 0:34:46 – 0:37:35

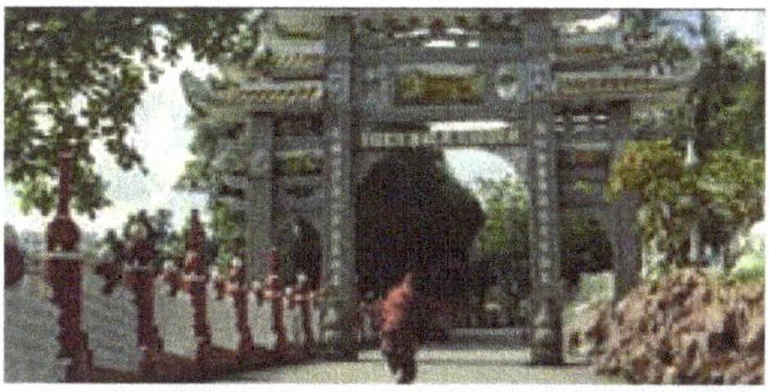
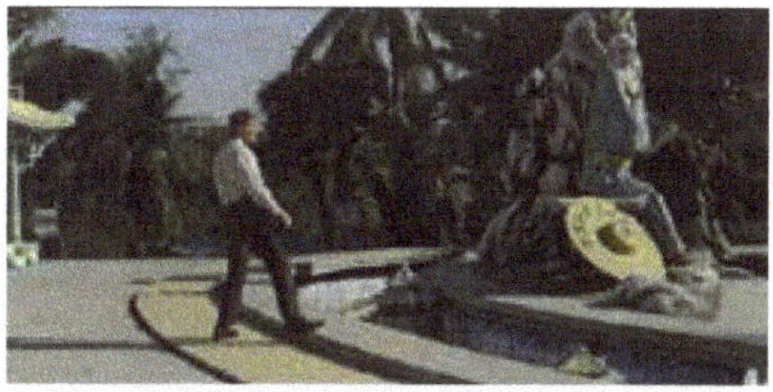
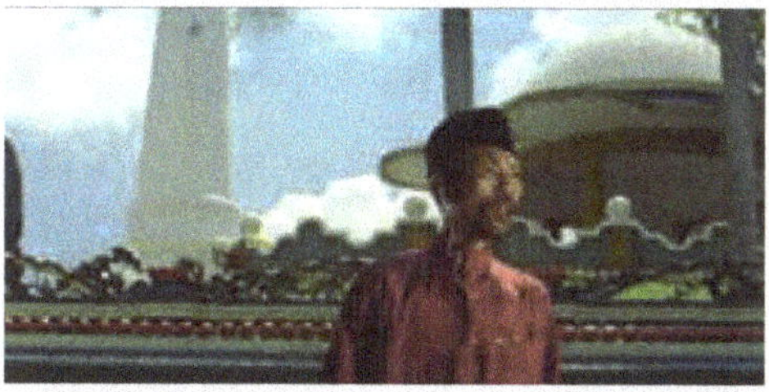
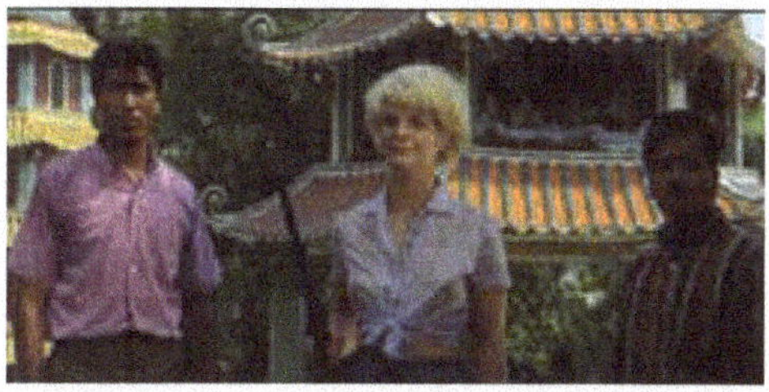
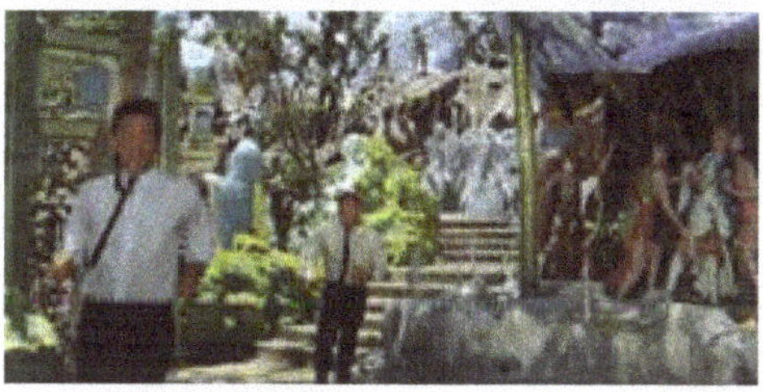
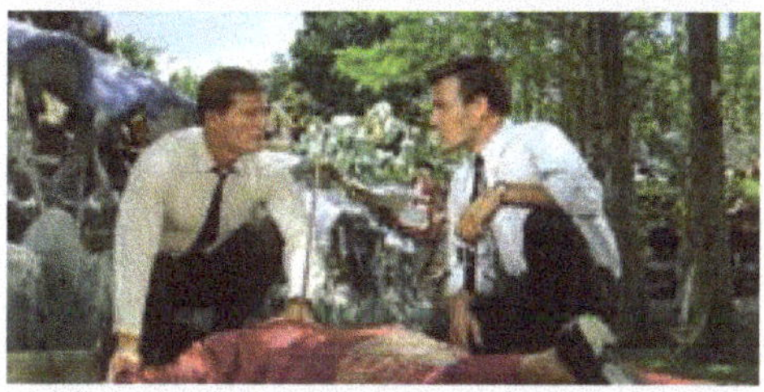
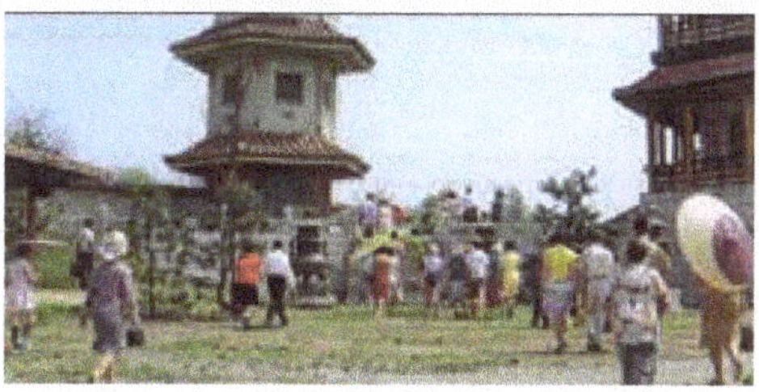
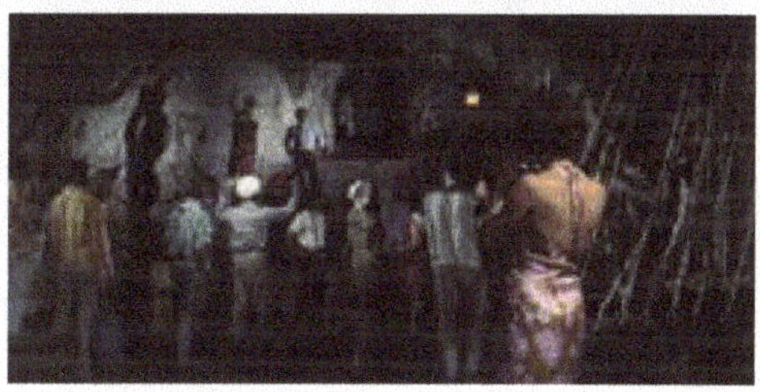

FIVE ASHORE IN SINGAPORE AKA CINQ GARS POUR SINGAPOUR AKA CINQUE MARINES PER SINGAPORE (1966)

LOCATION *Collyer Quay*

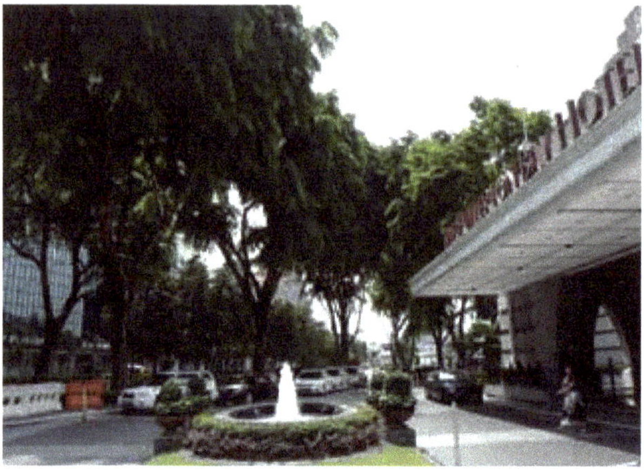

A WILD BUNCH OF MARINES led by Marc Michel and Sean Flynn stir up fights and brawls in public places in order to find their colleagues who disappeared mysteriously somewhere on the island. As historian Ben Slater observes, despite its loose spy plot 007-style – concocted by top Italian scribe Sergio Amidei following a pulp novel by French writer Jean Bruce – and its old-fashioned co-production conventions, *Five Ashore in Singapore* is frequently able to catch a 'tantalizingly real Singapore'. One year after its independence, the whole nation seems bursting with energy and *joie de vivre*. In its busy port avenues as well as along its crowded Chinatown sleazy bars, cinemas and food stalls, most people are staring amazed at these US 'tourists' treating them as Vietnamese enemies or sometimes allies. Producer Jean-Pierre Kalfon and director Bernard Toublanc-Michel, rooted as they are in the *nouvelle vague*'s stylistic approach, fancy to improvise most scenes on the spot. The frantic rhythm of bedlam – from a wild trishaw race to various brutal attacks and ambushes – owes much to 'Jessy Greek', alias Enzo Musumeci Greco, a renowned action director who also plays the bespectacled Chinese villain wearing a fez and an immaculate suit. This swordmaster who had taught Errol Flynn to spar, gets a chance to train the star's son Sean in this last film adventure. ➺***Lorenzo Codelli***

Photo © Toh Hun Ping

Directed by Bernard Toublanc-Michel

Scene description: Five marines arrive at Collyer Quay

Timecode for scene: 0:10:05 – 0:11:16

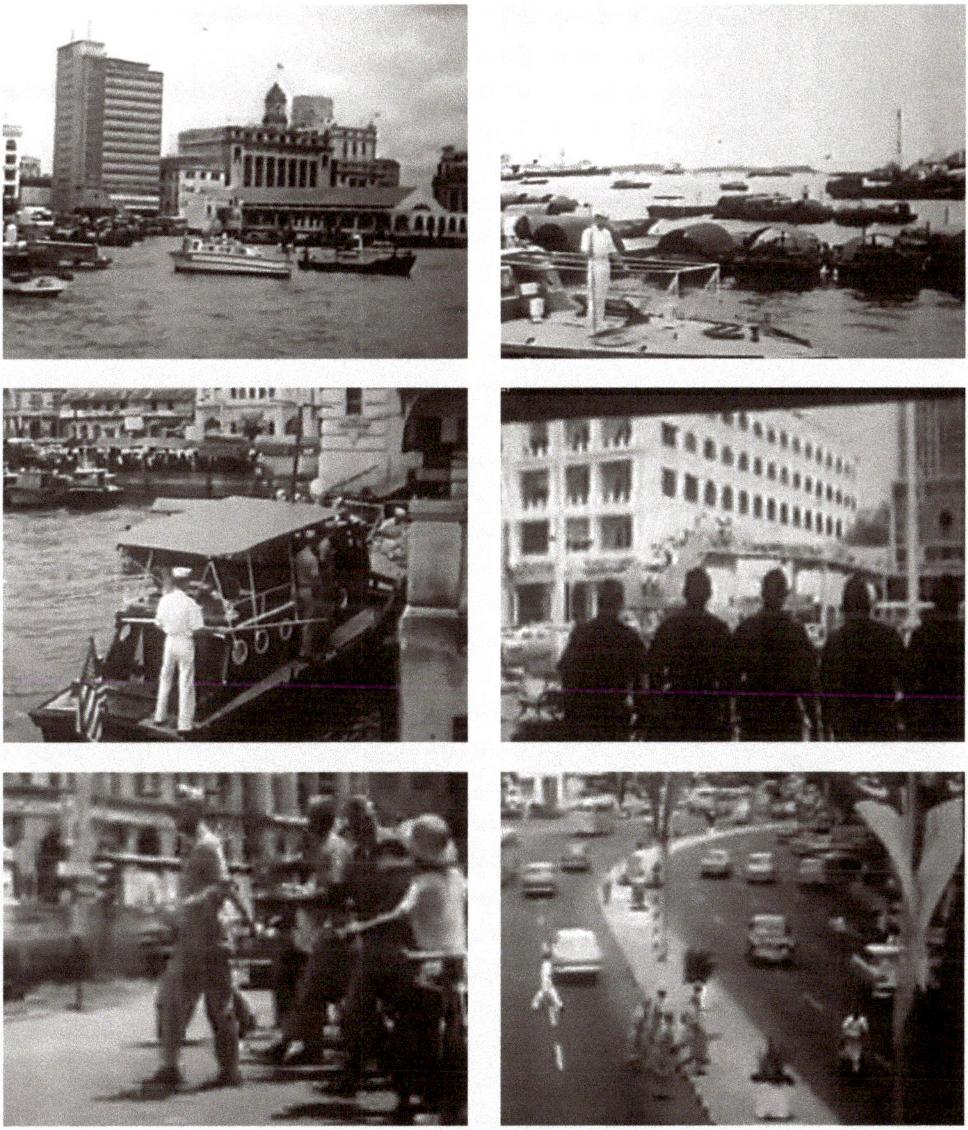

Images © 1966 Les Films Number One, Riganti Produzione Film

SPOTLIGHT

A HISTORY OF SAYING NO

Text by DANIEL HUI

Singapore International Film Festival and Censorship

SINGAPORE HAS LONG been known for its strict censorship laws. Yet, its cinema is currently experiencing a resurgence not seen since its heyday in the 1950s. Any discussion of this rapidly burgeoning film scene will be incomplete without examining the Singapore International Film Festival, which has almost single-handedly brought Singaporean cinema back into prominence since its inception. Founded in 1987 by Geoffrey Malone, the festival has been known for its long and storied battle with government censorship, and for its role in jumpstarting the careers of Singaporean auteurs such as Eric Khoo and Royston Tan. The festival had a policy of screening only uncensored films, bringing it into constant conflict with the censorship board.

Under the stewardship of Teo Swee Leng and Philip Cheah during its first twenty years, the Singapore International Film Festival had become known for its adventurous programming and its focus on Southeast Asian cinema. It quickly cultivated a cult following, screening local and foreign arthouse films in multiplexes such as Shaw Theatres and Golden Village. In 1991, the festival introduced the Silver Screen Awards with the aim of promoting film-making in Asia and paving the way for a Singaporean film industry. It was in the Singapore Short Films programme of this section where Khoo, eventually to become the first Singaporean film-maker selected to the Cannes Film Festival with *12 Storeys* (1997), had his first short films screened. However, the local censors did not immediately take to Khoo's provocative work. When the festival tried to programme his short film *Pain* (1994), it was immediately banned from public screening for its graphic portrayal of sadomasochism. Nevertheless, the festival still awarded it the Best Director and Special Achievement Awards, bringing it greater exposure to an international audience.

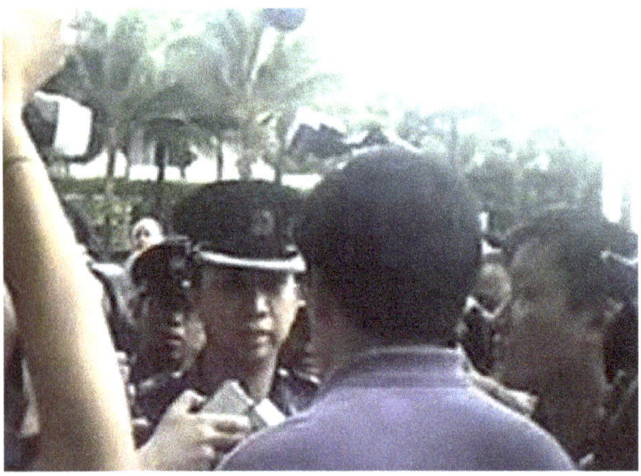

This would be the beginning of a trend that plagued the festival for years. In its drive to programme local films that showed a different reality from state-approved media, the festival repeatedly ran afoul of government censors. Films that contained sexually explicit (X'Ho's *Allen Ginsberg Gives Good Head* [2007]), political (Christina Mok, Mirabelle Ang and Tan Kai Syng's *A Vision of Persistence* [2001]) or gang-related (Royston Tan's *15* [2003]) content defied the censors' approval. The festival decided to refuse to screen censored films, and broadly publicized its withdrawal of these films. This created an unintended effect for the censors – instead of limiting public awareness of these films, the censors inadvertently created more publicity for the films.

This is especially true when the censors ordered the withdrawal of Martyn See's short

Opposite *Singapore Rebel* (2005) / **Below** *15* (2003)

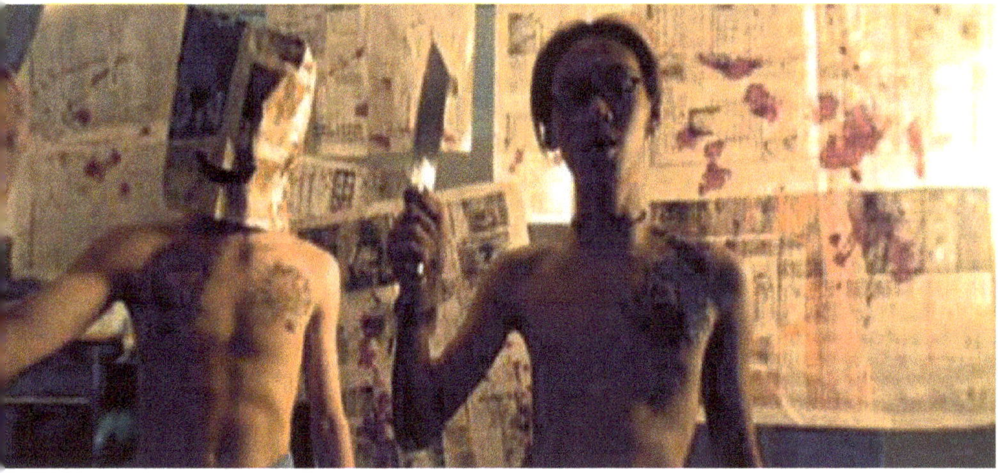

film, *Singapore Rebel* (2005), from the festival. The film, a portrait of prominent opposition politician Chee Soon Juan, was deemed a 'party political film' under Section 35(1) of the Films Act. This made it illegal for the festival to screen the film. See was placed under police investigation and forced to surrender his video camera and all footage he acquired during the shooting process. Because of the furore surrounding the film and the subsequent controversy that ensued, the film received extensive publicity in the press and even a response from Amnesty International Asia Pacific. The film was later circulated online and eventually posted on YouTube, garnering a large amount of views (over 360,000 views to date). The Media Development Authority (MDA) would later rescind the ban on *Singapore Rebel* and amend the Films Act, although the prohibition on making, distributing and exhibiting 'party political films' still exists. MDA has also since included more tiers to the ratings system it introduced in 1991, allowing more access to films that fall between adult-oriented cinema and family-friendly fare.

In its drive to programme local films that showed a different reality from state-approved media, the Singapore International Film Festival repeatedly ran afoul of government censors.

State censorship was not just restricted to Singaporean films, however. In the very first year of the festival, Singaporean censors had already demanded cuts to Istvan Szabo's Academy Award-winning *Mephisto* (1981) due to nudity. The film was subsequently withdrawn from the festival. This phenomenon would repeat itself year after year, with at least one film being either banned or withdrawn in protest of censorship. A well-known incident involves Ukrainian film-maker Kira Muratova travelling to Singapore for the screening of her film, *The Asthenic Syndrome* (1989), in the 1991 edition of the festival, only to realize that the Singaporean censors were demanding cuts to the film. Having fought against censorship in the Soviet Union all her life, she angrily demanded that her film be pulled from the festival, because she had not thought she would be faced with the same thing in the 'free world'.

Despite its constant battles with the state censors, the festival has staged successful coups with risky films that were unlikely to have been shown in Singapore. In 2000, the festival curated a groundbreaking program called 'Sex in Asian Cinema', showcasing Asian films that dealt with or featured sex. Although it still faced censorship – Jang Sun-woo's *Lies* (1999) was banned and Nagisa Oshima's *In the Realm of the Senses* (1976) was withdrawn due to cuts – the festival still managed to screen films that had never screened in Singapore before, such as Li Han Hsiang's seminal erotic film *Intimate Confessions of a Chinese Courtesan* (1972). The festival's 2003 retrospective of Pier Paolo Pasolini even showcased two films in the film-maker's famously sexually explicit *Trilogy of Life* (1971-1974), exposing Singaporean audiences to films that would have otherwise not made it to local cineplexes.

LOCATIONS MAP

SINGAPORE

maps are only to be taken as approximates

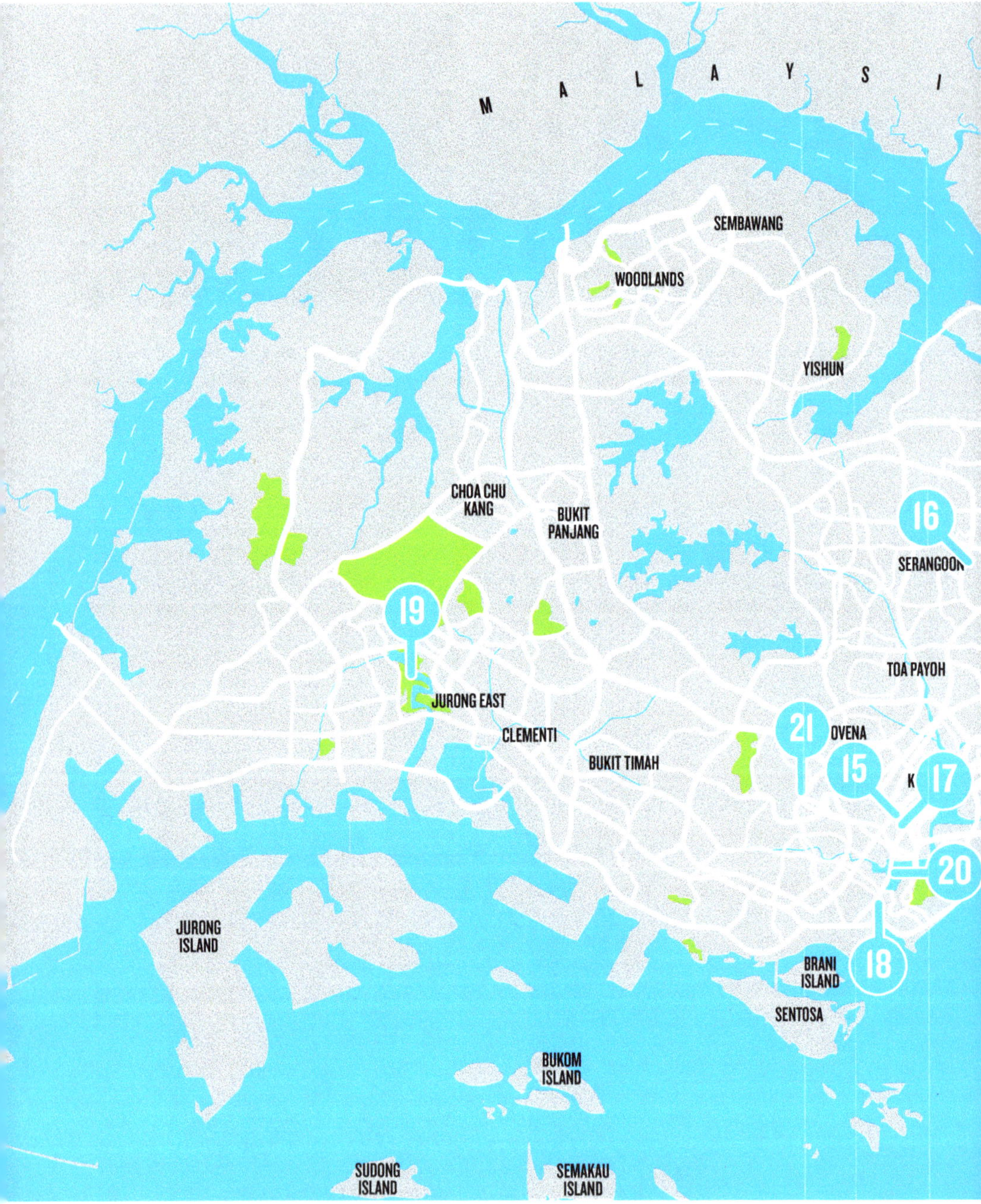

SINGAPORE LOCATIONS
SCENES 15-21

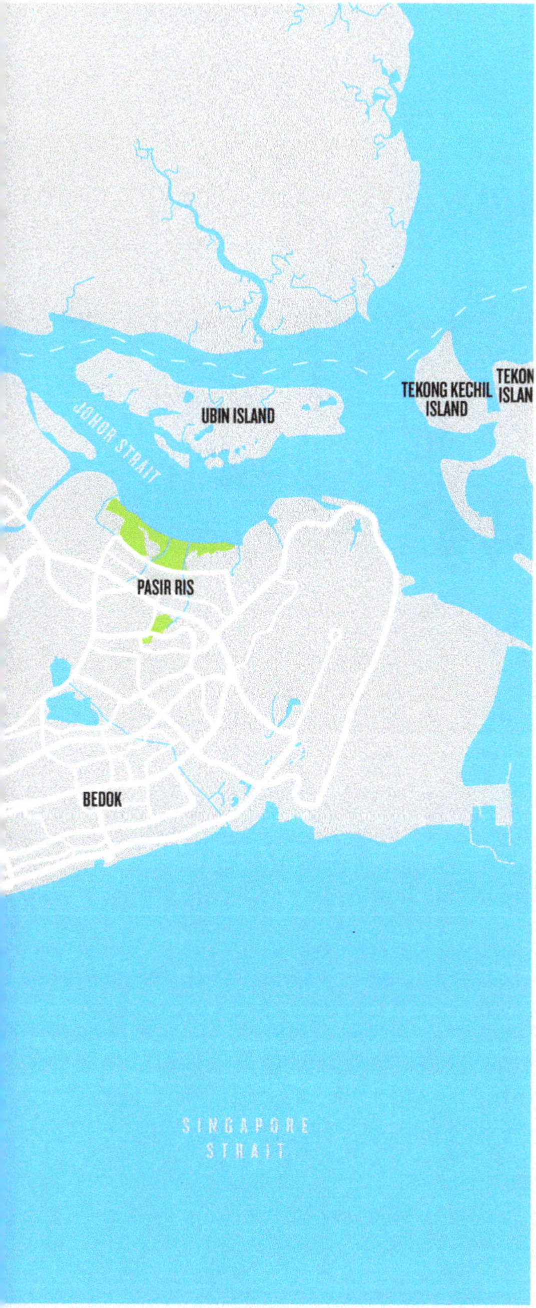

15.
PRETTY POLLY AKA A MATTER OF INNOCENCE (1967)
Bugis Street, Bugis Junction
page 48

16.
IN SEARCH OF THE UNRETURNED SOLDIERS IN MALAYSIA / MIKIKANHEI O OTTE (1971)
Paya Lebar Airport, Chinatown, Beach Road, Japanese Cemetery Park (Hougang), Changi Prison, Civilian War Memorial
page 50

17.
WIT'S END (1975)
Raffles Hotel, 1 Beach Road
page 52

18.
BLACK MAGIC 2 (1976)
Sidewalk opposite Shenton House, along Shenton Way, Central Business District
page 54

19.
THEY CALL HER... CLEOPATRA WONG (1978)
Chinese Gardens, Jurong
page 56

20.
SAINT JACK (1979)
Fullerton Quay, opposite the Fullerton Hotel
page 58

21.
THE LAST BLOOD (1990)
Orchard Road
page 60

PRETTY POLLY AKA A MATTER OF INNOCENCE (1967)

LOCATION

Bugis Street, Bugis Junction

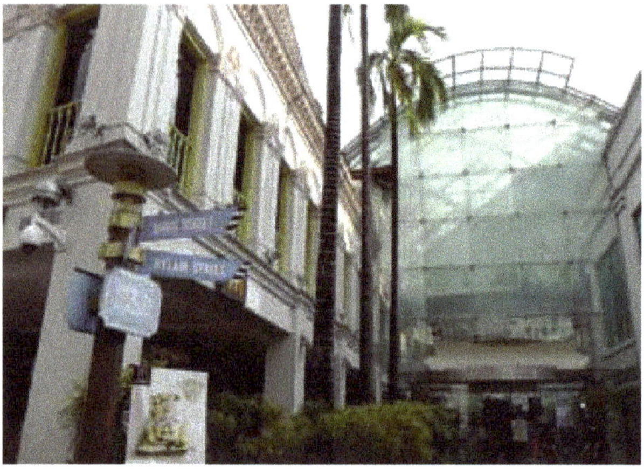

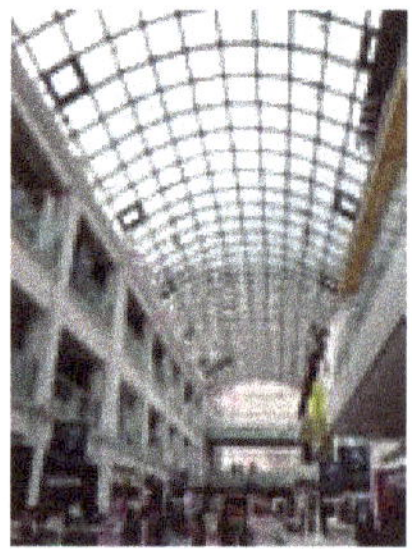

DESCRIBED IN 1957 by Dutch travel writer F.D. Ommanney as 'one of the most beautiful streets in the world', Bugis Street (often deliberately mispronounced 'Boogie Street'), was a very popular tourist attraction until it was closed in the 1980s. At night this back lane, not far from the city centre, was the site of open-air food and booze stalls, and a parade of 'ladies of the night' of ambivalent gender. Sailors and visitors flocked there, the girls became 'stars', and by the 1970s there were even Bugis Street postcards. Unsurprisingly, it fascinated visiting film-makers, and was memorably depicted in *Saint Jack* (Peter Bogdanovich, 1979) and nostalgically 'recreated' in Yonfan's *Bugis Street* (1995). One of the first films to feature the street was Guy Green's *Pretty Polly*, adapted from a short story, *Pretty Polly Barlow* by Noel Coward, published in 1964. The title character, played by former Disney starlet Hayley Mills, is a tourist (staying at Raffles Hotel) who begins a romance with a gigolo tour-guide, Amaz (Bollywood megastar, Sashi Kapoor). On her final night in Singapore, Amaz brings her to Bugis Street, describing it as 'an evil place'. As they arrive, documentary-style shots capture the bustle of the street and its glamorous, transgender denizens; bits of local colour are staged, such as a boy hustling tourists with a game of tic-tac-toe. As the long scene progresses a giddily tipsy Polly surrounded by various admirers, declares 'I've never been so happy in all my life.' It may have been 'evil', but it represented a freedom to live as you pleased. Sadly, today Bugis Street is covered by a shopping mall, and the 'New' Bugis Street, across the road, merely an emporium of tourist tat. ➻***Ben Slater***

Photo © Toh Hun Ping

Directed by Guy Green
Scene description: A visit to an evil, beautiful place
Timecode for scene: 1:09:06 – 1:16:50

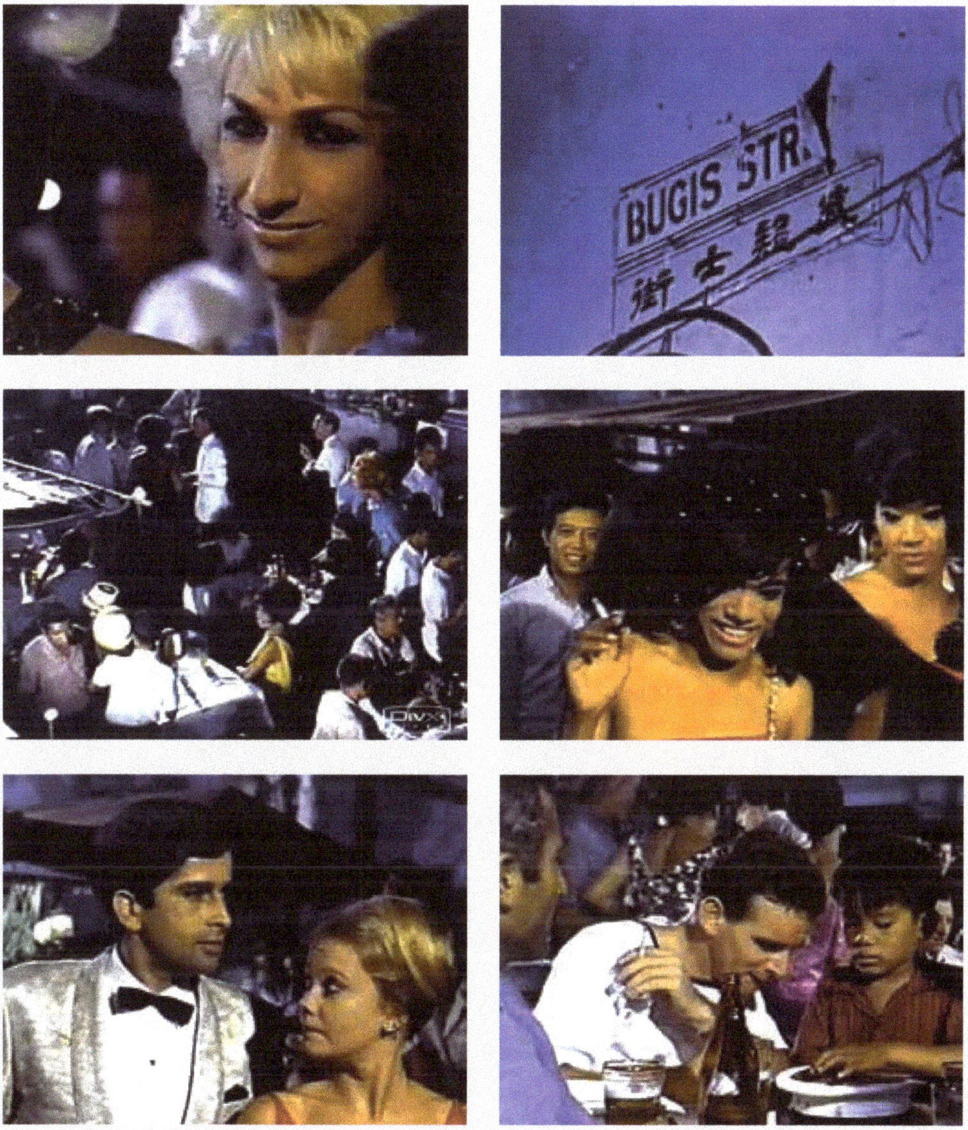

Images © 1967 Universal

IN SEARCH OF THE UNRETURNED SOLDIERS IN MALAYSIA / MIKIKANHEI O OTTE (1971)

LOCATION *Paya Lebar Airport, Chinatown, Beach Road, Japanese Cemetery Park (Hougang), Changi Prison, Civilian War Memorial*

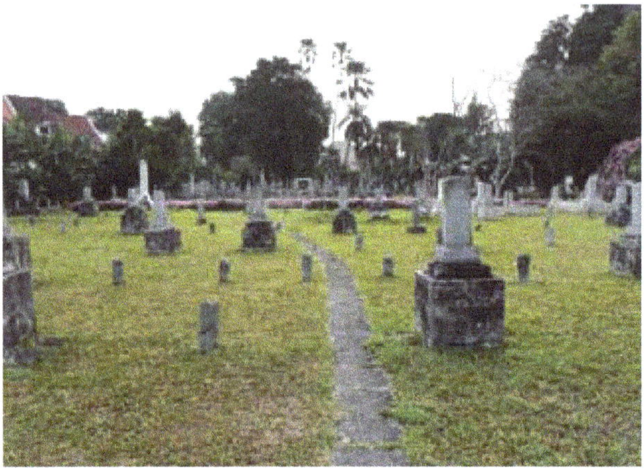

AFTER THE COMMERCIAL FAILURE of *The Profound Desire of the Gods* (1968), and the filming of a documentary, *History of Postwar Japan as Told by a Bar Hostess* (1970), Shohei Imamura decides to turn to television, which is currently hiring directors of the early-1960s generation to make documentaries. He directs seven between 1971 and 1979, before going back to feature film with *Vengeance is Mine* (1969), a masterpiece which will get him some national reputation and finally allow him access to international recognition thanks to festivals. All the documentaries are focused on one of his main concerns – to tell the story of the little, anonymous people, those forgotten by History, and who constitute the essence of the Japanese people. He thus focuses on the Japanese soldiers who refused to return to Japan after the defeat, or who did not know that their nation had lost the war, marginal men who sometimes openly violate the law. He also focuses on those prostitutes forced to serve soldiers outside of Japan, and who did not want to go back or were unable to afford a return ticket. All are victims of war who cannot – or do not want – to face what they often see as the decline of their nation. The prostitutes were landed in Singapore after being kidnapped in Japan and were then sent to other provinces, whereas the soldiers fled to Singapore at the end of the war to find work. Shohei Imamura is tracking their troubled destinies around the streets, the hotels and the war cemeteries of Singapore. ***Hubert Niogret***

Photo © Toh Hun Ping

Directed by Shohei Imamura
Scene description: The director goes all around town to meet some survivors
Timecode for scene: 0:0:01 – 0:19:08

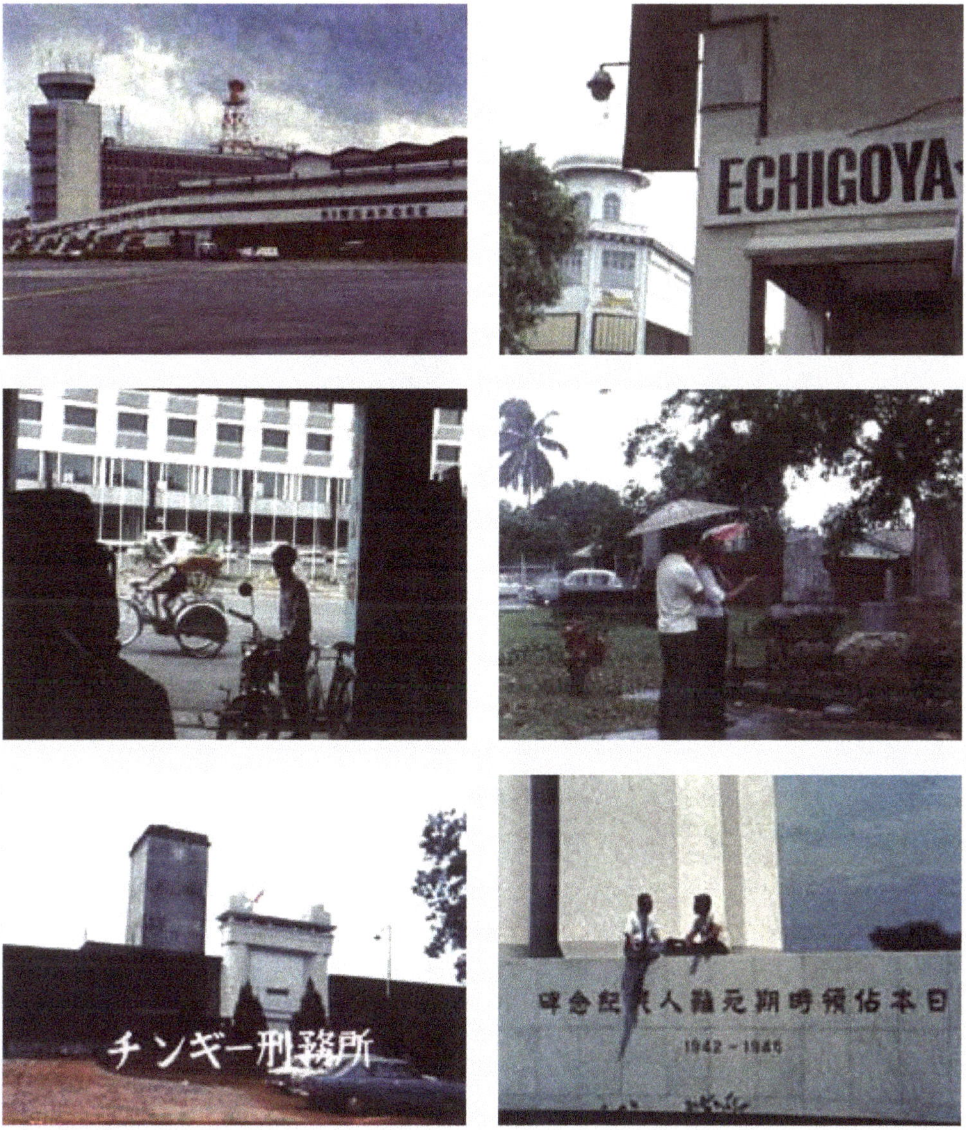

WIT'S END (1975)

LOCATION *Raffles Hotel, 1 Beach Road*

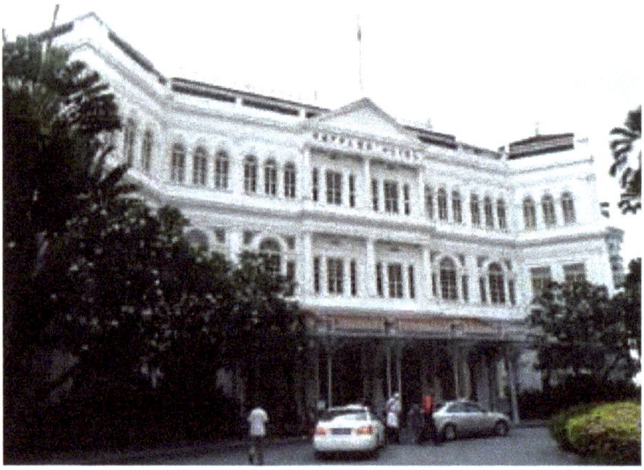

PROBABLY THE MOST peculiar film ever to be shot in Singapore was, until recently, one of the most forgotten. Available since the 1980s as a VHS under the (absurd) title *G.I. Executioner*, few realized that the B-movie, originally called *Wit's End*, had been entirely shot in Singapore on location in December 1969. The story, of a gone-to-seed Yank embroiled with gangsters and spies is a flimsy excuse for fights, chases and copious nudity. Incredibly, it had the support of Singapore's Cathay-Keris Studio, and among the myriad locations they shot in (Chinatown, Bugis Street, Arab Street, Collyer Quay, Upper East Coast Road), there's brief glimpses of Raffles Hotel. Founded at the end of the nineteenth century by a pair of Armenian traders, Raffles had an extraordinary 'Golden Age' in the pre-war years, feted as one of the great hotels of the world. From the 1960s to the 1980s, it retained its colonial charm, but had somewhat gone to seed. For *Wit's End*, they even show a prostitute soliciting in broad daylight right outside! Like most productions of the 1960s, they shot the interior and exterior of Raffles's temporary lobby, as the main entrance (grandly restored today, along with the rest of the building) was undergoing massive renovation during that period. In the scene, the hero has a hilariously stilted conversation with a British detective in the reception, complete with mural above the desk and 'RH' insignia on the carpet. Tellingly, the bedroom interiors and some of the exteriors were shot at Ocean View, a modern hotel miles away in the east of Singapore that looks absolutely nothing like Raffles. ➾ ***Ben Slater***

Photo © Toh Hun Ping

Directed by Joel M. Reed
Scene description: Bad acting in a famous hotel lobby
Timecodes for scene: 0:11:36 – 0:11:46 (the exterior shot); 0:48:02 – 0:48:39 (the interior and the Ocean View exterior)

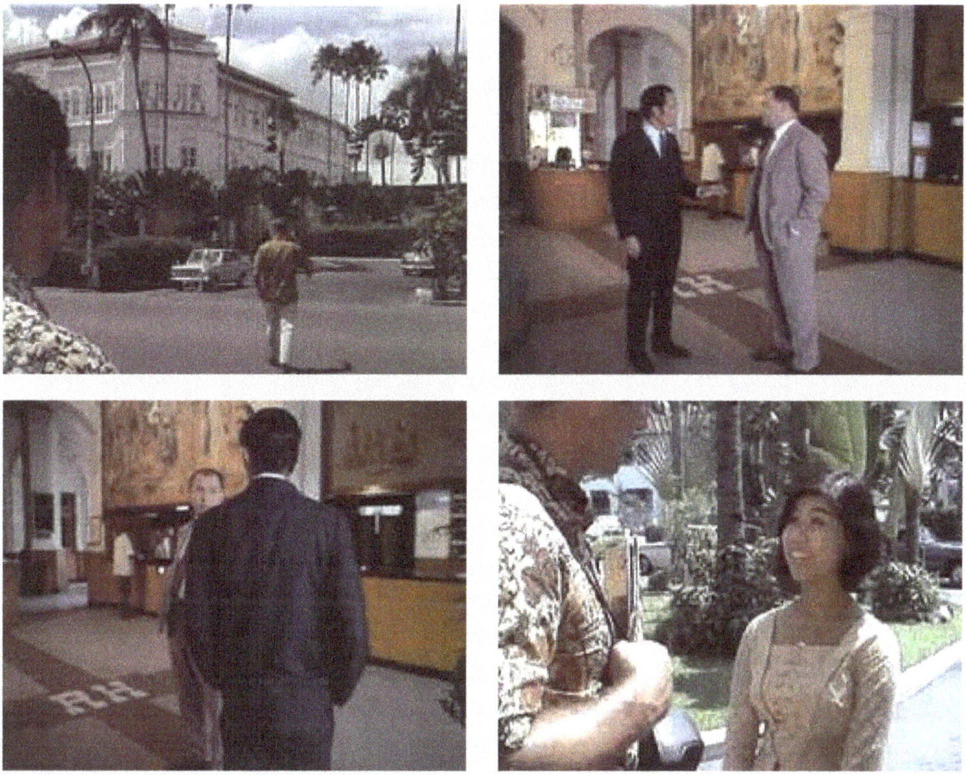

BLACK MAGIC 2 (1976)

LOCATION *Sidewalk opposite Shenton House, along Shenton Way, Central Business District*

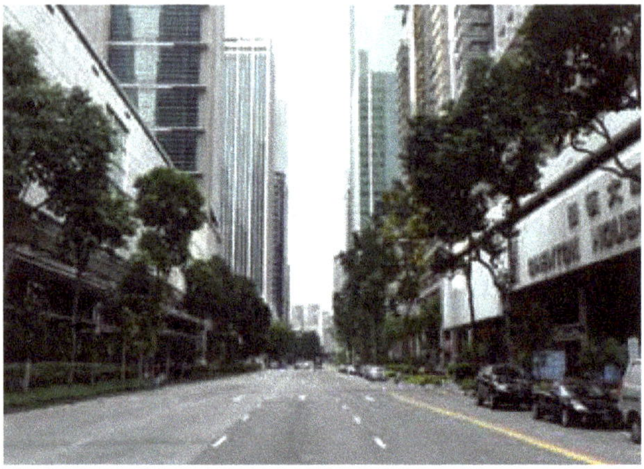

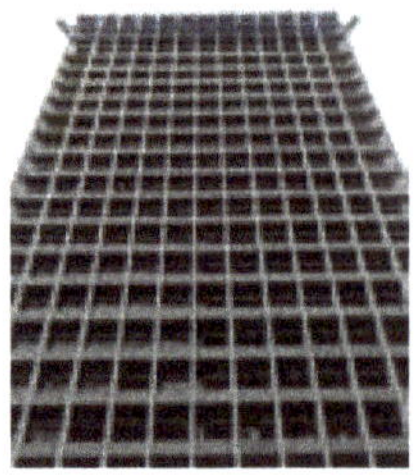

BLACK MAGIC 2 is a horror-exploitation cult thriller set in a nameless, modernized tropical city. Partly shot in Singapore, the film imagines the quintessential modern city as an urban locale besieged by rampant traditional witchcraft and evil sorcery. A group of doctors trained in western medicine are split between believing in the existence of occult 'black magic' – rumoured to be practised by witch doctors in South East Asia – or keeping faith with modern science to find the cure for the strange illnesses that victims in the city are afflicted with. In a particular scene shot along Shenton Way in the heart of Singapore's new financial district, a man is struck by a bout of delirium and vertigo, seemingly possessed by malicious spirits. He collapses amongst newly completed brutalist-style skyscrapers as his scalp and fingernails fall off, and his body dissolves into a mix of blood, soil and other gluey substances. Shenton Way opened in 1951 on land that was reclaimed from the old Telok Ayer Basin. It was dubbed 'Singapore's Wall Street' after many commercial financial institutions, such as the Development Bank of Singapore, based their operations there. If taken out of the diegetic context of the film, this scene of the spell-stricken man in Shenton Way could have been an expression of the underlying malaise felt by certain sections of the 1970s Singapore population – alienated by the rapidly modernizing and perpetually changing environs, and exasperated by the city-state's chase for the 'economic miracle' that was expected to be advanced by the burgeoning financial (greed) industry. ***Toh Hun Ping***

Photos © Toh Hun Ping

Directed by Ho Meng-hua
Scene description: Struck by a spell in Singapore's prime financial district
Timecode for scene: 0:41:23 – 0:42:58

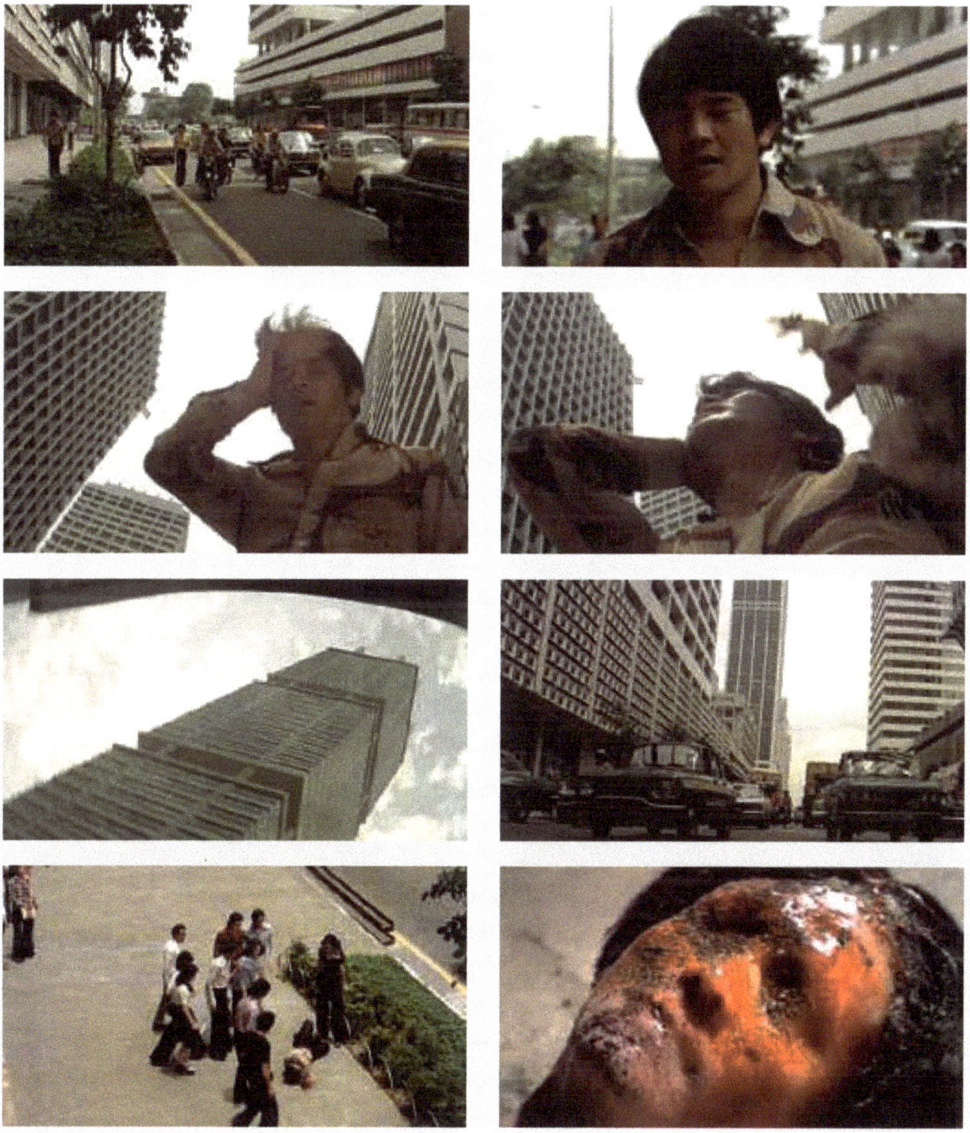

Images © 1976 Shaw Brothers (Hong Kong)

THEY CALL HER... CLEOPATRA WONG (1978)

LOCATION *Chinese Gardens, Jurong*

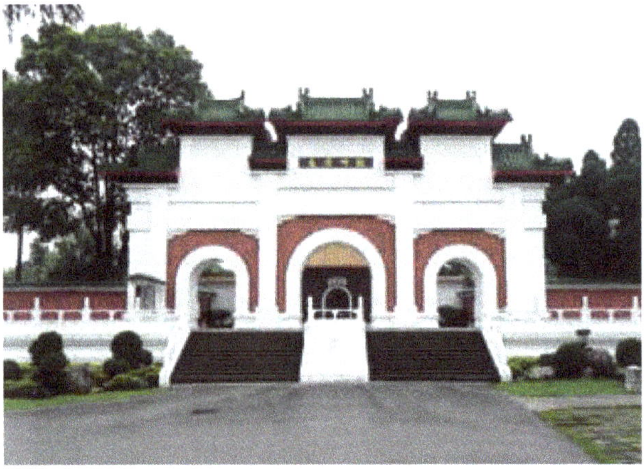

AN AMALGAMATION OF TV's *Charlie's Angels*, blaxploitation queen Cleopatra Jones and the Shaw Brothers' martial arts starlets, 'Cleopatra Wong' was the invention of an ambitious Filipino B-movie powerhouse, Bobby A. Suarez. He envisioned making English-language South East Asia-based action films that could be globally exported, and hooked up with Singaporean producer 'Sonny' Lim, first with *Bionic Boy* (1977), which featured a 9-year-old karate champ, and second with Cleo herself, played by a plucky young actress, Doris Yong, swiftly renamed 'Marrie Lee' (after Bruce Lee) in a trilogy (a fourth was shot but never completed), that has the surreal energy and demented logic of Saturday morning kids' cartoons. Suarez didn't spend a lot of money, but he had an army of 'goons' (Filipino movie parlance for tough guy stuntmen), a vast catalogue of funky soundtrack music and an eye for attractive backdrops. Cleo's mission begins in Singapore, investigating counterfeit cash (that threatens to destablize the ASEAN nations), and this brings her from Payar Lebar Airport to Orchard Road, along the Padang, the (now demolished) Seaview Hotel on East Coast Road, onto the cable car to Sentosa, from where she's improbably driven to Chinese Gardens in Jurong, the lair of the villain, and actually a peaceful civic park opened in 1975. Here, the snarling bad-guy challenges Cleo's fighting skills with Indian wrestlers and an entire Judo school, before she makes a superhuman leap over the wall, and escapes on a motorbike. Despite the film's (and the sequels') success, in a few years Suarez and Lim would part ways, as would Suarez and Yong, and Singapore would miss out on being at the heart of this extraordinary B-movie universe. It was the last Singapore-produced feature film for over a decade. ➻***Ben Slater***

Directed by George Richardson aka Bobby A. Suarez
Scene description: Cleo versus the Goons at Chinese Gardens
Timecode for scene: 0:16:10 – 0:21:53

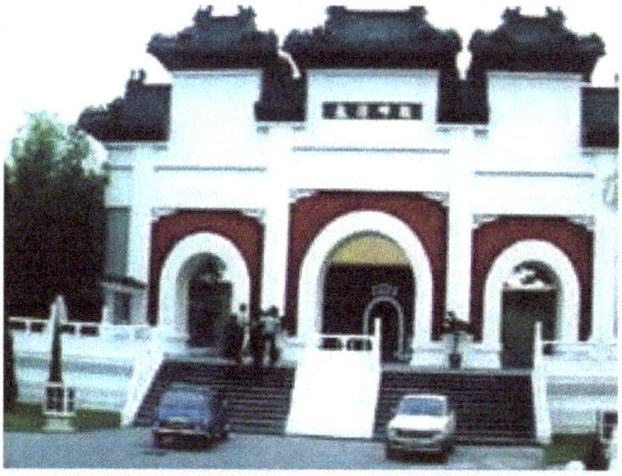

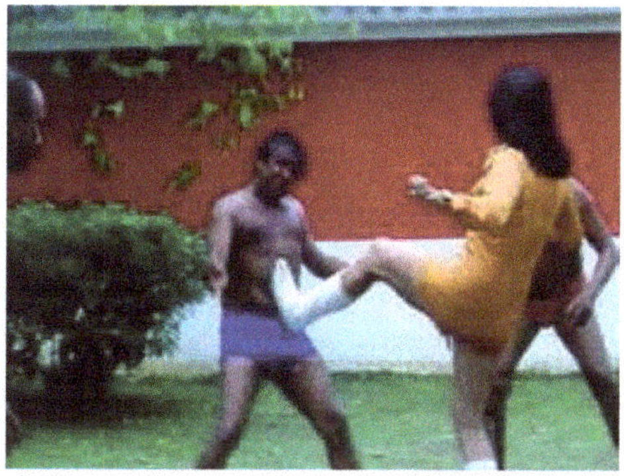

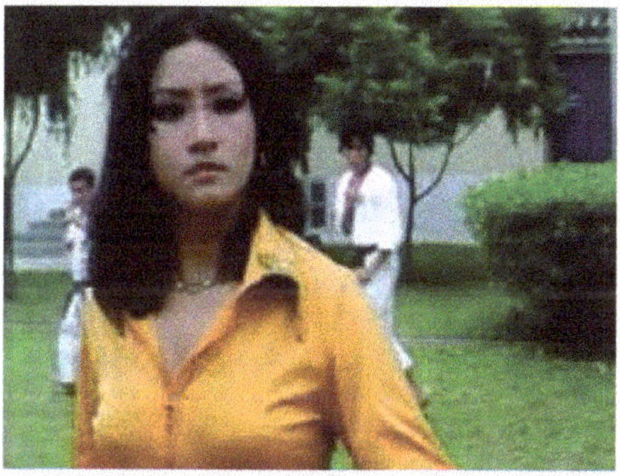

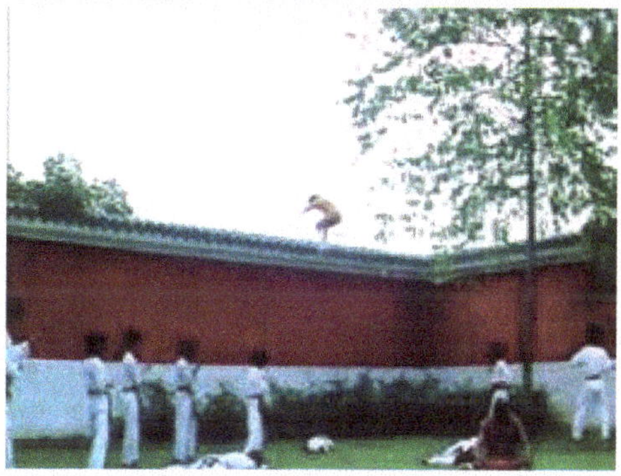

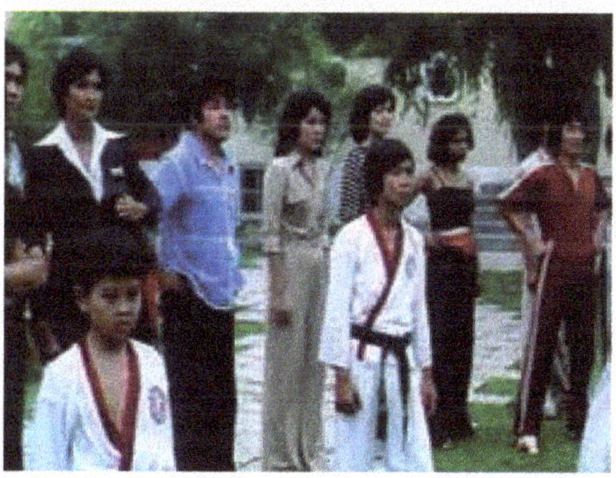

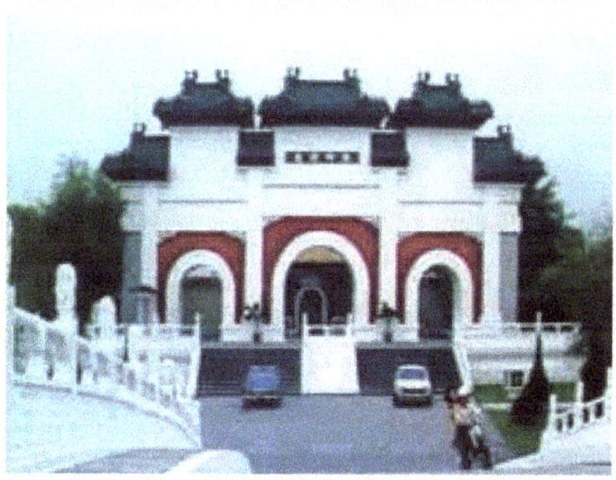

SAINT JACK (1979)

LOCATION *Fullerton Quay, opposite the Fullerton Hotel*

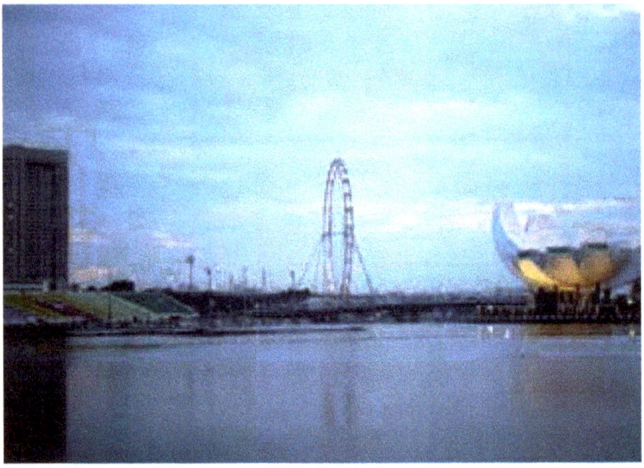

BANNED FOR NEARLY THIRTY YEARS in Singapore, Peter Bogdanovich's adaptation of Paul Theroux's 1973 novel of the same name is the most notorious film shot in the Lion City. In telling the story of an American pimp (Jack Flowers played by Ben Gazzara) hustling across the landscape of the post-independence republic, Bogdanovich was determined to show what he believed to be 'the real Singapore' and illicitly shot the entire film on location. The old waterfront, facing the sea, was still a working harbour in 1978 (when the film was made) and appears twice. Towards the end, Jack goes to pass incriminating photographs to the smug CIA spook Eddie Schuman (Bogdanovich himself). They're supposed to meet at the quayside directly in front of the magnificent colonial General Post Office (now the luxury Fullerton Hotel). Eddie nonchalantly waits on a bench beside the Fullerton Road sign, behind him are dozens of bumboats. Jack crosses to the traffic island but goes no further, calling out 'Fuck it' and heading back the way he came, thus saving his soul. Two days after filming wrapped, Bogdanovich returned at dawn with cinematographer Robby Müller, and created the 360-degree pan which became the film's opening sequence. We move from the boats on the bay around to the vehicles on the streets, listening to the sounds of Singapore waking up. A mysterious and foreboding shot, it perfectly expresses the city-state – from the sea onto the land, from the past into the future. Today the traffic's still there, but the boats are long gone, replaced by a hotel-casino complex that Jack could only dream about.
→ *Ben Slater*

Photo © Toh Hun Ping

Directed by Peter Bogdanovich

Scene description: Jack Flowers saves his soul/the opening titles

Timecodes for scene: 0:00:09 – 0:01:43 (opening titles); 1:50:00 – 1:50:58 (Jack saves his soul)

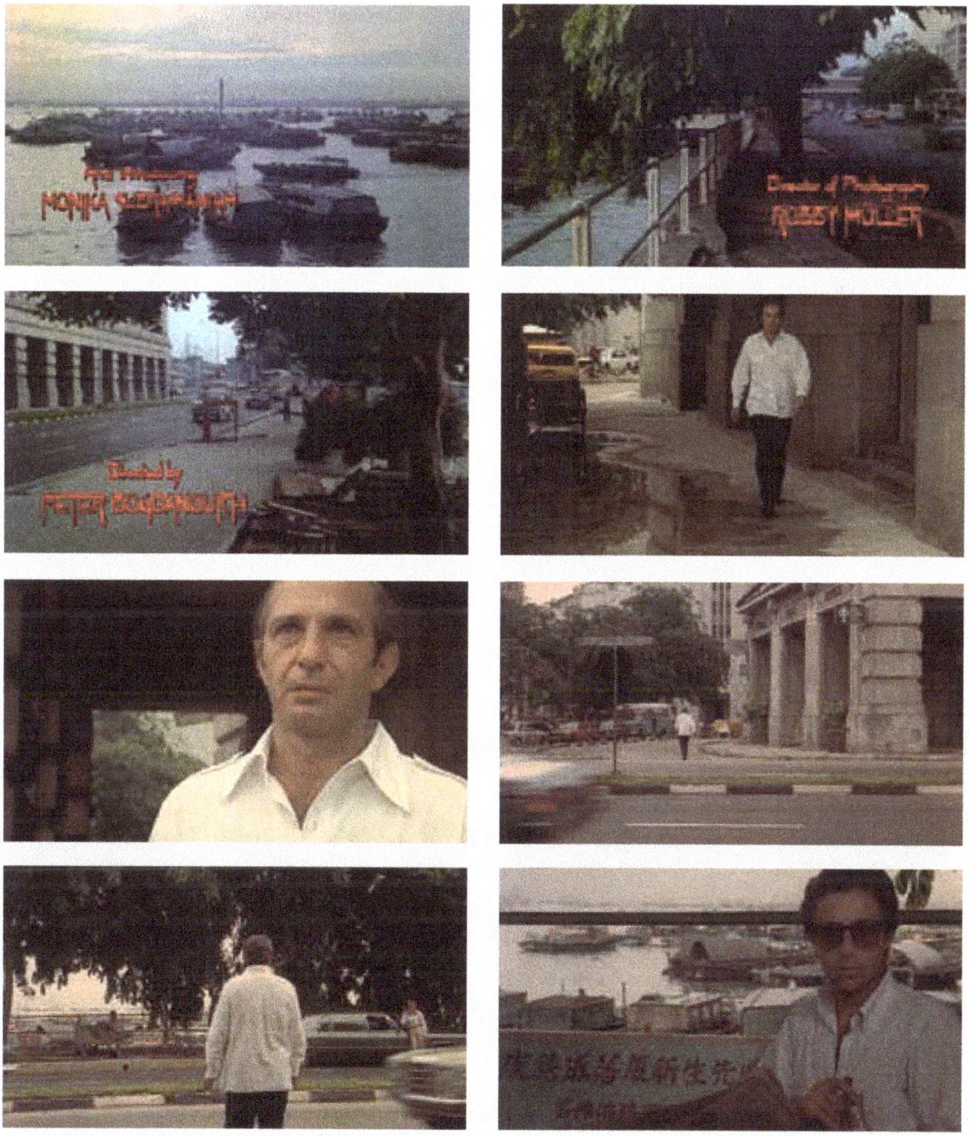

THE LAST BLOOD (1990)

LOCATION *Orchard Road*

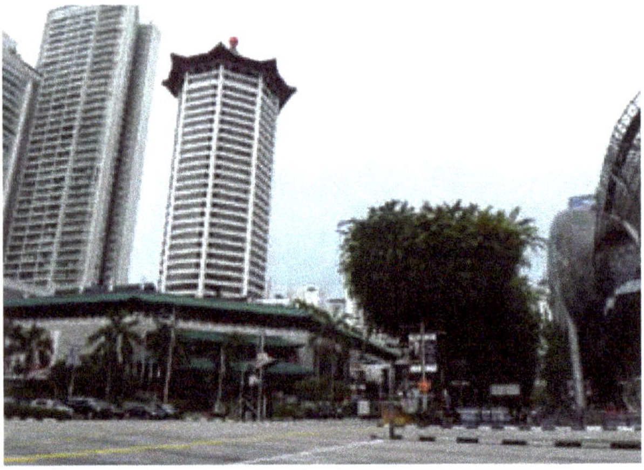

AT THE TURN OF THE 1990S, Singapore's Economic Development Board (EDB) began to attract Hong Kong film companies to set up branches locally, with an eye to the anticipated 'migration wave' from Hong Kong before the 1997 handover to China. *The Last Blood* was produced by one such company (Movie Impact) and was the first EDB-backed collaborative production that was largely shot on location in Singapore. Written and directed by the prolific schlockmeister Wong Jing, this comedic, gun-friendly action flick is a somewhat crass response to the global issues of the day (international terrorism, Tibetan sovereignty). Lui Tai (Alan Tam) is an Interpol agent tasked to stop Japanese Red Army terrorists from assassinating a religious leader 'Daka Lama' (a thinly veiled reference to the Dalai Lama). He crosses paths with Bee (Andy Lau), whose girlfriend is a victim of the terrorists' homicidal exploits. They are pursuing the sole surviving person in Singapore who shares a rare blood-type with Daka Lama and Bee's girlfriend, both dying from gunshot wounds. The pyro-laden chase leads them to some of Singapore's most promotion-worthy tourist spots – Sentosa, Padang, Raffles Place, Singapore River... and Orchard Road, the internationally renowned shopping district, where a (real) countdown party is taking place to celebrate the country's 25th anniversary of independence. Once a year , between 1988 and 1991, Orchard Road would be pedestrianized for 'Swing Singapore', a government-sanctioned street bash that welcomed toiling, hardworking citizens to let their hair down, while indulging in nation-building propaganda. The film returns to the Orchard Road party after the villains are killed in the final shootout. A happy ending ensues, complete with more pyrotechnics, balloons, confetti and all. ➻ ***Toh Hun Ping***

Directed by Wong Jing
Scene description: Spotting the wanted man in a National Day party crowd
Timecodes for scene: 0:55:55 – 0:57:30; 1:27:27 – 1:27:55

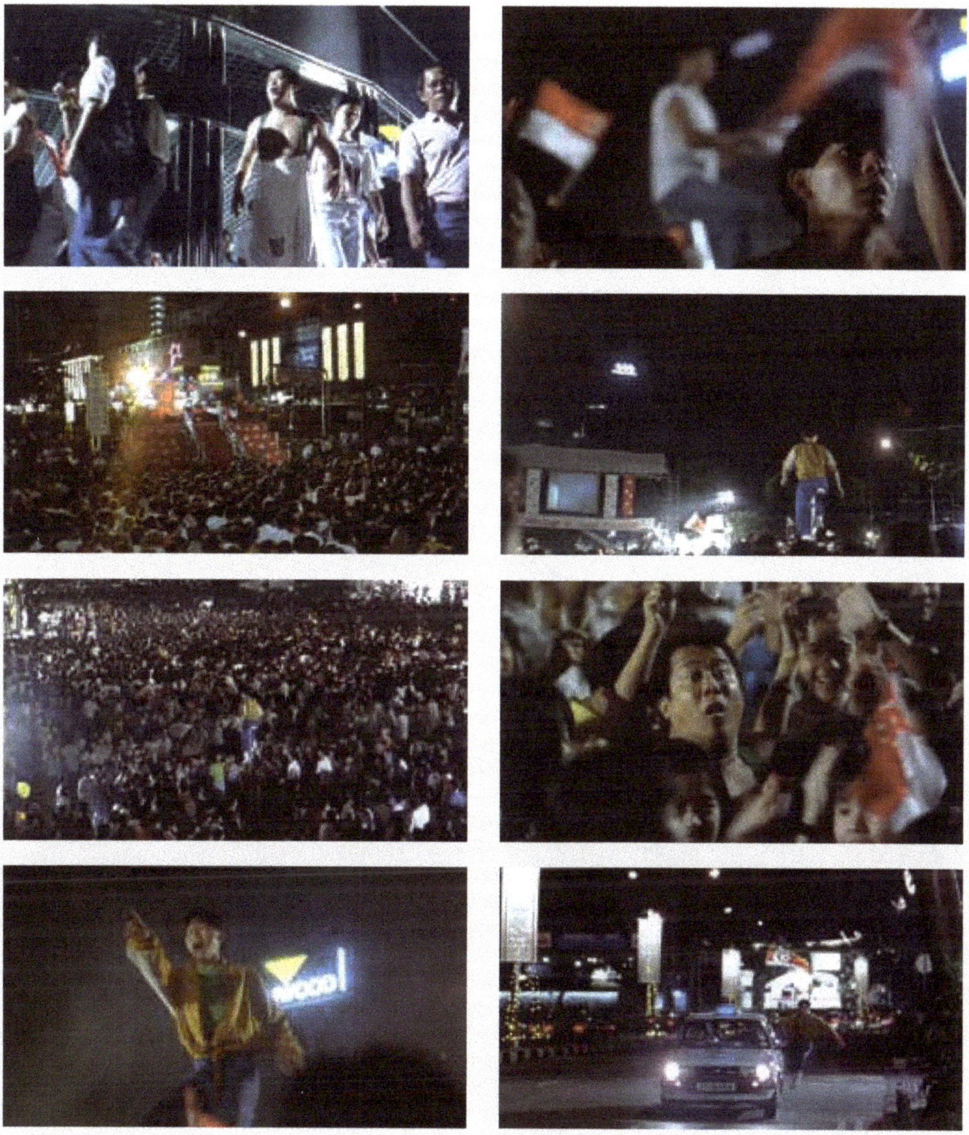

SPOTLIGHT

ERIC KHOO

Text by SILVIA WONG

An (Un)typically Singaporean View

IN A COUNTRY WHERE EATING is a serious business, food is a recurrent theme for Singapore auteur Eric Khoo. The titular *Mee Pok Man* (1995) runs a noodle stall; the elderly widower in *Be with Me* (2005) finds a life purpose again through cooking homemade dishes for the blind-and-deaf Theresa Chan; and Hainanese curry rice with multiple layers of sauces becomes a main inspiration in his latest telemovie *Recipe* (2013)..

As a foodie himself, Khoo is particularly drawn to old coffee shops and eating places which bring back memories of his childhood from a bygone age. One of his favourite filming locations is the Mee Pok Man coffee shop, easily one of the oldest in Singapore, which serves as the main set where a noodle seller meets and falls in love with a low-class prostitute.

'Landscape is crucial. It adds flavour to storytelling and characterization,' says Khoo who effectively put Singapore on the international film scene through his feature debut *Mee Pok Man* which was screened in over thirty film festivals, including Venice and Berlin. It also won prizes at Busan, Fukuoka and Singapore.

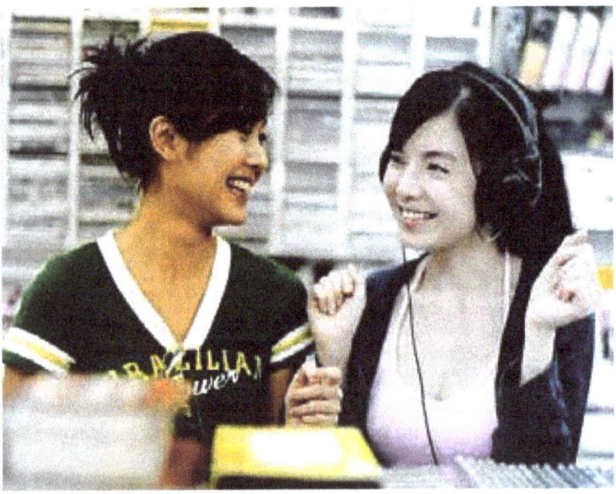

When envisioning the atmosphere for the film, 'it's deliberate to capture the old flair of Singapore – to create a world that is not Orchard Road,' he adds. 'Only at the end of the film did we show Shenton Way and modern buildings as a contrast to the rest of the film.' *Mee Pok Man* also featured plenty of exteriors of red-light district Geylang.

The world in which his characters inhabit is often government flats built by the Housing and Development Board (HDB). His second feature *12 Storeys* (1997) follows three families who live in a typical HDB block which is 12-storey high with a long common corridor on each level.

It was Khoo's plan to use just one location, cutting down on the downtime from location move. An ideal place was found on Stirling Road with HDB blocks 172–74 ending up as the primary filming location. Much of the film's interiors (including the entire story of the sister's keeper) and exteriors (including the outdoor playground and the coffee shop) were shot here. The other two locations Kim Tian Road in Tiong Bahru and Shunfu Road near Thompson were used only as the interiors for the China bride story and for the old lady story respectively.

12 Storeys became the first Singapore film to travel to the Cannes Film Festival when it was played at Un Certain Regard in 1997. But Khoo then took a long break from the director's chair to focus on producing, such as local box office hits *Liang Po Po:The Movie* and *One Leg Kicking*, Royston Tan's first feature *15* (2003), as well as TV series *Drive* and *Seventh Month*.

After a hiatus of eight years, Khoo returned to the big screen with *Be with Me* which was selected as the opening film of Directors' Fortnight, a sidebar of the Cannes Film Festival. Unlike his previous films, this time he aimed to create a different architecture by putting diverse locations together to reflect the stories involving characters

Opposite *Be With Me* (2005) / **Below** *My Magic* (2008)

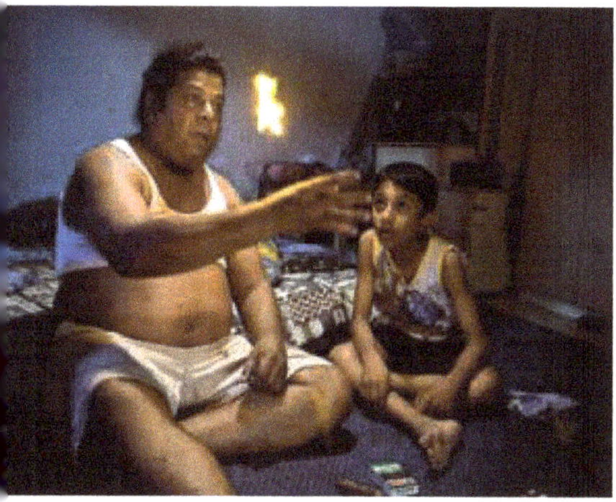

from three generations. These include a 1950s-style terrace house near Patterson Road for the teenager; an HDB on Farrer Road for the middle-aged security guard; and an old provision shop in Tiong Bahru for the ageing couple.

As an old residential estate in which the old coffee shop and the fresh food market described in *Mee Pok Man* are situated, Tiong Bahru holds a special place in Khoo's heart. He spent a good deal of his childhood in the area which was where his maternal grandmother used to live. He also likes its 1940s art deco architecture.

If *Be with Me* presents a nice-looking map of Singapore, *My Magic* (2008) brought him back to the earlier hard world as illustrated in his first two films. The protagonist is a dark and gloomy figure and his HDB was shot in a tiny one-room flat on Mei Ling Road near Queenstown. Where he performs as a magician was filmed in Orchard Towers, a sleazy transgender pub with murals painted on the wall. Exterior shots were taken in Little India along Serangoon Road.

The American painter Edward Hopper has much influence over Khoo. 'He is a master at mood lighting and atmosphere. I love the loneliness his paintings evoke. Both *Mee Pok Man* and *My Magic* were inspired by his works,' says Khoo who named his eldest son after the reclusive painter. (Khoo's production outfit Zhao Wei Films, in turn, is named after his son's Chinese name.)

While *My Magic* took Khoo's career to new heights as it was the first film from Singapore screened in competition at Cannes, his production budget remained modest. The film was shot in a short nine days.

Given the shoestring budget, it is important 'to go into a space where pretty much everything is there and limit the work for art direction,' Khoo says. Equally important for him is filming on location, which is a cheaper alternative to building sets in Singapore.

With the rapid social and economic developments, Singapore's cityscape is fast changing. Many of the locations featured in Khoo's films have since disappeared. The HDB blocks on Stirling Road have been demolished for redevelopment; the terrace house near Patterson Road is now a luxury condominium complex; and the provision shop has become a bakery.

With the rapid social and economic developments, Singapore's cityscape is fast changing. Many of the locations featured in Khoo's films have since disappeared.

One iconic building, the New 7th Storey Hotel, provided its exterior for the opening credits of *Mee Pok Man*. Once the tallest hotel in the Rochoer Road area when it was built in 1953, it had to close its doors in 2008 to make way for MRT (Mass Rapid Transit) expansion.

One location even disappeared almost overnight. The scene in which *Mee Pok Man* is beaten up by the gangsters was filmed in a back alley between two rows of shophouses in Newton Circus. When Khoo and his team went back for pick-up shots one week later, one row of shophouses was demolished. While the other row was still standing, the alleyway was no longer there. Now it is vacant land.

All is not lost fortunately. The Mee Pok Man coffee shop, located at Moh Guan Terrace, is designated as part of the Tiong Bahru Heritage Trail by the National Heritage Board. It is still operating as a noodle place in the morning although a Japanese yakitori restaurant takes over at night. Also still in business is the old Hainanese curry rice stall at Beo Crescent, which was featured in *Recipe* along with its wonderful food.

In addition to Zhao Wei Films which produced all his films, Khoo set up a new production company, Gorylah Pictures, in 2009 with post-production house Infinite Frameworks. Specializing in genre films, Gorylah Pictures has recently produced films shot in Singapore (*Ghost Child*) as well as abroad (*Darah* and *23:59* were filmed in Indonesia and Malaysia respectively). ✢

N

LOCATIONS MAP

SINGAPORE

maps are only to be taken as approximates

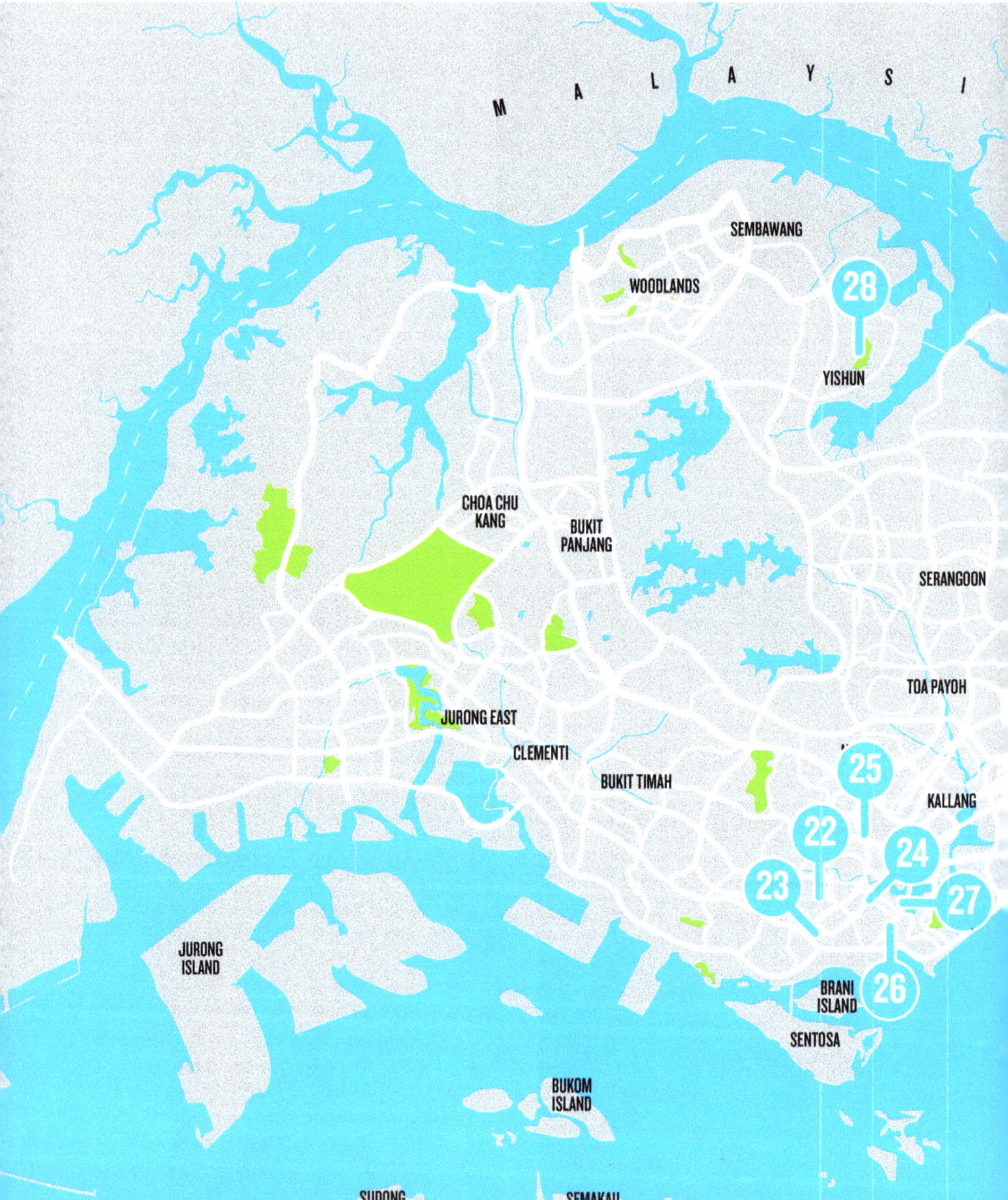

SINGAPORE LOCATIONS
SCENES 22-28

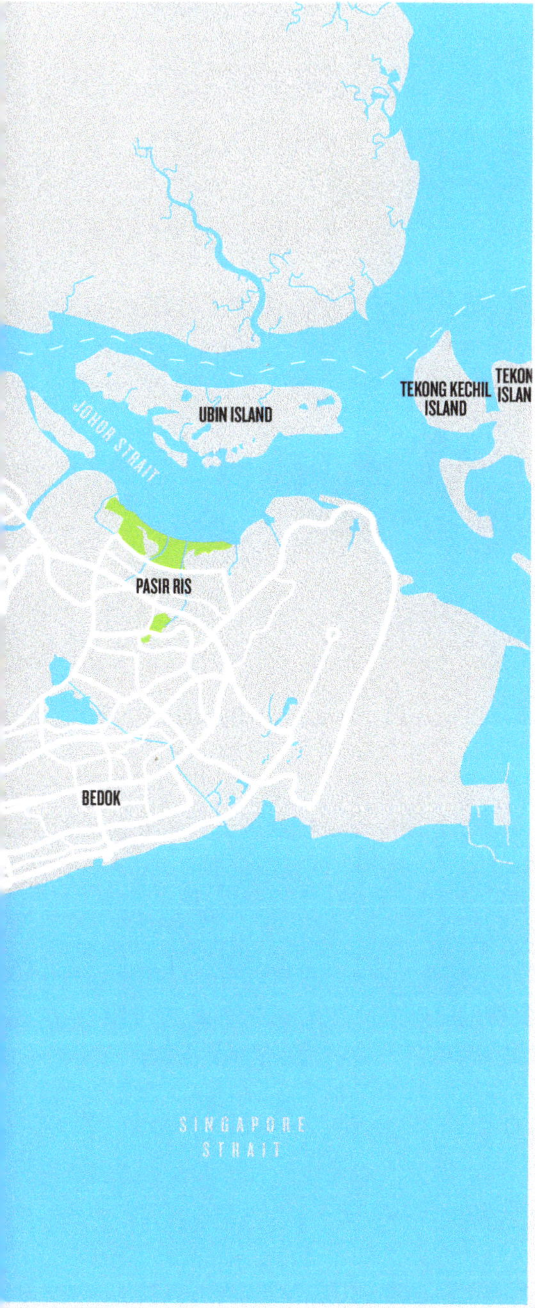

22.
MEE POK MAN (1995)
Hua Bee, Block 78, Moh Guan Terrace, Tiong Bahru
page 66

23.
THE ROAD LESS TRAVELLED (1997)
The 50's Bar at Tanjong Pagar Road/railway tracks near Tanjong Pagar Railway Station
page 68

24.
FOREVER FEVER (1998)
The Majestic, Eu Tong Sen Street, Chinatown
page 70

25.
EATING AIR (1999)
The CTE (Central Expressway) tunnels
page 72

26.
ROGUE TRADER (1999)
The Singapore Exchange (SGX)
page 74

27.
FULLTIME KILLER/
CHUEN JIK SAT SAU (2001)
Raffles Place MRT and Marina South
page 74

28.
15 (THE SHORT FILM) (2002)
Yishun Park, Yishun Avenue 11
page 76

MEE POK MAN (1995)

LOCATION *Hua Bee, Block 78, Moh Guan Terrace, Tiong Bahru*

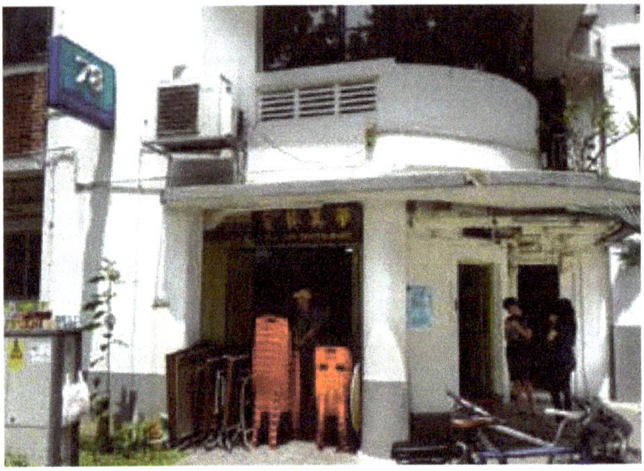

KICK-STARTING THE 'indie' film scene in Singapore in the mid-1990s (after a drought on film-making in the 1980s), Eric Khoo's *Mee Pok Man* is a brutal exploration of local low-life, relentlessly up-ending notions of Singapore as sanitized and sedate. The place where the title character slings his *mee* (noodles) is Hua Bee, a half-century old *kopitiam* (coffee shop or cooked-food cafe) currently enshrined in nostalgia for 'the old days' (and the heritage of Tiong Bahru where it resides), but there's no trace of that in the film's long opening sequence. We begin with in-your-face images of raw meat, cooked meat, naked female flesh (yes, that's meat too!) over a blistering punk track by the Opposition Party (a local band). Then we find ourselves in a squalid bathroom as a stoned prostitute lights a cigarette post-heroin fix. She makes her way back inside Hua Bee to join her friends, working girls gathered for a late-night 'supper' of noodles delivered by the Man (played by musician Joe Ng) who drops his bowls at the mere sight of one of the girls, Bunny (Michelle Goh). As they tease Bunny about sleeping with the 'idiot' noodle seller, they have no idea how much he yearns to save her from her pimp (veteran actor, Lim Kay Tong), who arrives at the end of the scene. Khoo's debut feature was a riff on Martin Scorsese's *Taxi Driver* (1976), yet the film takes an even nastier, almost gothic turn, and remains the quintessential vision of Singapore's 'dark side'. ➾ ***Ben Slater***

Photo © Toh Hun Ping

Directed by Eric Khoo
Scene description: Meat, flesh and noodles with chilli
Timecode for scene: 0:00:00 – 0:07:21

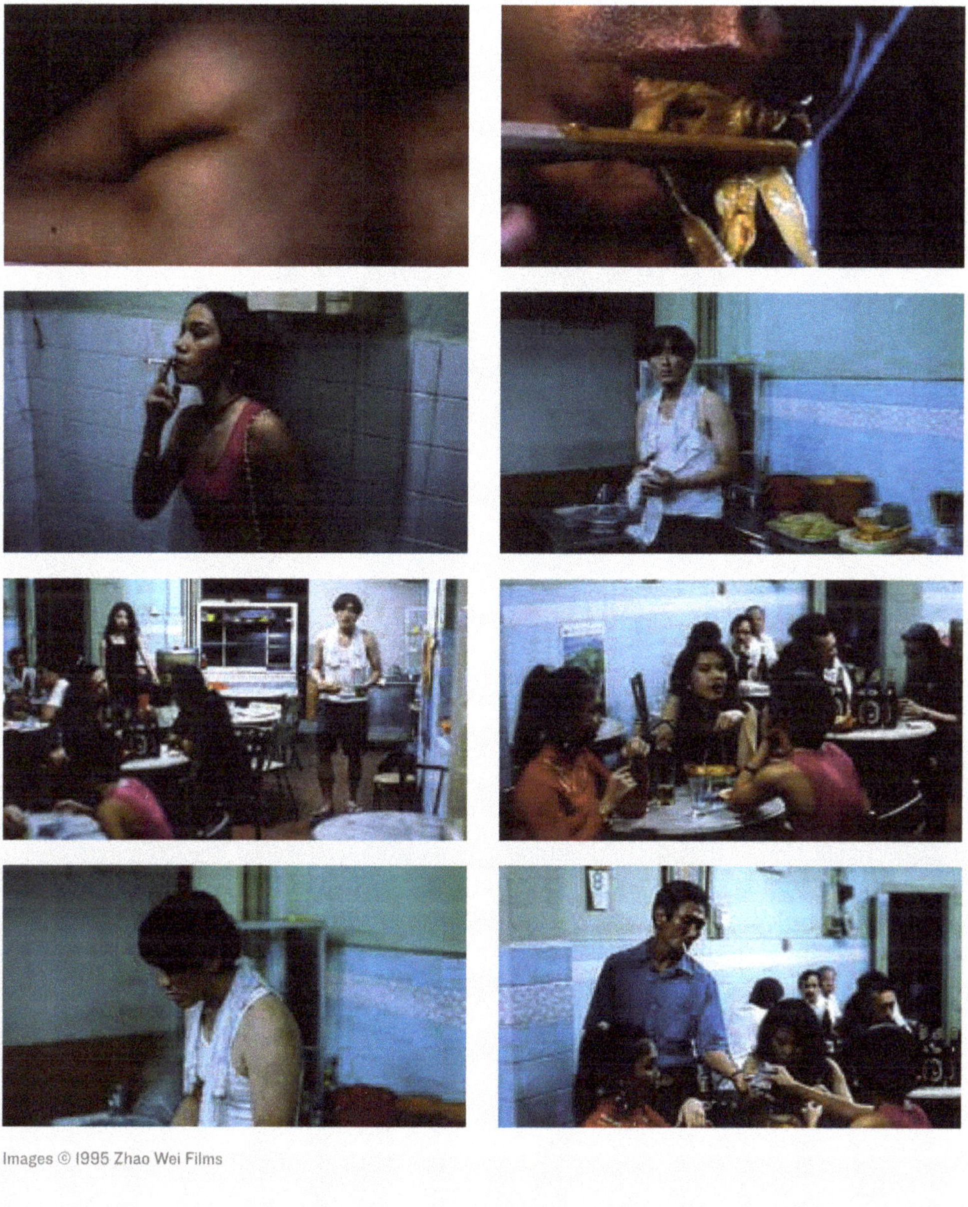

THE ROAD LESS TRAVELLED (1997)

LOCATION *The 50's Bar at Tanjong Pagar Road/ railway tracks near Tanjong Pagar Railway Station*

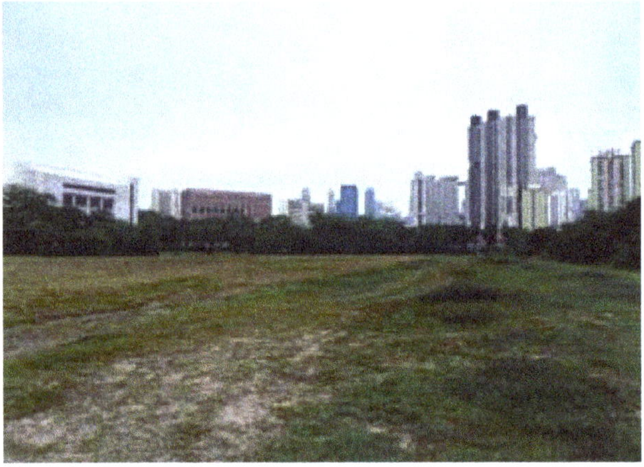

'XINYAO' (a Chinese term for 'Singapore songs') is a homegrown music movement which was highly popular in the 1980s as its Mandarin songs written about idealism, love, local memories and environs found recognition among the mainstream audience. 'Xinyao' became increasingly commercialized in the 1990s as 'xinyao' artistes competed for attention with a new wave of overseas pop idols. It was in this context that director Lim Suat Yen situated *The Road Less Travelled*, a film about a group of youths – including three 'xinyao' singers – who struggle to reconcile their dreams and love for their art with the pragmatic preoccupations of their parents, the music industry and the society-at-large. In an extended sequence from the film, Tianren, an aspiring 'xinyao' singer-songwriter, performs to an unappreciative crowd in a music lounge (the 50's Bar in downtown Tanjong Pagar). Dejected, he reveals to his friends that his parents are sending him abroad to study, which effectively ends his music career in Singapore. They drive to a faraway 'countryside' (Choa Chu Kang) to spend the night, and at dawn they return to Tanjong Pagar at the railway tracks near the old train station, where Tianren splits ways with his company of artiste-friends. The secluded railway tracks become metaphors for the 'less travelled' artistic paths which Tianren abandons, and other protagonists persist in following. These tracks were removed when Malaysian-run (KTM or Keretapi Tanah Melayu) train services between Tanjong Pagar and Woodlands ceased in July 2011. Continuing the metaphor, these absent railway tracks now represent, perhaps, the perpetual dearth of opportunities (paths) for homegrown artistic talents to pursue their true aspirations and prosper here in Singapore. ⇒ ***Toh Hun Ping***

Photo © Toh Hun Ping

Directed by Lim Suat Yen
Scene description: Final farewell to a friend who gives up his music career
Timecode for scene: 0:39:51 – 0:40:47

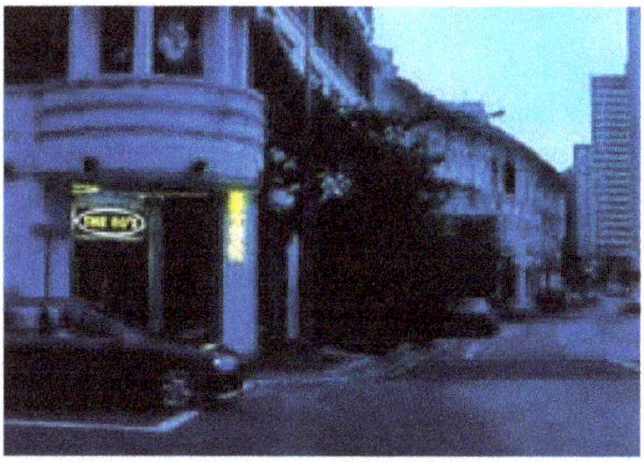
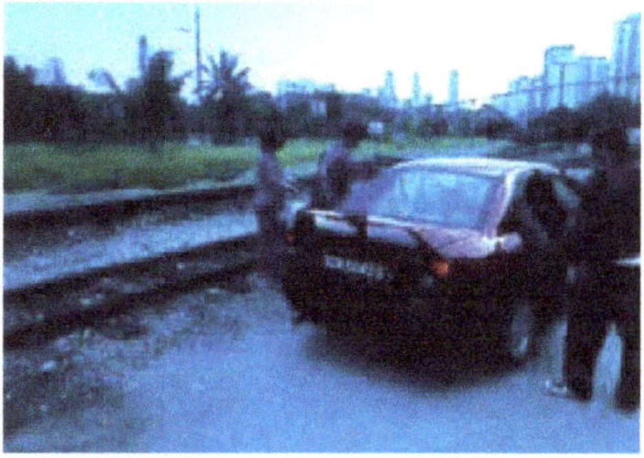
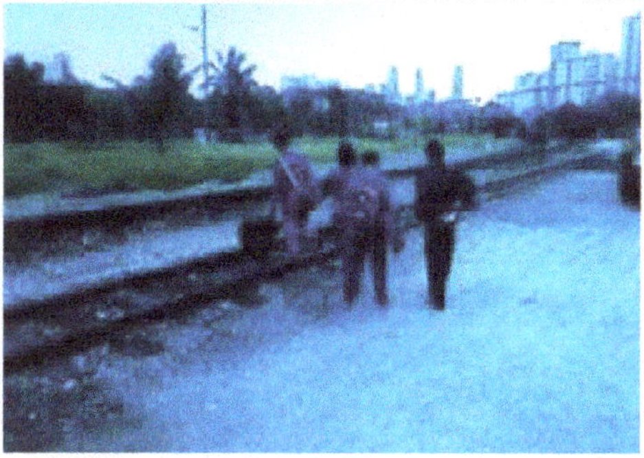
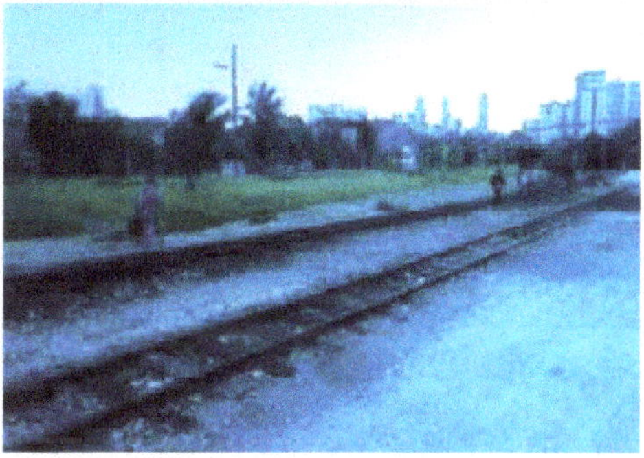

FOREVER FEVER AKA THAT'S THE WAY I LIKE IT (1998)

LOCATION *The Majestic, Eu Tong Sen Street, Chinatown*

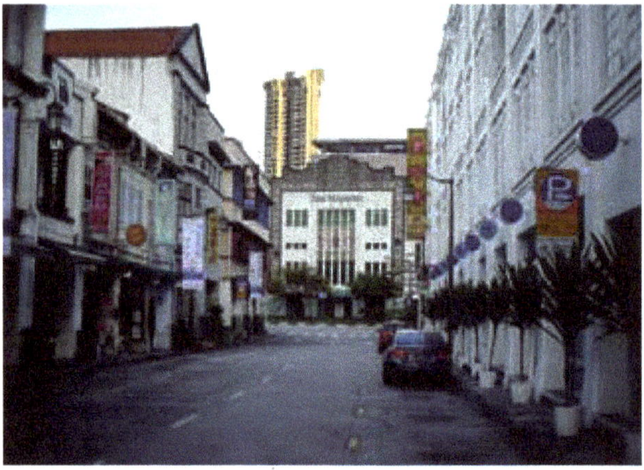

IT'S THE 1970S and the life of a young, uncouth supermarket shelf-stacker, Hock, is transformed when he's dragged to see an American film about a man... who can dance. Although its title is disguised (presumably for copyright reasons), few will mistake the film-within-a-film as anything other than *Saturday Night Fever* (1977), and its Italian American hero (who later steps out of the screen to advise Hock) as a stand-in for John Travolta. Made as Singapore's local film revival was picking up speed, *Forever Fever* is a mostly English (or rather 'Singlish') language comedy written and directed by theatre doyen Glen Goei and starring actors from a burgeoning performing arts scene. Hock (Adrian Pang) is initially reluctant to see 'the Fever show', at the Majestic Theatre, with its magnificent art deco facade, designed by Singapore's premier colonial architects, Swan & Maclaren. Originally a Cantonese opera house, it became a cinema before the war, and continued to show mostly Chinese films until the late 1990s. It was an icon of cinematic glamour in the midst of the chaotic bustle of Chinatown. Once inside (interiors were filmed in a now-defunct cinema in Jurong) Hock shifts from boredom to amazement and the sequence ends with a fantasy projection of himself on the big screen as Travolta 'strutting' down Mosque Street with the Majestic in the background. It's unlikely that *Saturday Night Fever* would even have played there in 1978 (when it was released in Singapore), but for an elegy to an era in which a trip to the cinema could change your life, the Majestic is the perfect location. ➡ ***Ben Slater***

Photo © Toh Hun Ping

Directed by Glen Goei

Scene description: : Catching the fever of cinema

Timecode for scene: 0:13:17 – 0:15:22

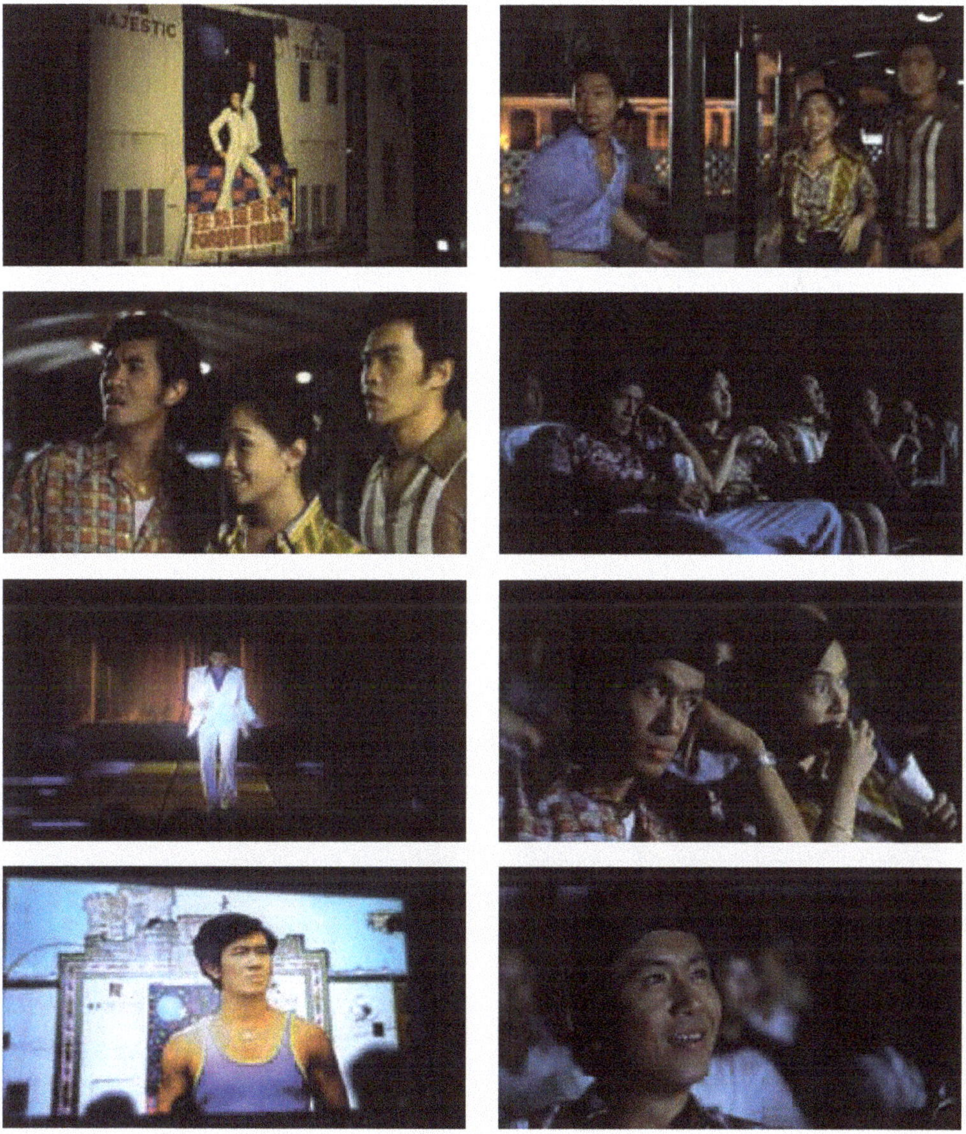

Images © 1998 TigerTiger Productions

EATING AIR (1999)

LOCATION

The CTE (Central Expressway) tunnels

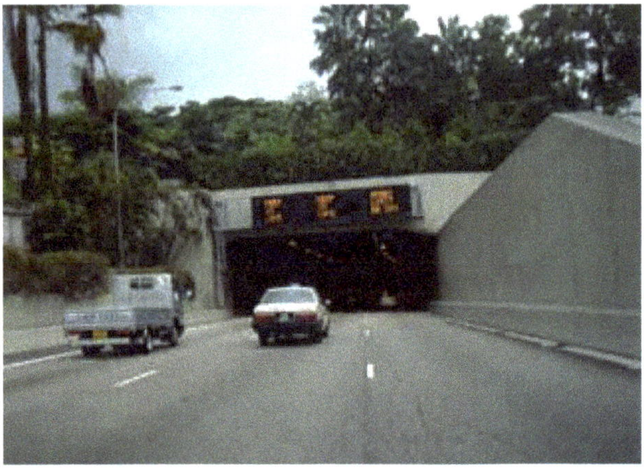

BOLDLY DESCRIBING THEIR FILM as 'a motorcycle kung fu love story', *Eating Air*'s directors Jasmine Ng and Kelvin Tong, used style, fantasy and a blast of youthful energy to vividly depict a landscape already starting to look mundane after the Singapore film revival in the 1990s. Hong Kong cinema was a big influence, from the period martial arts flicks that the hero Ah Boy fantasizes about, to the gangster movies that his best (and doomed) buddy Ah Gu seeks to emulate, and Wong Kar Wai's neon-lit urban romanticism looms over the tentative courtship between Ah Boy and the quiet, Ah Girl. The film's action is played out in shopping malls, games arcades and HDB (Housing and Development Board) flats, but going underground there's a key location revisited several times. The CTE tunnels were opened in 1991 as the final stage of a network that linked the city centre with many densely populated housing estates. An entire lane was closed for filming (in the middle of the night) and the production took full advantage of this. The film opens with Ah Boy and Ah Gu coolly sharing a cigarette as they ride their bikes parallel down the tunnel, Ah Boy and Ah Girl's romance is expressed through their journeys under the green-blue neon, and in the film's tragic climax, Ah Boy hopelessly confronts the gang that brutally beat Ah Gu. Finding her lover's body, Ah Girl picks up his helmet and walks through the tunnel in a long, unbroken shot. The tunnel becomes a place for escape, the scene of a crime and a route out towards possibility. ➾***Ben Slater***

Photo © Mailer diablo (wikimedia commons)

Directed by Jasmine Ng and Kelvin Tong

Scene description: Life ends and begins beneath the city

Timecode for scene: 1:34:56 – 1:38:65

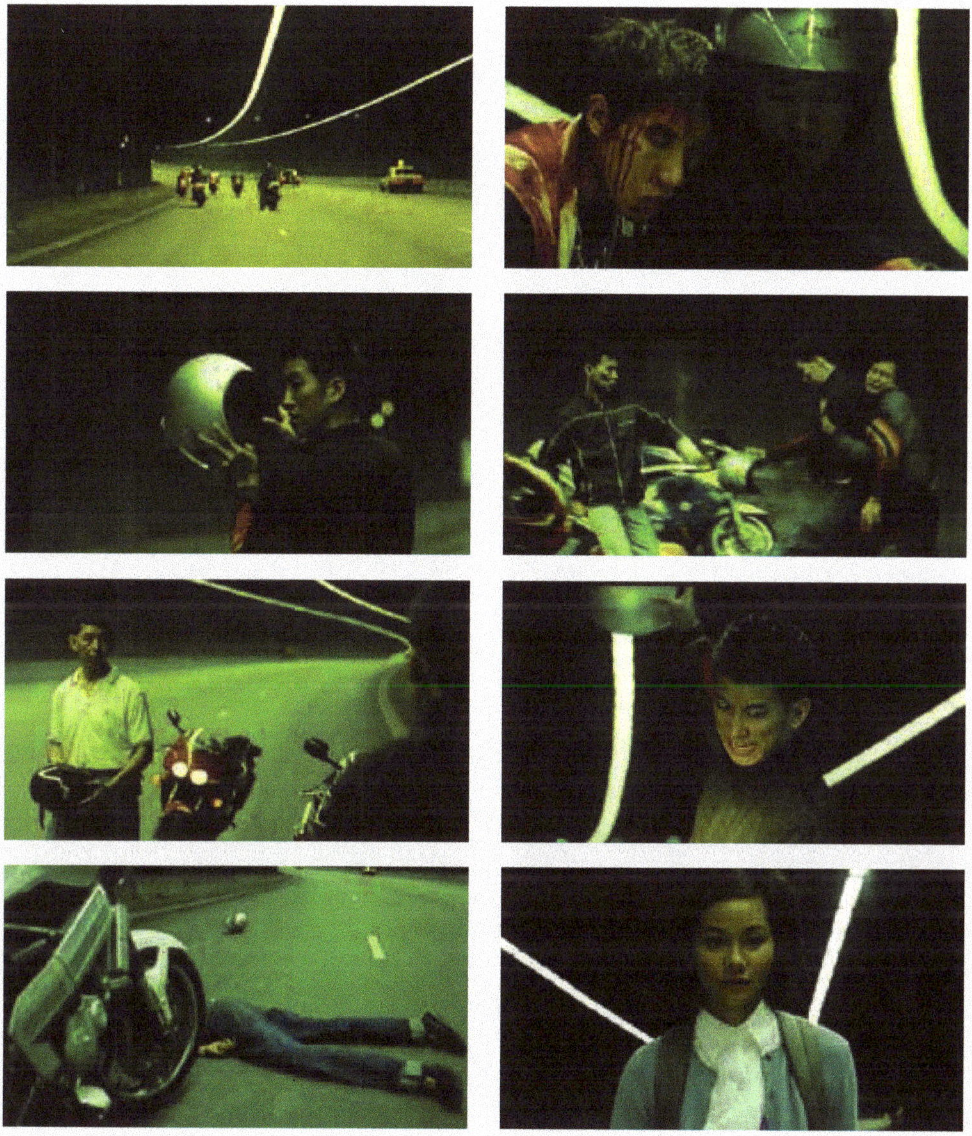

ROGUE TRADER (1999)

LOCATION *The Singapore Exchange (SGX)*

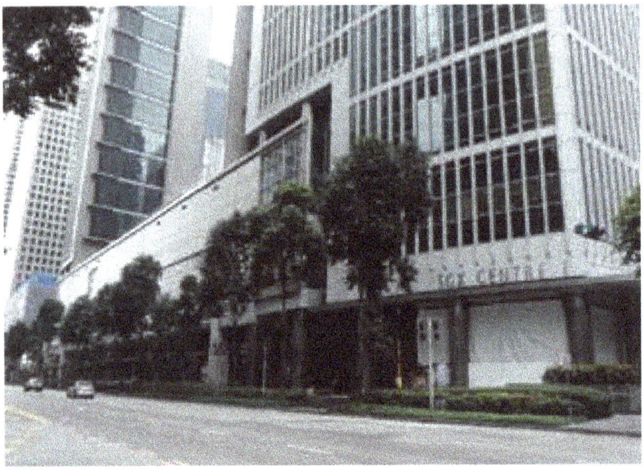

IN 1995, Britain's oldest investment bank, Barings collapsed when it was discovered that a young futures broker had been hiding extraordinary losses (over a billion dollars worth), while running the company's apparently successful trading in Singapore. For a brief moment, Nick Leeson and his exploits were international front-page news, where he was dubbed the 'Rogue Trader'. This became the title of Leeson's own book and James Dearden's adaptation of the same year. With Ewan McGregor as our (anti)hero, the film portrays Leeson as an essentially good guy whose attempts to cover up his team's mistakes lead him down a crazy rabbit hole of lies. Dearden's crew shot for only ten days in Singapore, capturing views of the futuristic skyline of the Central Business District. Permission was denied to shoot in the story's most important location, the trading floor for what was then the Singapore Stock Exchange (SIMEX), where, before his fall, Leeson was nicknamed 'The King of the Exchange'. A detailed studio recreation was built at Pinewood Studio, and it's amusing to watch McGregor and his Singaporean colleagues stride through Raffles Place, wearing their signature yellow-and-black jackets, and onto the studio set on the other side of the world, accompanied by a cover version of the Beatles's 1963 hit 'Money'. A far more compelling version of the tale is told by Adam Curtis in his 1996 documentary *25 Million Pounds*, featuring an interview with an utterly unrepentant Leeson in prison, and a few seconds of precious footage shot on the actual SIMEX trading floor at the height of his deception. All the traders stare anxiously at the screens, waiting for the numbers, but Leeson looks elsewhere, chewing gum, a faint smile – a man who knows it's all a fraud. ➾ ***Ben Slater***

Photo © Toh Hun Ping

Directed by James Dearden
Scene description: Nick and his team join the chaos of the trading floor
Timecode for scene: 0:11:01 – 0:13:00

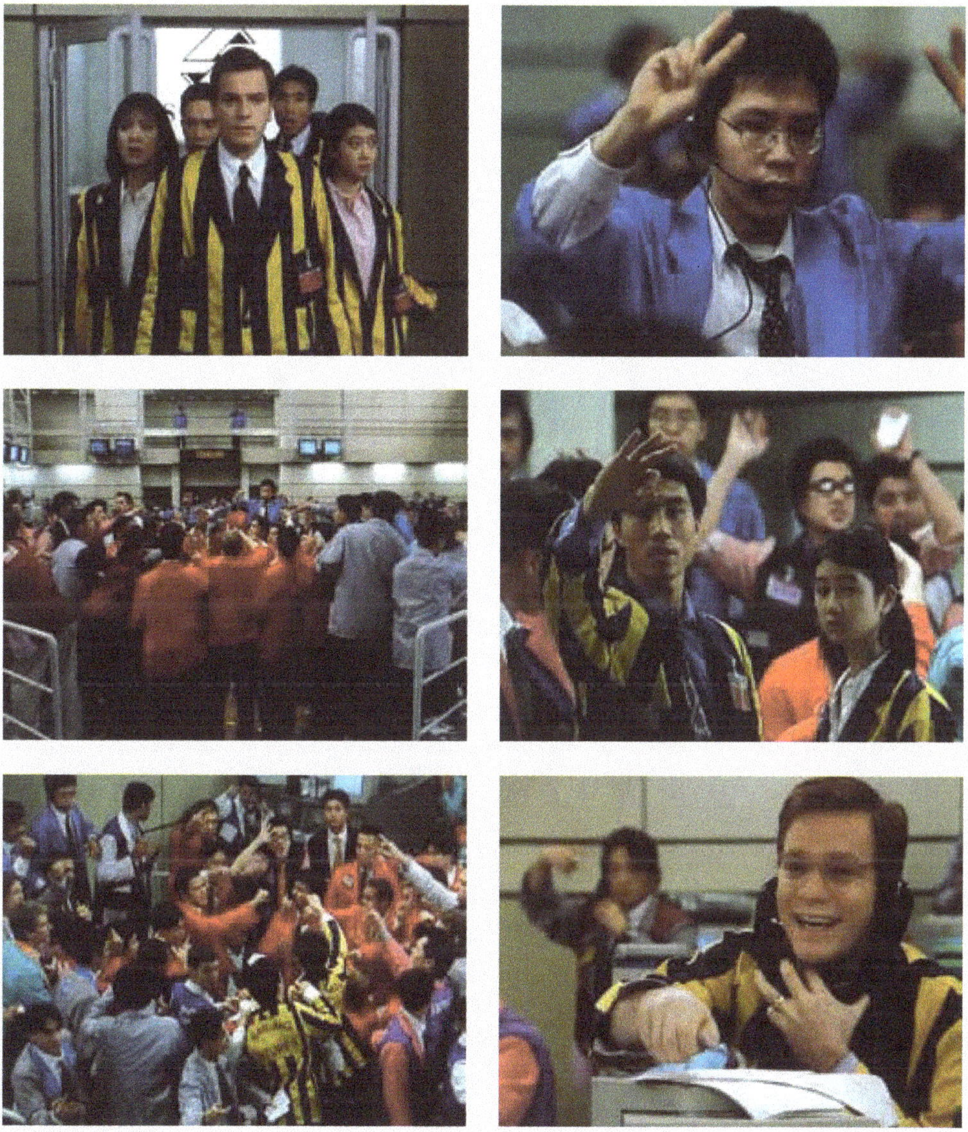

FULLTIME KILLER/CHUEN JIK SAT SAU (2001)

LOCATION *Raffles Place MRT and Marina South*

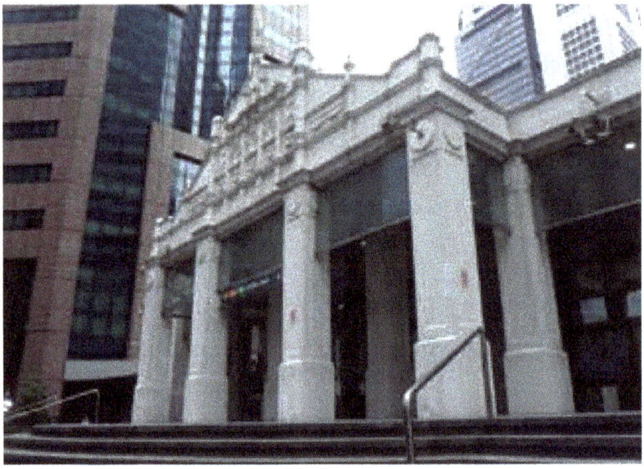

CAN YOU MAKE crime and action movies in a country with low crime and rarely any action? After independence, Singapore's government purged the city-state of organized crime and illegal weapons, leaving Singaporean film-makers reluctant to tackle a genre that thrives on gangsters and guns. Hong Kong directors working on location have had no such qualms. In Johnnie To's deeply self-reflexive *Fulltime Killer* one of the film's itinerant hit men, Tok (Andy Lau) encounters a Singapore-based crime boss (Lam Suet) operating out of Harry's Bar along Boat Quay (a famous expat drinking hole), where, bizarrely, the Cantonese actors speak to each other in English. The major Singapore set-piece takes place, according to a title on-screen, at Outram Park MRT Station, but signage shows it's Raffles Place Station beneath the Business District. Tok slides down the side of the escalator (an infraction that would surely result in instant arrest), and stalks his female target as she steps off a train (along with some appropriately multi-racial extras). It's a trap. After dispatching his two would-be assassins, Tok flees from the local cops onto the tracks and presses himself against a tunnel wall while a train screams past (a dangerously realistic stunt), before emerging in the green fields of Marina South (passing a publicity blimp for the Singapore telco Starhub), a landscape now completely transformed into a tourist attraction, Gardens on the Bay. In the context of law-abiding Singapore it's all utterly absurd, but the hyper-stylized action and archetypal characters prove that we can be thrilled even by the ridiculous. ➾ ***Ben Slater***

Photo © Toh Hun Ping

Directed by Johnnie To

Scene description: Action movie mayhem in an MRT (Mass Rapid Transit) Station

Timecode for scene: 0:44:37 – 0:48:30

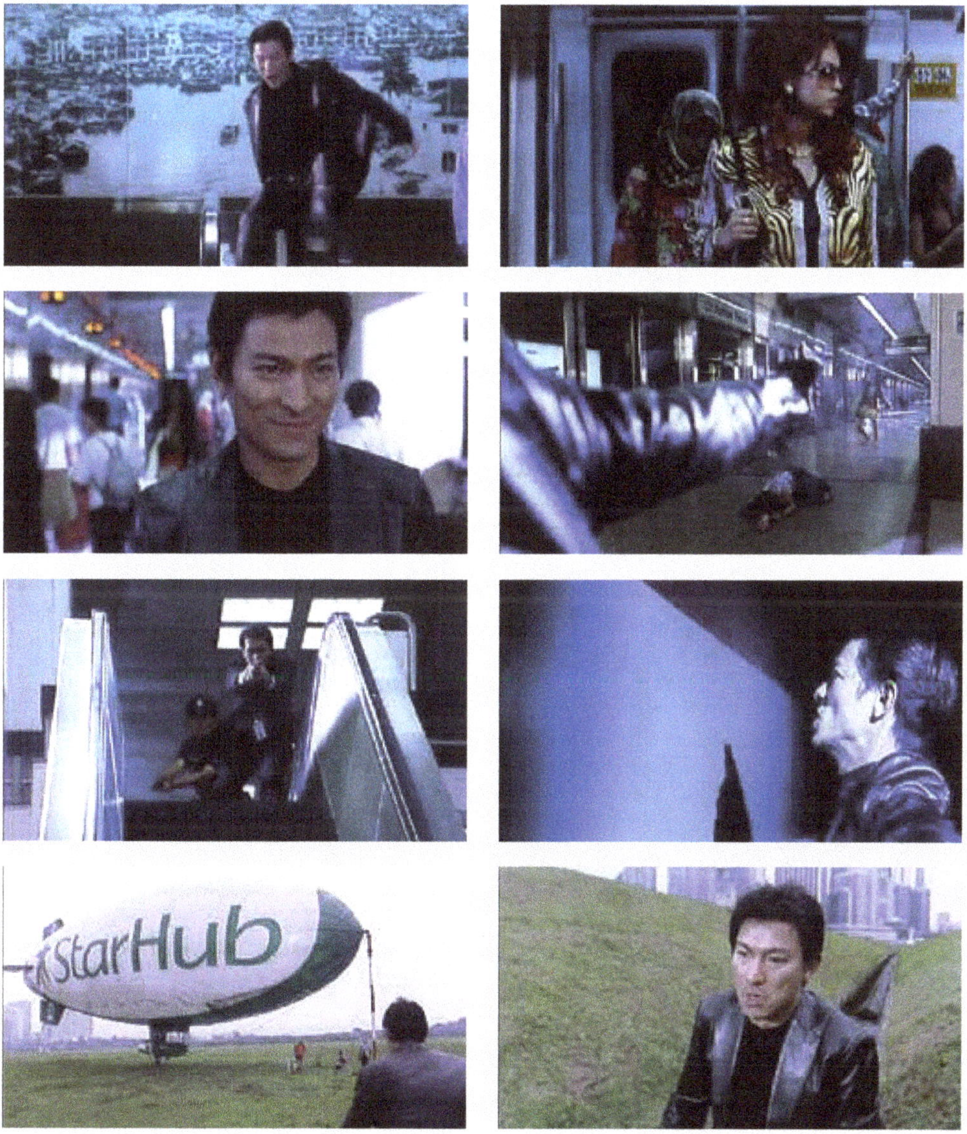

Images © 2001 Teamwork/Milky Way Image

15 (THE SHORT FILM) (2002)

LOCATION *Yishun Park, Yishun Avenue 11*

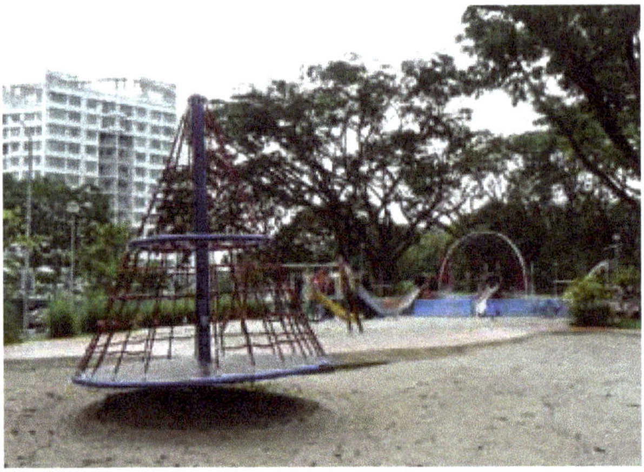

OLD PLAYGROUNDS are hard to find in Singapore these days. Bloggers write about them with nostalgia. So nostalgic are these old playgrounds, young local designers have taken to them for inspiration to make pins, bags and other knick-knacks. This scene in *15* was shot in a merry-go-round but we don't see it. There are no little children running around but what is captured is the carelessness of youth and the feeling of transience that only being in that time of your life can bring. We see the faces of the three young teenage characters of the film the day before their school test pondering about their future – will they fail their maths test? Will they get married? Will they be friends forever? We see the sunny sky peeking out from the lush greenery of the trees. This old playground where this scene was shot is a rare find in Singapore these days. They are replaced by less adventurous playgrounds with safety polysoft surfaces that are supposed to lessen the impact of a child's fall. The lost of hope these teenagers share in this scene is placed suitably in this playground as one realizes that in the end, they are still young boys with years ahead of them. If only they would get off this ride and move on to another. 'I don't dare think about the future,' says Melvin, one of the boys. **→ *Wahyuni A. Hadi***

Directed by Royston Tan
Scene description: The three main protagonists have a heart-to-heart the day before their school test
Timecode for scene: 0:12:58 – 0:14:28

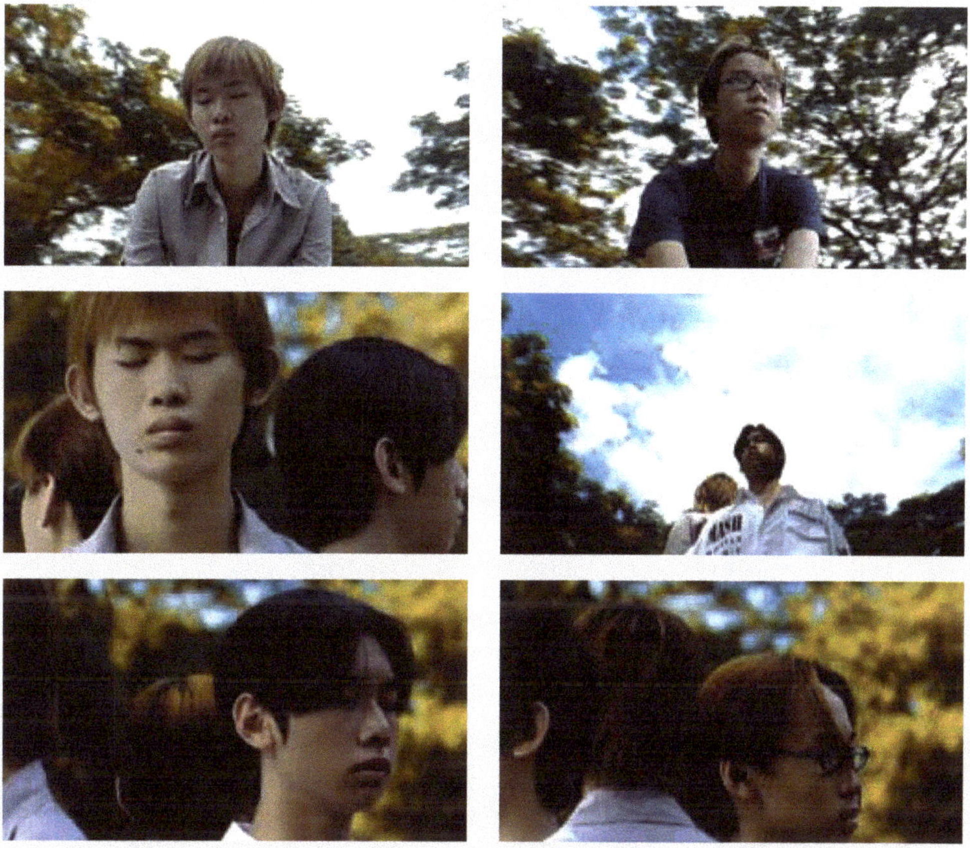

SPOTLIGHT

THE CULTURAL MATERIALISM OF SINGAPORE IN JACK NEO'S CINEMA

Text by STEPHEN TEO

SINGAPORE IS A CITY of business and consumerism. If there is a single film director who can be said to represent this maxim, it is probably Jack Neo. His films have been consistent box office hits, and that success is in itself very revealing of the kind of values that Neo depicts. Neo's characters are usually 'Ah Bengs' (the nickname for lowly educated but streetwise Chinese Singaporeans) who live in the heartlands and are utterly obsessed with money, or with not having enough of it. His first huge success was, after all, entitled *Money No Enough* (1998) – and he has gone on to expand on the money-obsession in *I Not Stupid* (2002), *Homerun* (2003), *The Best Bet* (2004), *Ah Long Pte Ltd* (2007).

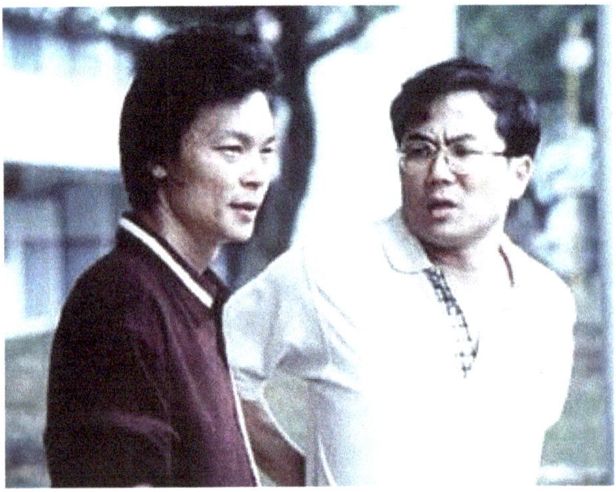

Neo clothes this materialistic concern with comic touches and slapstick humour. Yet he is able to handle themes that emanate out of the money obsession, such as the lack of civic consciousness and the state of unhappiness that is inherent in heartlander families, who must pay special attention towards educating their children so that they can succeed in the rat race (this is the basis of *I Not Stupid*, which is probably his best film). This ability to entertain and to provide a social dimension to his films make Neo a rare type among Singapore's film-makers. Within the community of Singaporean film-makers, Neo is a kind of *enfant terrible*, a precocious talent (he acts, writes and directs) and an intense media personality and celebrity who often comments on current affairs as a public intellectual (a scandal in 2010 arising out of his private life has since kept him very quiet). In comparison with Neo, the films of his contemporaries like Eric Khoo, Royston Tan, Kelvin Tong, and more recently, Anthony Chen (whose film *Ilo, Ilo* was awarded the 2013 Caméra d'Or prize in the 2013 Cannes Film Festival, and went on to win the Best Picture Award at the Golden Horse Awards – a rare honour for Singapore films) do not perform as robustly at the box office and are more sedate in style. Though they are better known internationally, Neo has superseded them all in terms of popularity and accessibility.

Neo can be seen then as an upstart film-maker whose entry into films came by way of his status as a well-known television entertainer and who went on to establish his own creative credentials

Opposite *Money No Enough* (1998) / **Below** *I Not Stupid* (2002)

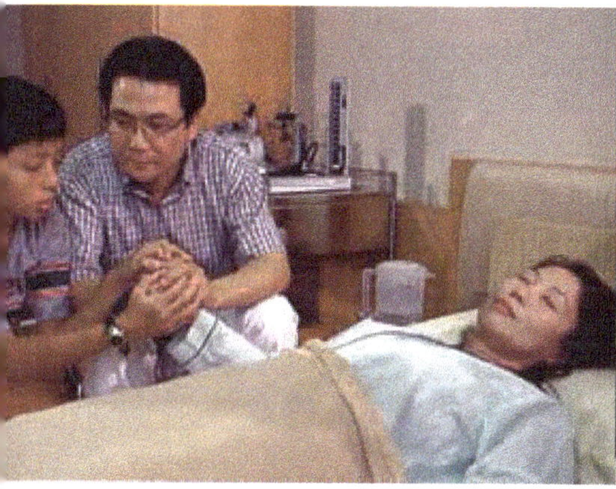

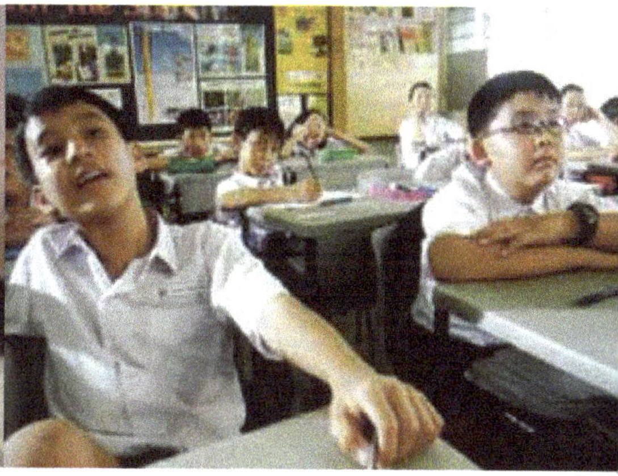

in the cinema while yet never losing his identity as a comedian-entertainer. As an actor, he appeared in Eric Khoo's *12 Storeys* (1997), and *Money No Enough*. On the latter film, he was in fact the major creative force, having written the screenplay, although he did not direct it. The box office success of *Money No Enough* sealed Neo's cinematic journey as an auteur-entertainer and he never looked back. It set the commercial formula for Neo's subsequent films which he went on to produce, direct, write and act in. Since then, *Ah Boys to Men*, released in two parts in 2012 (part one) and 2013 (part two), has become the highest grossing film ever made to date in the island republic (the previous record holder was *Money No Enough*).

Because of his commercial success, Neo represents a strand of film-making in Singapore that I would define as cultural-materialistic. This is evident in his style of film-making (his tendency to feature stars and to include product placement, his preference for comedies, etc.), and these materialistic instincts are responsible for the perception of his films as populist products par excellence in modern Singapore cinema. As such, Neo's works have mostly been neglected by international critics. Even on the home front, Neo's films are largely underappreciated or perhaps not even understood because of their perceived materialism. However, Neo defines Singaporean cinema as a cinema that deals largely with materialist values in a cultural manner. It is therefore a cinema of cultural materialism; one that reflects mainstream values. Cultural materialism is a process in which culture becomes entwined with capitalist economics. Neo's films depict the lifestyles of Singaporeans determined by a capitalistic consumerist culture, as well as the more social culture of what is usually known as *kiasu*, in local Hokkien parlance, indicating a fear of losing out and therefore taking every advantage as soon as possible to ensure that one wins or gets the material object sought after (Neo's films are therefore classic *kiasu* movies).

Within the community of Singaporean film-makers, Neo is a kind of *enfant terrible*, a precocious talent and an intense media personality.

This cultural reworking of capitalism and materialism is the key to understanding Neo's films. Through these films we can see Singapore as a mature society of late-capitalist development. Cultural materialism is a kind of ideology that befits the city-state, one which prides itself in attaining First World status within a generation from its previous Third World existence. Many people criticize Singapore as materialistic, meaning that it is a self-seeking society, lacking civic values, and these concerns are also reflected in Neo's films. They function as a critique of Singapore while at the same time lauding its strengths as a social entity. Neo's protagonists are typical Singaporeans whose preeminent purpose in life is to work hard and make money. They celebrate materialism as a necessary evil but they are not bereft of humanity which cries out to be recognized. ⁜

LOCATIONS MAP

SINGAPORE

maps are only to be taken as approximates

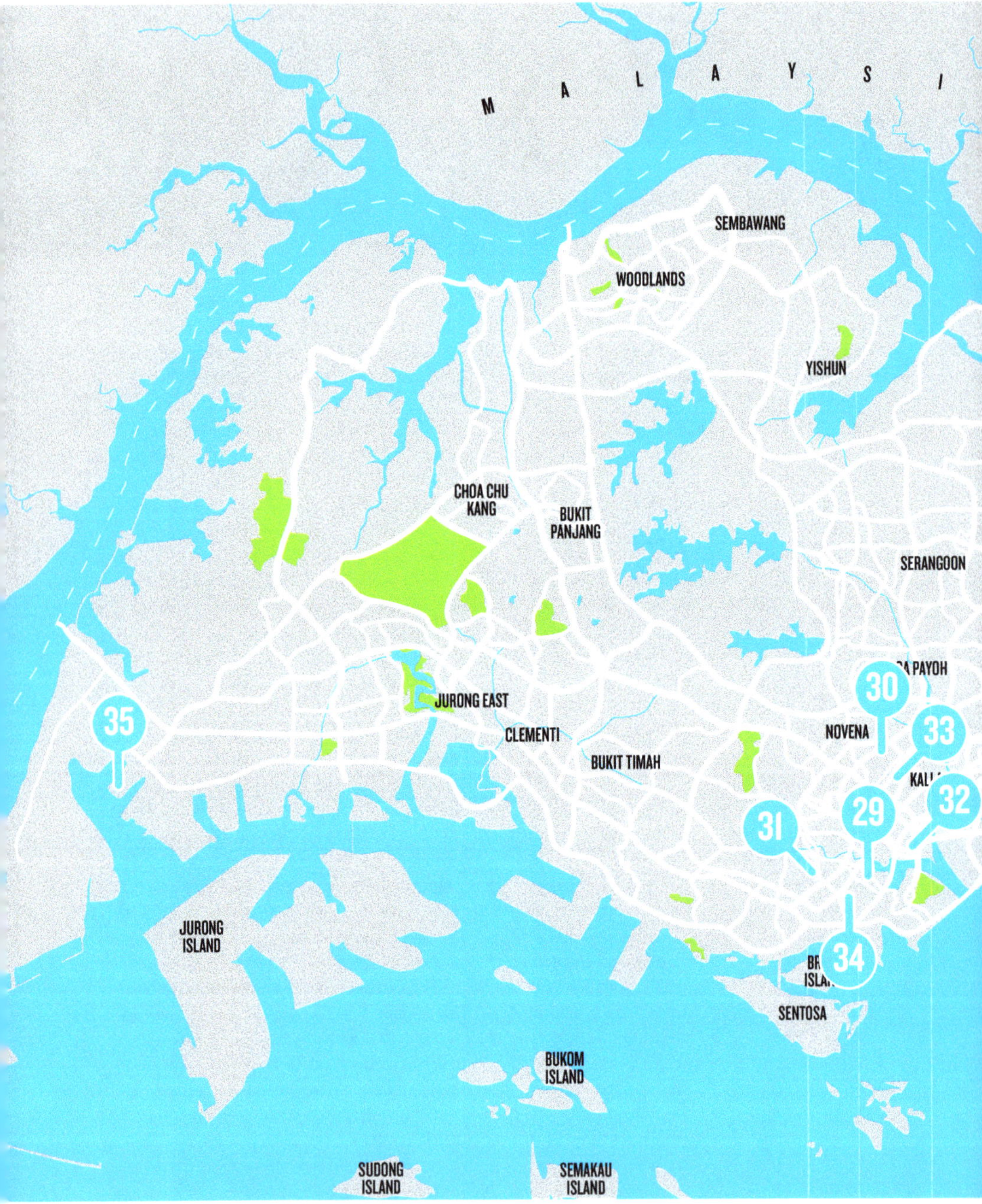

SINGAPORE LOCATIONS
SCENES 29-35

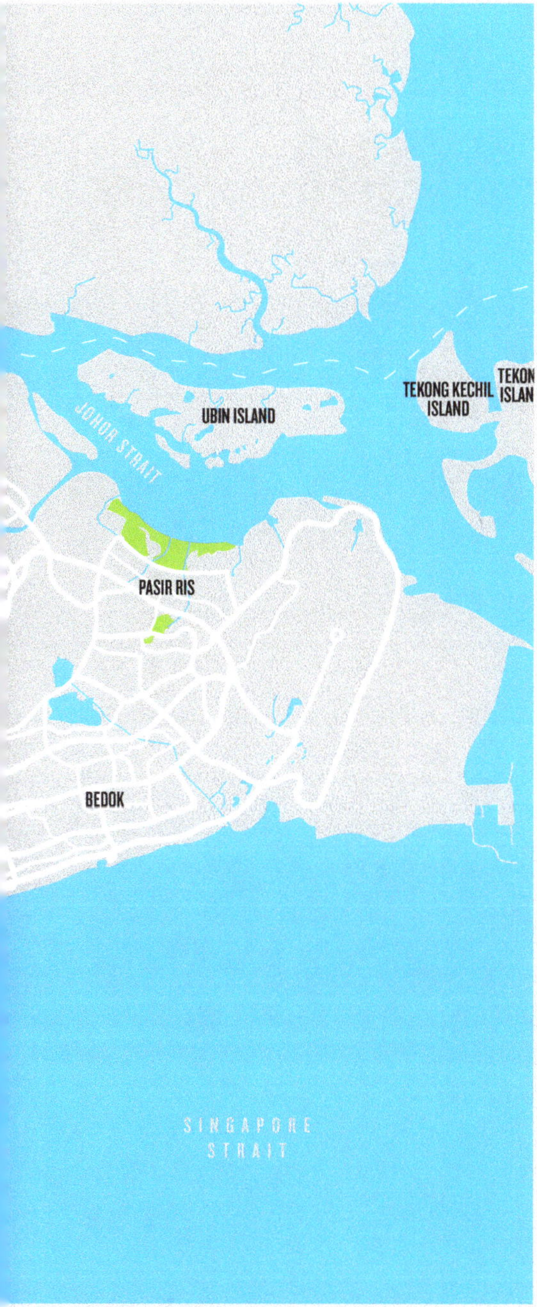

29.
CUT (2004)
Underground car park of China Square Central, Chinatown
page 84

30.
SINGAPORE GAGA (2005)
Void deck, Block 51, Kent Road
page 86

31.
BE WITH ME (2005)
Guan Hin provision shop, Block 55, Tiong Bahru Road, Unit 01–57
page 88

32.
KRRISH (2006)
Marina Bay, Financial District, Sentosa
page 90

33.
GONE SHOPPING (2007)
Mustafa Centre, 145 Syed Alwi Road, Little India
page 92

34.
DREAMS FROM THE THIRD WORLD (2008)
Former Tropical Hotel at the junction of Keong Saik Road and Teck Lim Road (now Park 22 Hotel)
page 94

35.
LOST IMAGES: FILMS FROM THE IVAN POLUNIN ARCHIVE (2009)
A kelong and the Tuas Market (now shipyards and industrial estates)
page 96

CUT (2004)

LOCATION *Underground car park of China Square Central, Chinatown*

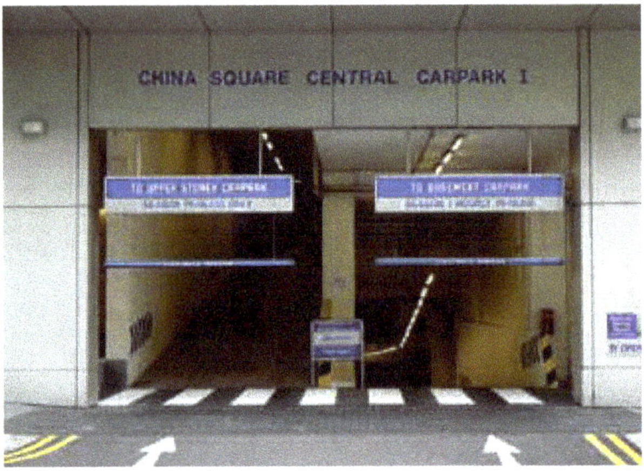

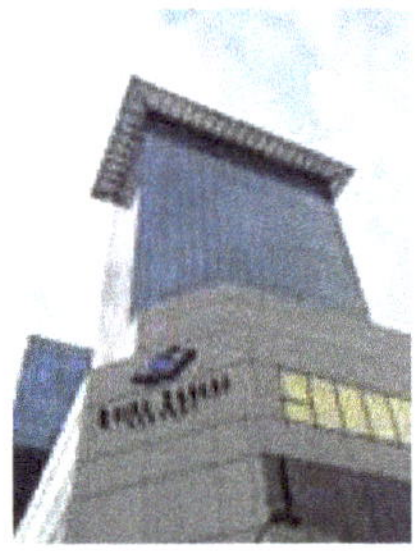

FOLLOWING IN THE STEPS of Federico Fellini, who devoted to his 'beloved' censors a Swiftian satire with *The Temptations of Doctor Antonio/ Le tentazioni del dottor Antonio* (from the 1962 anthology film *Boccaccio 70*), Royston Tan took his own kind of sweet revenge. The butchering of his internationally acclaimed feature *15*, pushed him to use his own money to produce a lavish musical short titled *Cut*. An irresistible lampoon of Amy Chua, the notorious mastermind of the omnivorous censorship. Playing a jolly superfan, Jonathan Lim sings to her: 'How about street gang leader Royston Tan's *15*? 27 cuts! Your highest record! I am so proud of you!' Neo Swee Lin, embodying the powerful cutting lady, sings a new kind of national anthem: 'This is Singapore, censorship is free!' Before premiering it at the Singapore International Film Festival, Royston Tan said to the press: 'The film was done in a spirit of fun, so no one should take offence.' The all-singing, all-dancing, 180 members cast includes the who's who of the local creative community such as Eric Khoo, Beatrice Chia, Geoff Ang. And Bugs Bunny, aka Royston Tan, whose *Cut* was miraculously screened uncut at the Festival's opening.
➾Lorenzo Codelli

Photos © Toh Hun Ping

Directed by Royston Tan
Scene description: A ballet celebrating censorship
Timecode for scene: 0:05:98 – 0:08:94

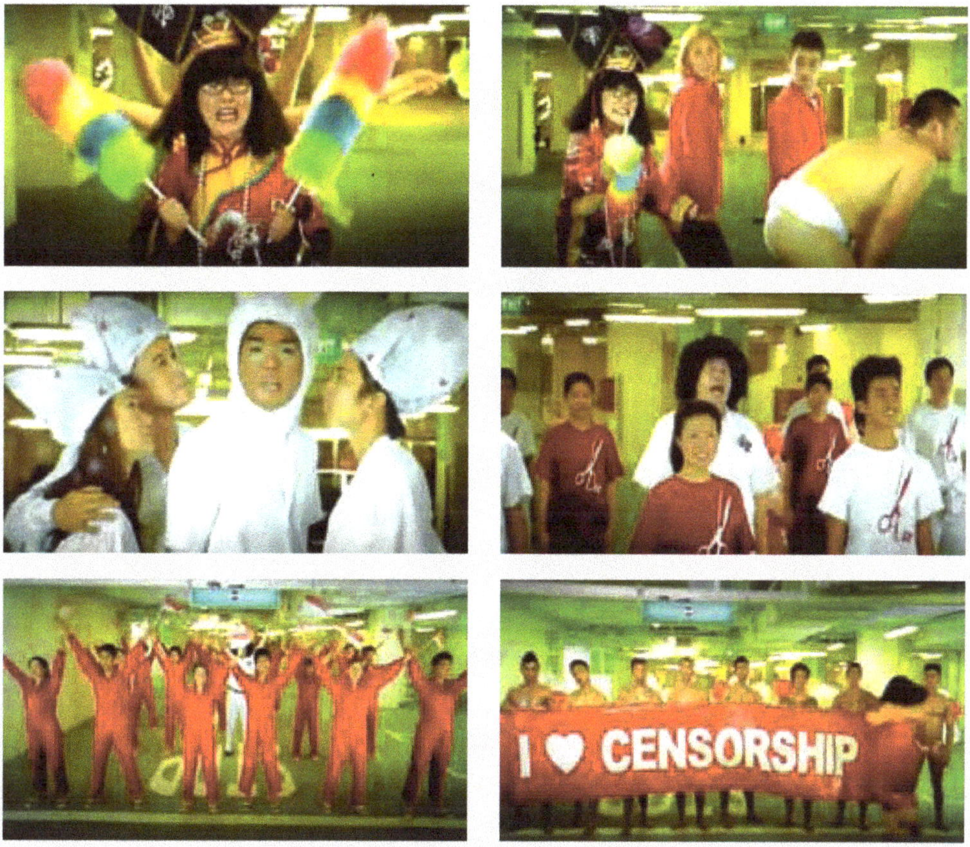

SINGAPORE GAGA (2005)

LOCATION *Void deck, Block 51, Kent Road*

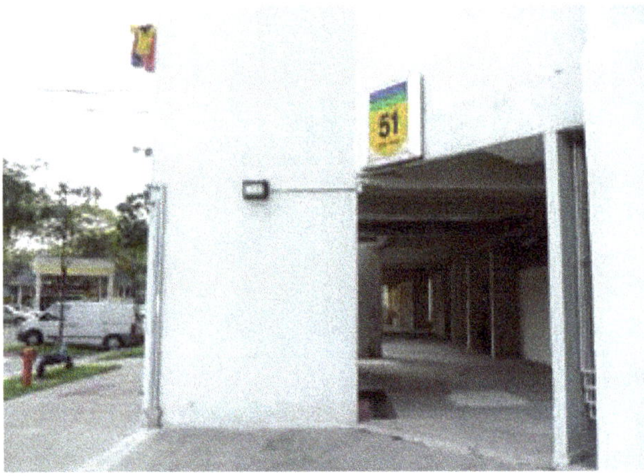

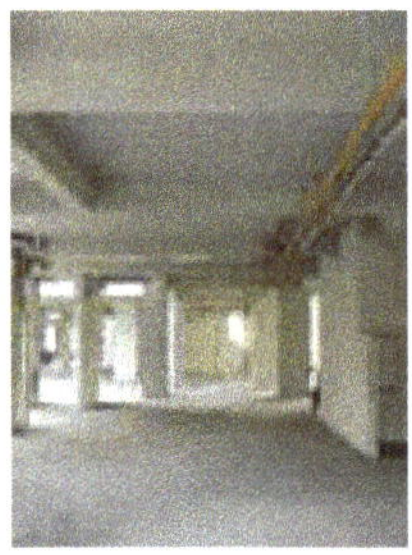

HOME TO OVER 80 per cent of Singaporeans is the HDB flat (Housing and Development Board, Singapore's public housing). The void deck, an empty area beneath the apartment block, is as ordinary as it comes. Its grey cement floor and plain pillars with signs that indicate there is to be no playing football limit the activity of the space. The space is left empty so that residents can hold communal gatherings that require a fairly large area, more often than not, weddings and funerals. When a wedding or funeral is held at a void deck, one may see the accompaniment of a banquet, karaoke, gambling tables or solemn religious music from a stereo. One's joy or sadness is shared openly with the hundreds that live in the same few blocks of flat with you. When not in use, the void deck is often quiet. Any sound made echoes through – the sound of footsteps, laughter or a mobile phone beep. It is then that it comes alive. Trust film-maker Tan Pin Pin to bring alive an HDB void deck by placing renowned pianist Margaret Leng Tan and her toy piano there. Dressed elegantly in black, Margaret performs John Cage's 'silent' composition, *4'33"*. We are mesmerized by the image of Margaret performing so still and we hear the accompanying ambient sound. Tan Pin Pin has transformed this place that no one really notices into a performing stage. If we could have that privilege every day, what wonderful things would happen? At the end of the performance, Margaret takes a bow. And we hear the silent 'applause'. ➾ ***Wahyuni A. Hadi***

Directed by Tan Pin Pin
Scene description: Pianist Margaret Leng Tan performs 4'33"
Timecode for scene: 0:16:20 – 0:20:15

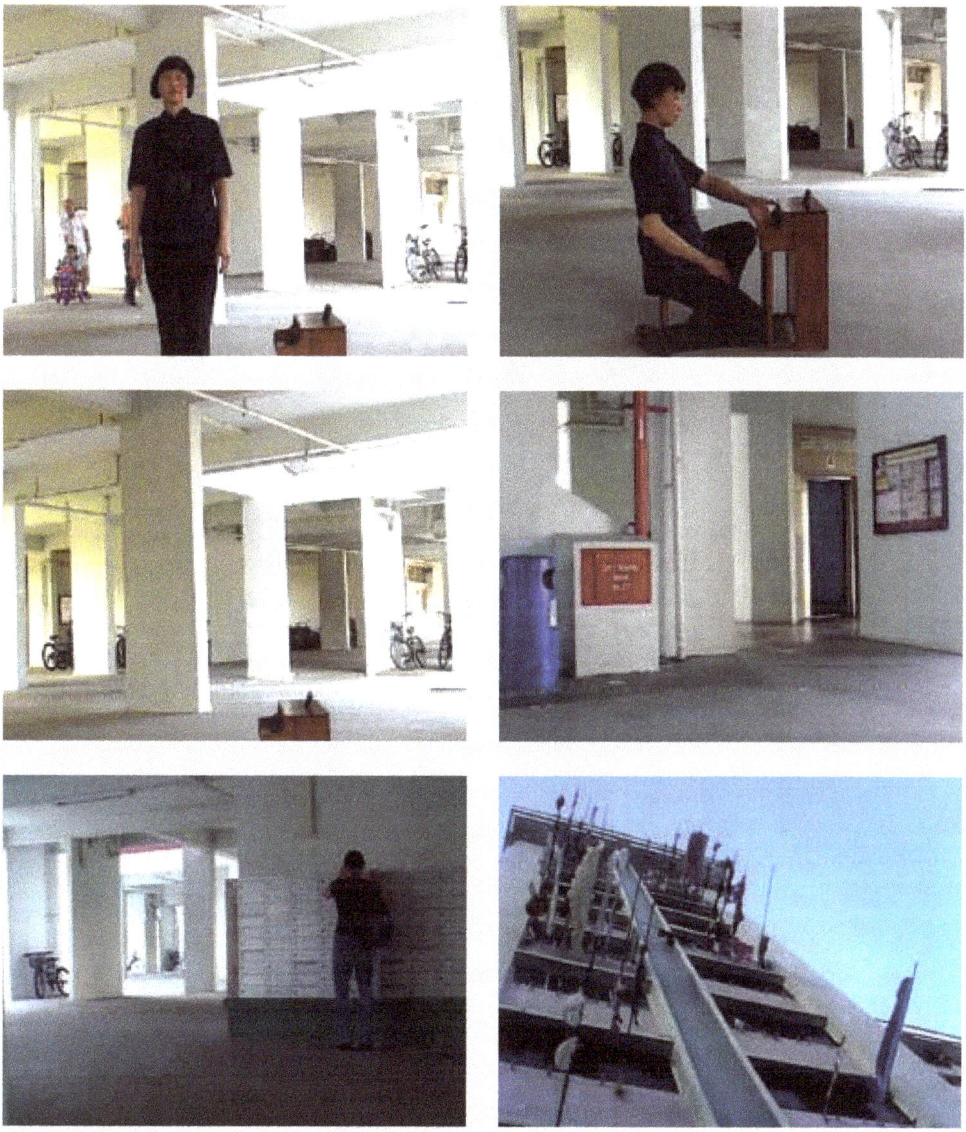

BE WITH ME (2005)

LOCATION *Guan Hin provision shop, Block 55, Tiong Bahru Road, Unit 01-57*

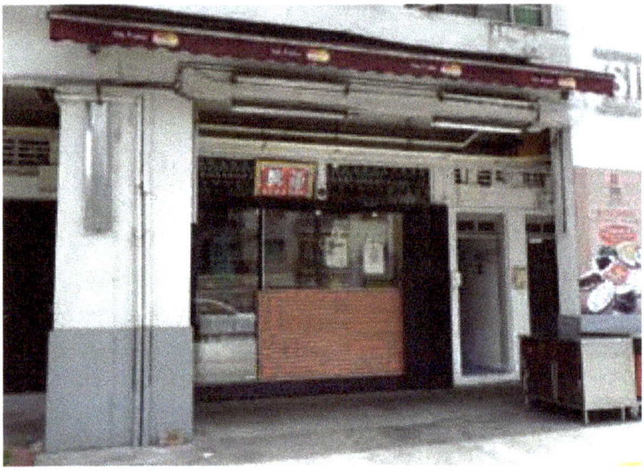

THE FILM OPENS AT DAWN. An old man is slowly closing his small grocery shop with his assistant. Eric Khoo loves to shoot inside such doomed, haunted buildings. In his third film, people are defined by what they do, who they love, where they live and where they stay. The shop owner's wife passed away, but he goes on living as if she was still with him. A security guard is helplessly in love with a beautiful business woman who works in the tower he watches. Two teenage girls meet on the web, fall in love and split up. All these characters share the same goal: *to be with someone*. Around them Singapore is creating loneliness. Highways run impassibly like rivers of cars. The city is an aquarium, a world of glass and frustration. The security guard tries to get his fantasy through windows and screens, nothing but a shadow on a cold surface. In the residential areas, windows and doors are locked by metal gates. Khoo's characters are both free and jailed. They walk, they dance, they take the bus. But at some point they find themselves behind bars, staring at the unreachable, sometimes with tears in their eyes. The only character who actually communicates is a blind and deaf woman. Theresa Chan touches the food, the face of the people she meets. Her *real life* is all about feeling. And as we get to know her, we realize that she is giving a soul to the city. And 'Be with me' really means 'Hold my hand', help me cross the avenue to the other side. ➾ ***Adrien Gombeaud***

Photo © Toh Hun Ping

Directed by Eric Khoo
Scene description: An old shop owner closes his grocery
Timecode for scene: 0:0:25 – 1:27:44

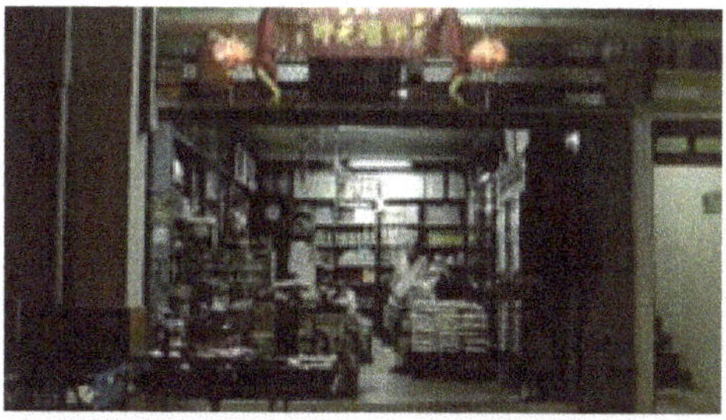

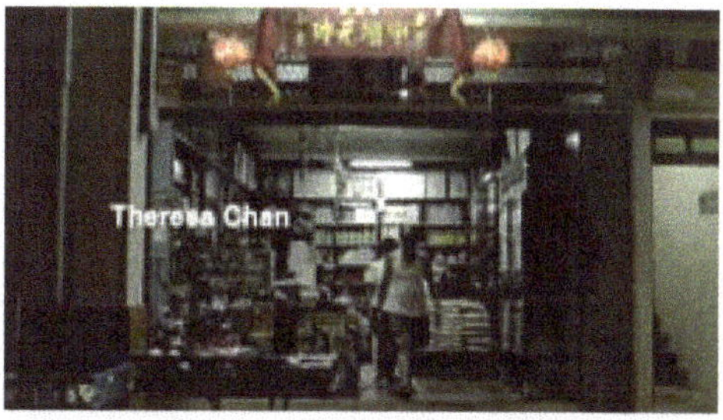

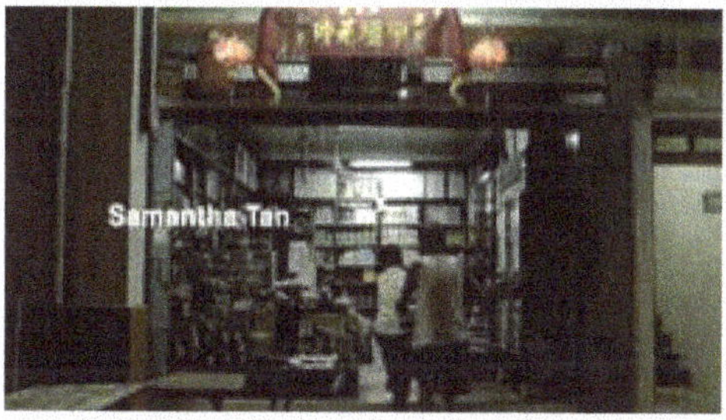

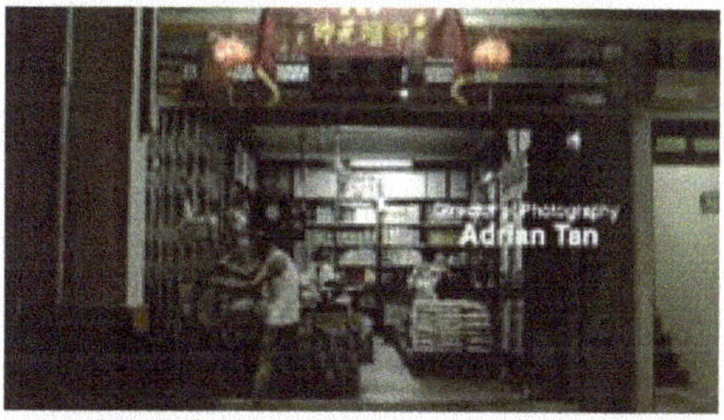

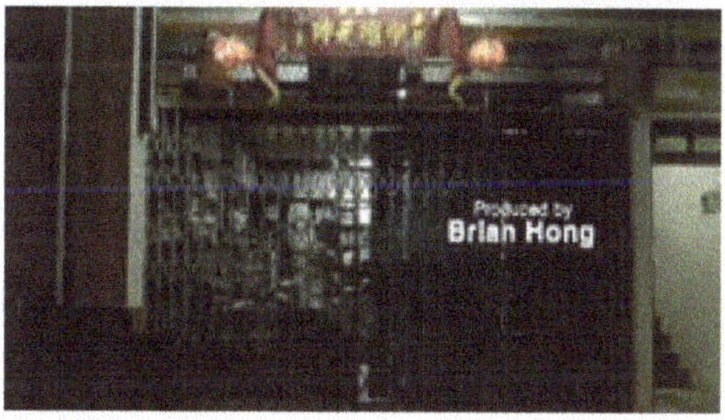

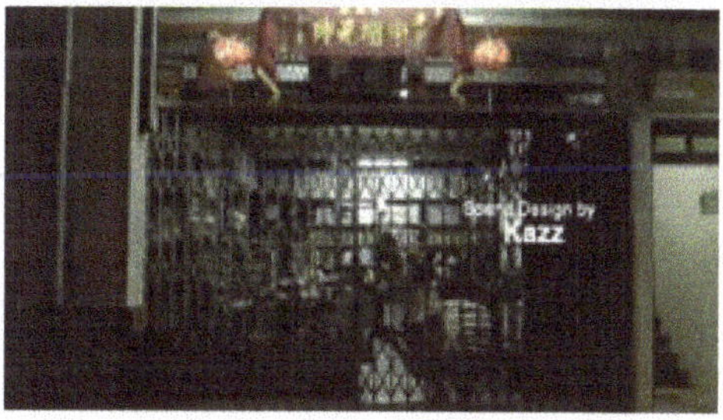

KRRISH (2006)

LOCATION *Marina Bay, Financial District, Sentosa*

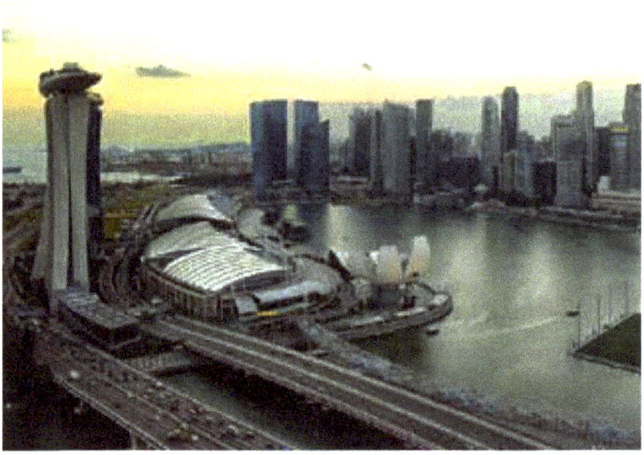

SUPERSTARS SHAMMI KAPOOR and Padmini started a Bollywood invasion of Singapore in 1960 (*Singapore*, by Shakti Samanta), tracing the path for Shashi Kapoor, Aishwarya Rai, Akshay Kumar and the like. Their flame is kept alive on a daily basis by some lively theatres in the Little India neighbourhood showing new Hindi and Tamil hits. The Singapore Tourist Board, which supported *Krrish*, must have been more than fulfilled by superhero Hrithik Roshan's kinetic jumping up spectacular landmarks, as well as by his sweeping choreography with gorgeous Priyanka Chopra. Intoning 'Koi Tumsa Nahin' ('There's no one like you') the romantic couple seem to fly like seagulls from Marina Bay – before its facelift – to the Financial District, the National Library, the Botanic Gardens, Sentosa beaches. Since 2006 how many astonishing vistas have radically changed for better or worse? **Lorenzo Codelli**

Photo © chensiyuan (wikimedia commons)

Directed by Rakesh Roshan

Scene description: The two fiancés sing and dance all over town

Timecode for scene: 1:59:48 – 2:04:45

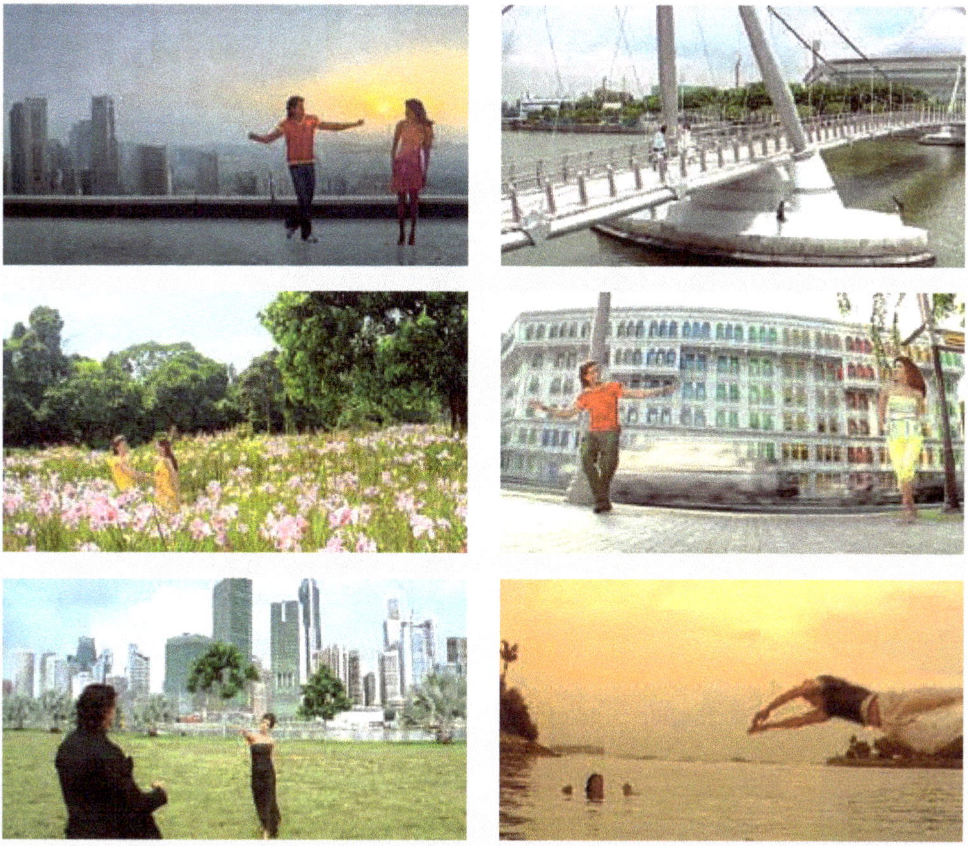

GONE SHOPPING (2007)

LOCATION *Mustafa Centre, 145 Syed Alwi Road, Little India*

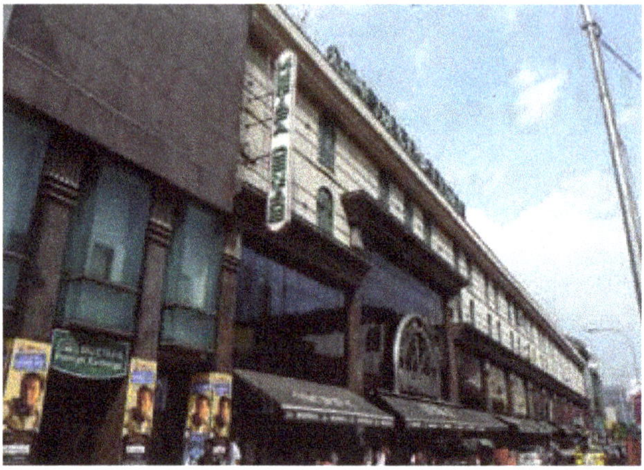

MUSTAFA CENTRE is a 24-hour departmental store located in Little India. Mustafa is one-of-a-kind in Singapore. It offers everything from jewellery to groceries to electronics to clothing to toys. Imagine walking through from one department to another. At its exit points, small food stores sell hot savoury snacks to keep you going through the night. In the day, middle-aged women and tourists do grocery and souvenir shopping. Come night, Mustafa becomes a place for the insomniac, bored teenagers or 'another dreamer' as described in Wee Li Lin's film, *Gone Shopping*. Mustafa is the kind of saving-grace place one needs. Forgot an anniversary? Have a hankering for a late night cook-in? Anybody desperately in need of something at the odd hour? Mustafa is the place. But more than that, it has become a local iconic place over time. Singaporeans often refer to it with fondness and delight. It has a strange sense of excessiveness to it. Do we need a 24-hour shop where we can buy gold, a television set or a little Merlion globe? Unlikely. But oh how fun it is when we do. It is the kind of absurdity that Singapore needs. It injects us with imagination. In *Gone Shopping*, a little girl is lost from her parents and a young woman is lost emotionally. They are both dreamers and want to escape their reality at Mustafa. 'I want to stay in my dream,' says the character named Clara. She falls asleep and dreams of kissing the man of her dreams.
→ *Wahyuni A. Hadi*

Photo © Toh Hun Ping

Directed by Wee Li Lin

Scene description: Clara (Kym Ng) goes to Mustafa Centre to shop in the late night and meets little Renu (Sonya Nair)
Timecode for scene: 0:31:36 – 0:41:10

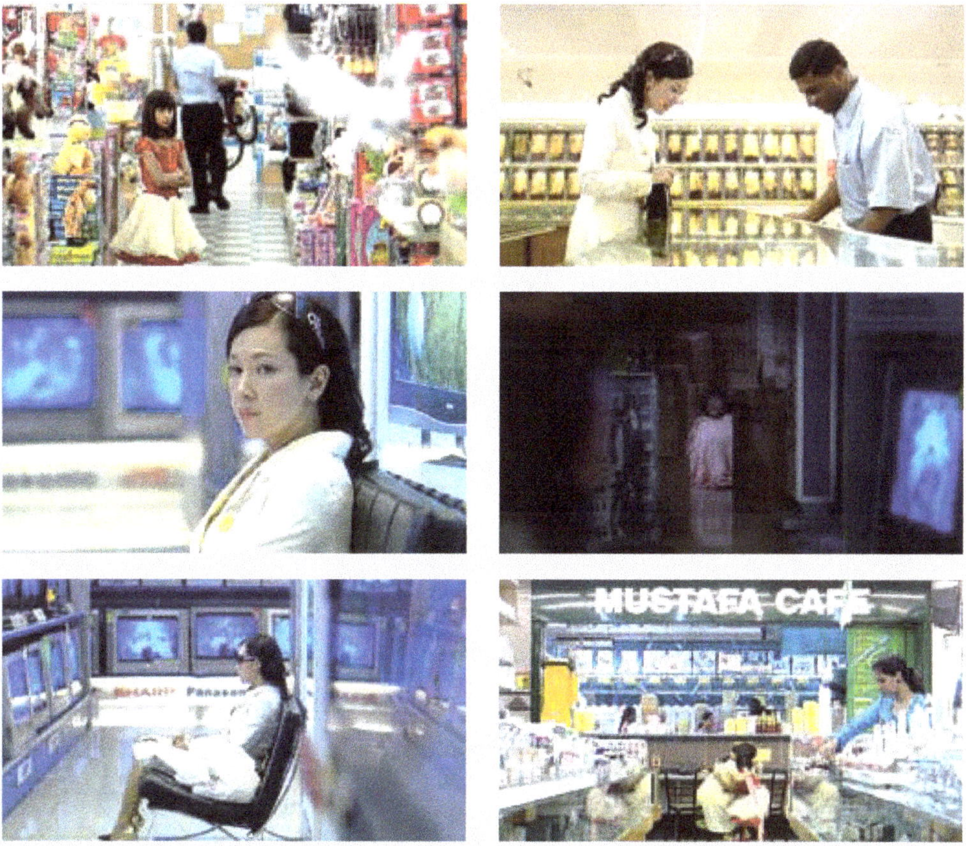

DREAMS FROM THE THIRD WORLD (2008)

LOCATION

Former Tropical Hotel at the junction of Keong Saik Road and Teck Lim Road (now Park 22 Hotel)

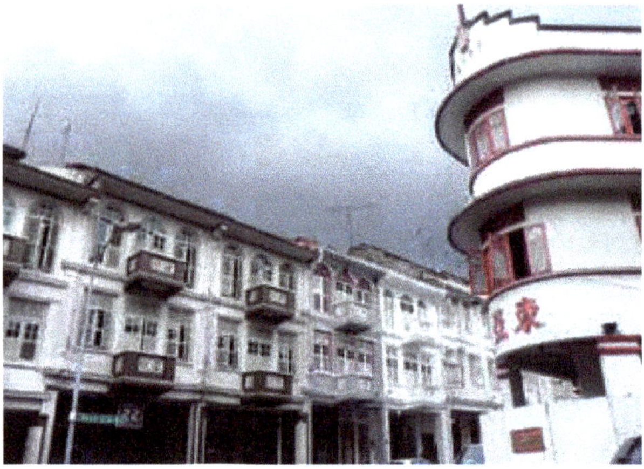

DREAMS FROM THE THIRD WORLD was shot purposely in one of Singapore's oldest red-light districts, Keong Saik Road, in Chinatown. This location reverberates with Singapore film history. Joel M. Reed's *Wit's End* (1975) was the first American film to be entirely shot on location in Singapore in 1969 and the Keong Saik Road area features prominently in the final scenes. Coincidentally, many years later from the 1990s till the noughties, it was also the office location of the Singapore International Film Festival. Leon, the protagonist, decides to follow the path of the artist, that of a film-maker. He then finds that his whole upper-middle-class world starts to collapse. When he decides to make a sex film, the prostitute he hires, at Keong Saik Road, is at first impressed by his wealth. But Leon's money is quickly depleted. Soon he is reduced almost to a beggar and he has to steal food from his own cast member. Using the locations of the short-time rooms there, the film is almost a paean to the faded glory of this once-glorious red-light (prostitution) hub of the 1960s. The setting reinforces the notion that artists in Singapore have to prostitute themselves. The fact that today the area has been cleaned up with only two prostitution houses remaining, suggests also that even the oldest profession in the world can be stripped of its passion in Singapore. Both artists and prostitutes have to struggle to regain their passion. ***Philip Cheah***

Directed by Kan Lume

Scene description: The porn film-maker and his actress

Timecode for scene: 0:37:50 – 0:46:46

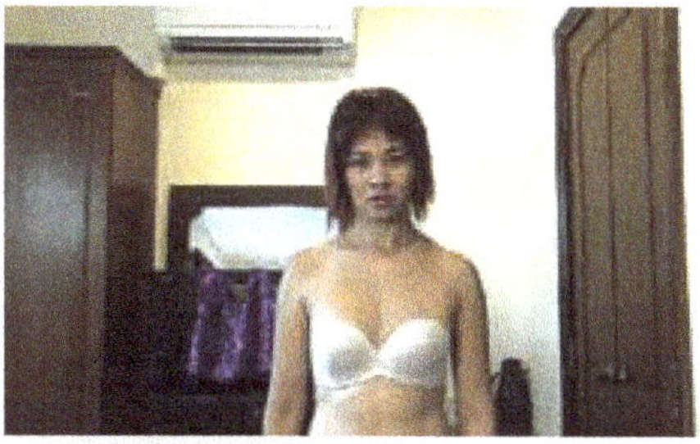

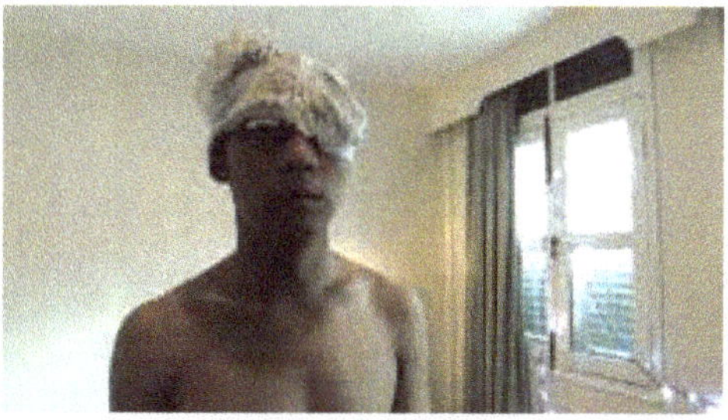

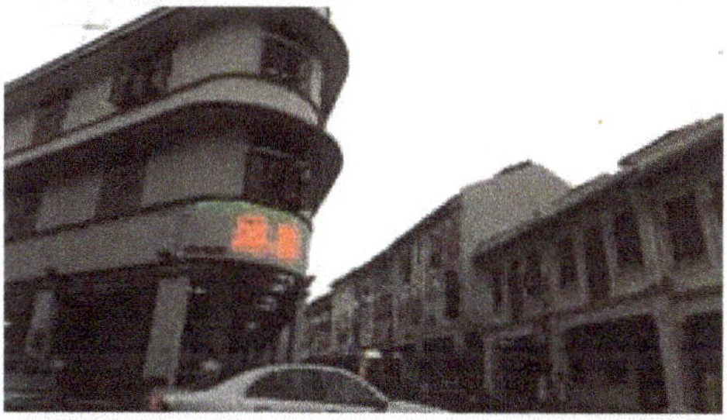

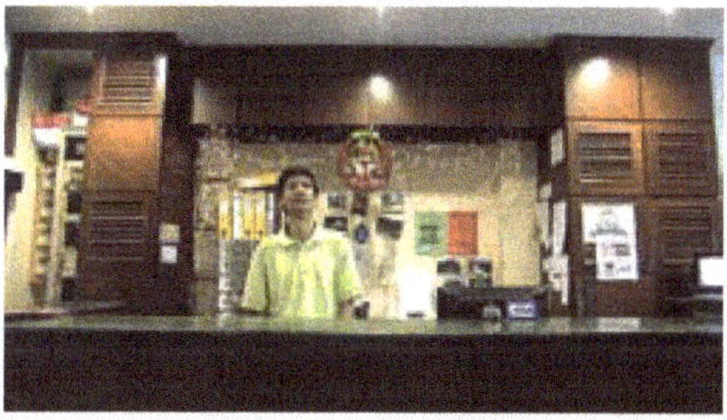

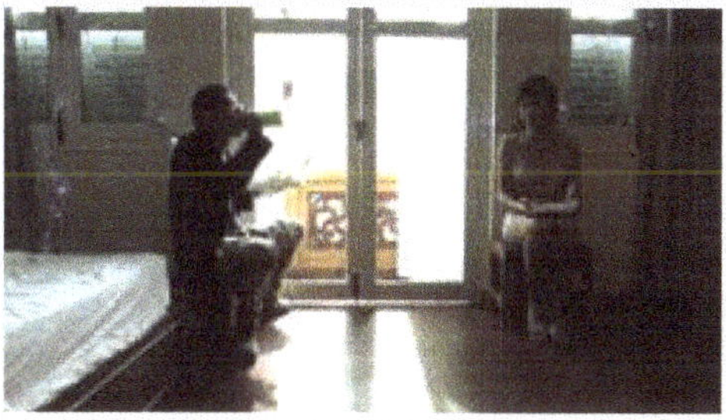

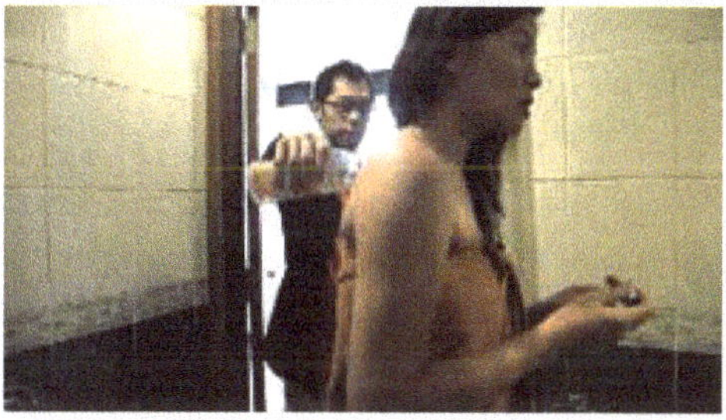

LOST IMAGES: FILMS FROM THE IVAN POLUNIN ARCHIVE (2009)

LOCATION

A kelong and the Tuas Market (now shipyards and industrial estates)

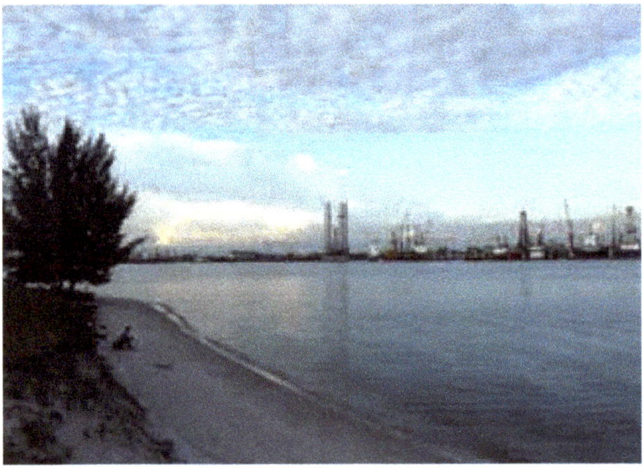

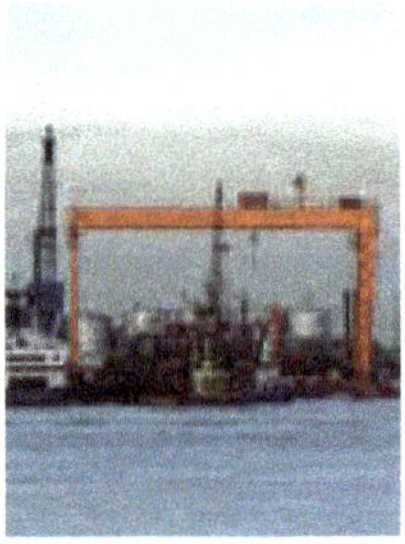

DOCTOR IVAN POLUNIN (b.1920–d.2010), a medical lecturer since 1952 at the University of Malaya in Singapore – later renamed National University of Singapore – was an extraordinary self-made film-maker who shot all over the island, and elsewhere, for his own pleasure as well as researching diseases, and was frequently hired by the BBC too. His wide collection of 16mm reels was rediscovered thanks to Tan Pin Pin's feature documentary *Invisible City* (2007). He devoted his old age to restoring over 100 hours of rushes, mostly made by 30 seconds-long shots. In this wonderful anthology commentated by, and starring himself, the Peter Ustinov-like physician is following the ever-smiling natives thriving in a pre-industrial Eden free of any *tabus*. During the colonial 1950s and the 'liberating' 1960s, the blue sea still looks as generous and productive as the luxuriant plantations, both granting bountiful nutrition. Polunin's camera shares Robert Flaherty's deep empathy towards the fishermen and their daily labours on their fragile offshore *kelongs*. He helps to build one ironically using his heavy weight. According to Tan Pin Pin, 'Polunin was a good visual storyteller in terms of the nuts and bolts of the event. All the more important because it is in *colour* – suddenly there was life, and *thriving life* as that! He was also a naturalist, and extremely familiar with the flora and fauna of South-east Asia. He was really a renaissance man.'
Lorenzo Codelli

Photos © Toh Hun Ping

Directed by Peter Leslie Lamb

Scene description: Fishermen living on offshore platforms bring their catch to the fish market

Timecode for scene: 0:30:56 – 0:35:14

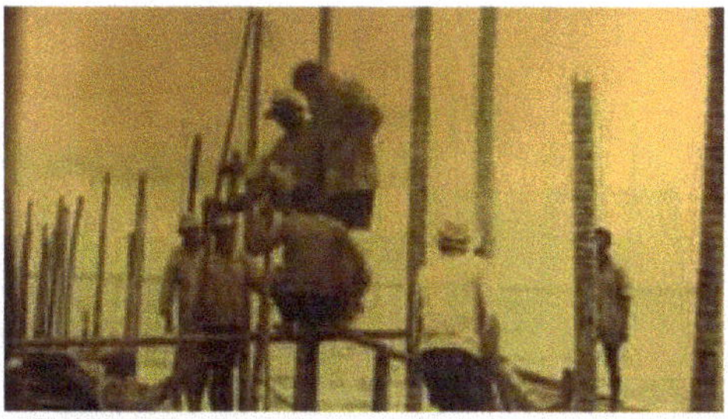

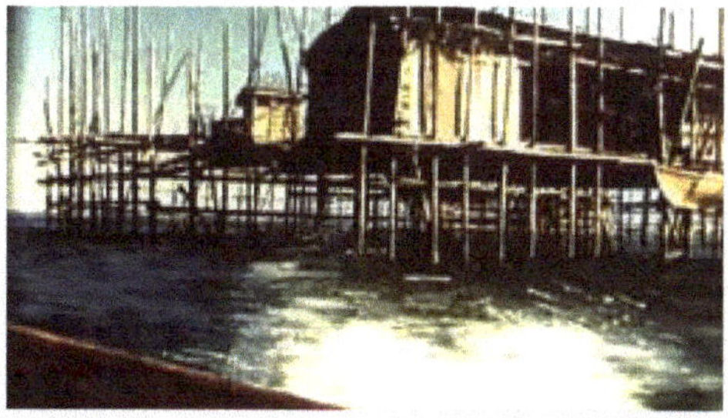

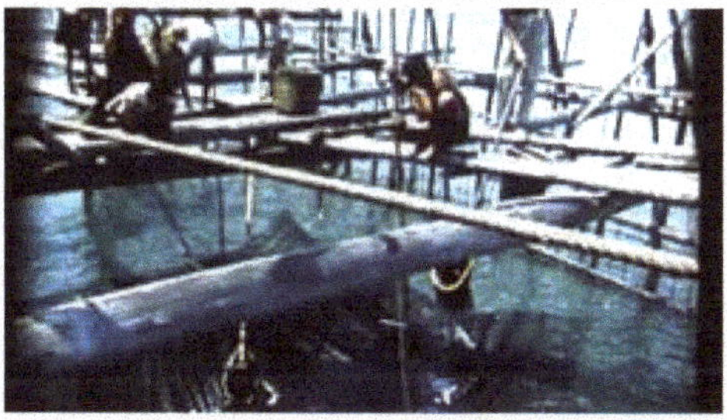

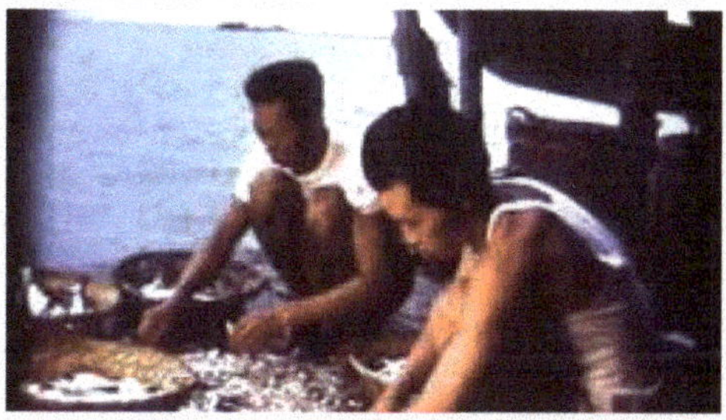

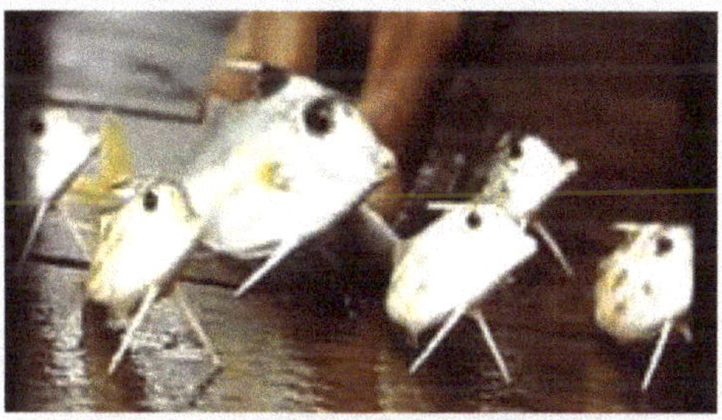

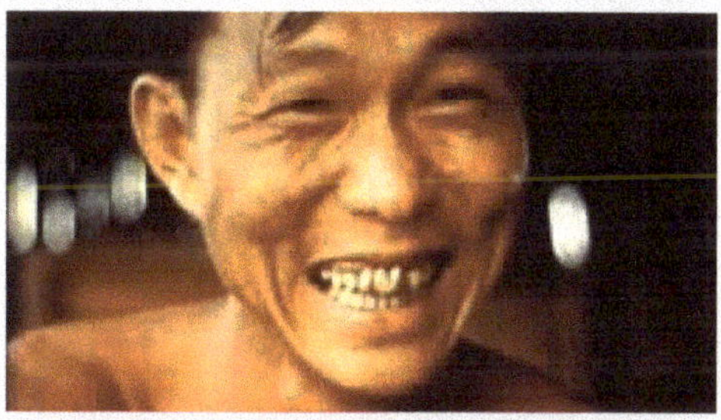

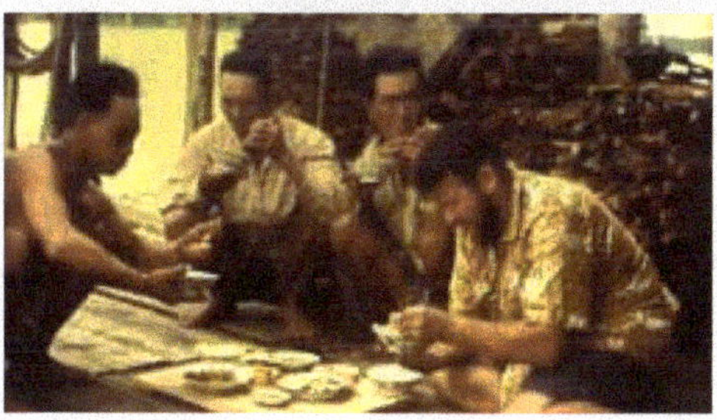

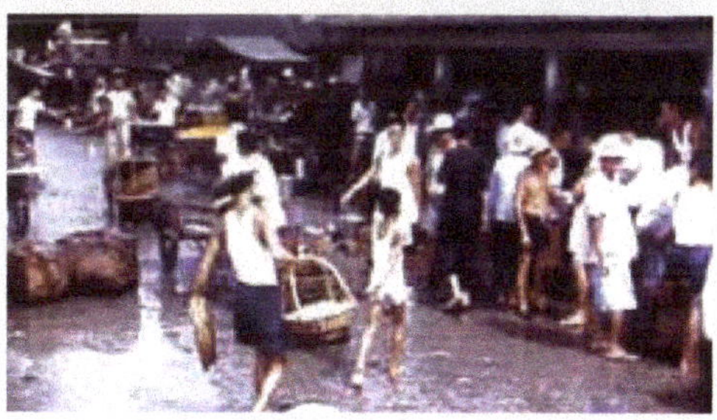

SPOTLIGHT

HDB FLATS

Text by WARREN SIN

A View of Public Housing in Singapore Cinema

Of course, movies aren't about the places. They are about stories. If we are noticing the location, we are not really watching the movie. It is what's upfront that counts.

– THOM ANDERSON, *LOS ANGELES PLAYS ITSELF*

THE HOUSING DEVELOPMENT BOARD (HDB) provides public housing for up to 80 per cent of Singaporeans in the form of flats located in housing estates which are self-contained satellite towns with schools, supermarkets, clinics, food centres and sports and recreational facilities. With the Housing Development Board providing public housing to the majority of the country's citizens, it is only contingent that HDB blocks of flats occupy a sizeable amount of screen-time in the local cinema. While the blocks vary in design and functionality, the flats are classified on the basis of size and number of rooms. Size is usually denoted by terms such as four-room, five-room, and is based on the number of bedrooms inclusive of the living room. Newer five-room flats come with only three bedrooms and a dining room. On average, the size of the flats range from 23 square metres to 130 square metres.

A survey of Singapore films reveals that HDB flats are often portrayed as a backdrop. At times, if rather infrequently, HDB flats surface as a character, and seldom, if ever, have they been considered as a subject.

The most notable early instance of the HDB flat in a Singapore film can be traced back to Cathay-Keris's sole Mandarin production, *Lion City* (1960). The appearance of which must be startling in an age of *kampong* (village) living. The *kampong* was the backdrop of many Malay films made in that era. An entire generation of stories revolves in and around the *kampong*, encompassing all genres from melodrama to horror and everything in between. At times the *kampong* itself becomes a character, most memorably in Hussein Haniff's *Jiran Sekampong* (1965). In the studio era, it is not difficult to pre-suppose the keen representation of the HDB flats as a force of modernity. While the idea of public housing is explicitly optimistic in *Lion City*, the few times HDB flats peered over the filmic horizon in the studio era, they loomed as stark reminders of things to come: the massive public housing project spearheaded by HDB from as early as the 1960s. At the end of K. M. Basker's social comedy *Satay* (1958), the titular little orphan is at a literal crossroads in his life as he has run away from his foster parents: hedged in on one side of the road by familiar middle-class semi-detached houses with decorous garden spaces, and on the other by impersonal newly built flats. In Liao Jiekai's sprawling debut film *Red Dragonflies* (2010), stately vertical HDB flats can be seen peering over the immense greenery of nature. At the threshold between the order of man-made structures and the chaos of nature is created imbuing a phenomenological concern as to the ways in which the film is perceived.

Films that dispensed with genre expectations are in a better position to revel in the locations and atmosphere. Ho Tzu Nyen's *Here* (2009) is bookended by the spatial relationship between the lead character and his surroundings, a sparsely decorated, nondescript HDB flat. The sparseness of the flat is broken up by two visual flourishes that define the spatial condition between character and environment. A glowing orb of orange light and accentuation of a series of cracks on the ceiling provide cues that integrate the exterior with the interior, giving psychological depth to the unfolding act of violence that is to follow. The idea of home is inexplicably linked with the notion of self. In this instance, the flat has obvious connotations of the character's unhinged state of mind. The scene's brilliance lies in the placid

Below *Ilo Ilo* (2013)

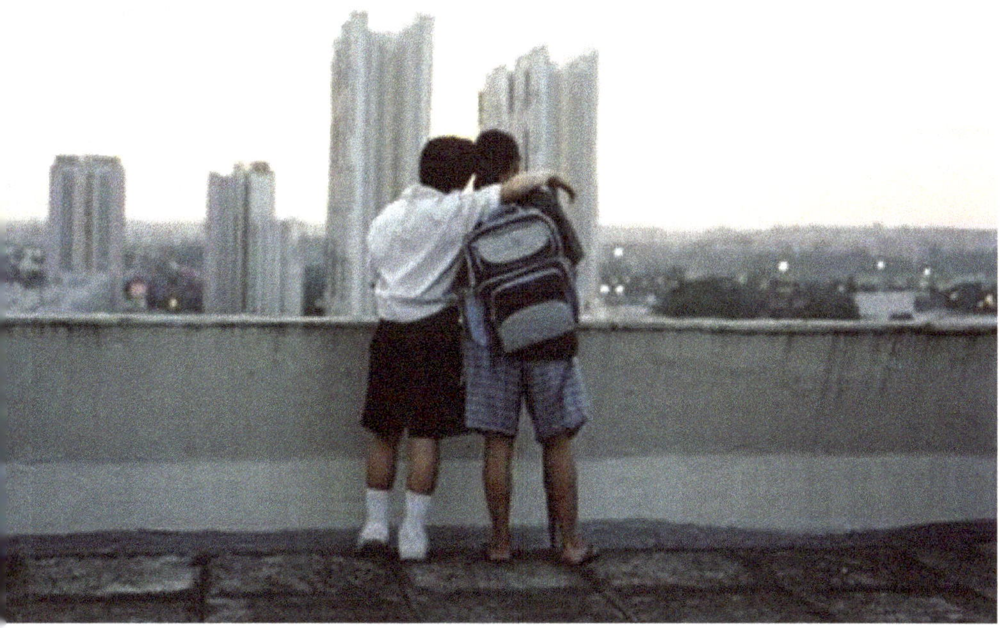

Above © 2013 Fisheye Pictures

performance of the actor counterpointed by the turmoil of the inanimate environment. In Sherman Ong's *Flooding in the Time of Drought* (2009), much of the film takes place in the various spaces within HDB flats where immigrants from diverse nationalities engage in conversations about life and concerns in Singapore. The cacophony of voices reveals different social orders living in the same space trying to make sense of their environment. The scenes are framed as static portraits as the characters inhabit intimate spaces in their newly adopted homeland. The subjects are often framed in relation to the angular design of a typical flat. In a Singaporean film devoid of any Singapore characters, the almost ubiquitous presence of the HDB flat and the framing device adopted by Ong breathe life into the environment. As the film progresses, the familiar environs of a HDB flat come together, giving rise to an impression of a living and breathing monolith in silent observation to the testimonials of its foreign inhabitants.

In a Singaporean film devoid of any Singapore characters, the almost ubiquitous presence of the HDB flat and the framing device adopted by Ong breathe life into the environment.

Here, the flat becomes a metaphorical character. Along the same tangent but on a completely different path, Eric Khoo's *12 Storeys* (1997) presents the titular twelve-storey flats as backdrop to the lives of four sets of characters. The film starts and ends with the block of flats at night illuminated by the cold fluorescent lights emitting from the common corridors and individual home units. One can just about imagine the block of flats as a behemoth in the depth of the ocean and the ensuing dramas played out by the parasites in the bowels of the immense beast.

A significant number of Singapore films include scenes shot on the rooftops of HDB blocks. Perhaps the location affords the film-makers considerable visual mileage with panoramic views of the rest of Singapore (most times dotted with even more towering HDB blocks). In Anthony Chen's *Ilo Ilo* (2013), a casual visit to the rooftop develops the ongoing relationship between Jia Ler and his Filipino maid Theresa that is the crux of the film. And in Kelvin Tong and Jasmine Ng's *Eating Air* (1999), the rooftop presents respite for the main protagonists Ah Boy and Ah Girl from their worldly troubles. So perhaps the highest point of one's dwellings represents the verticality of man's aspirations. ⁜

LOCATIONS MAP

SINGAPORE

maps are only to be taken as approximates

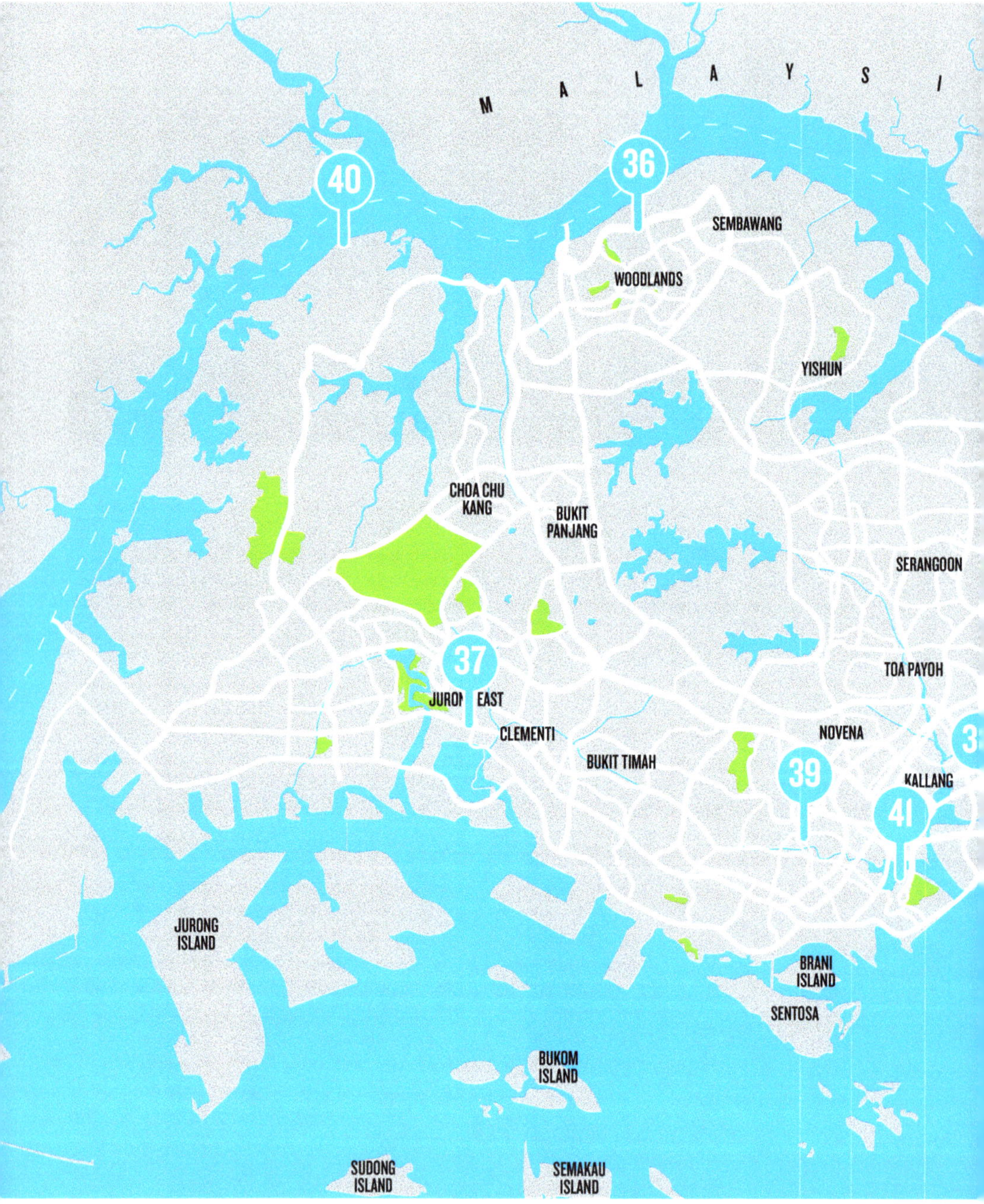

SINGAPORE LOCATIONS
SCENES 36-42

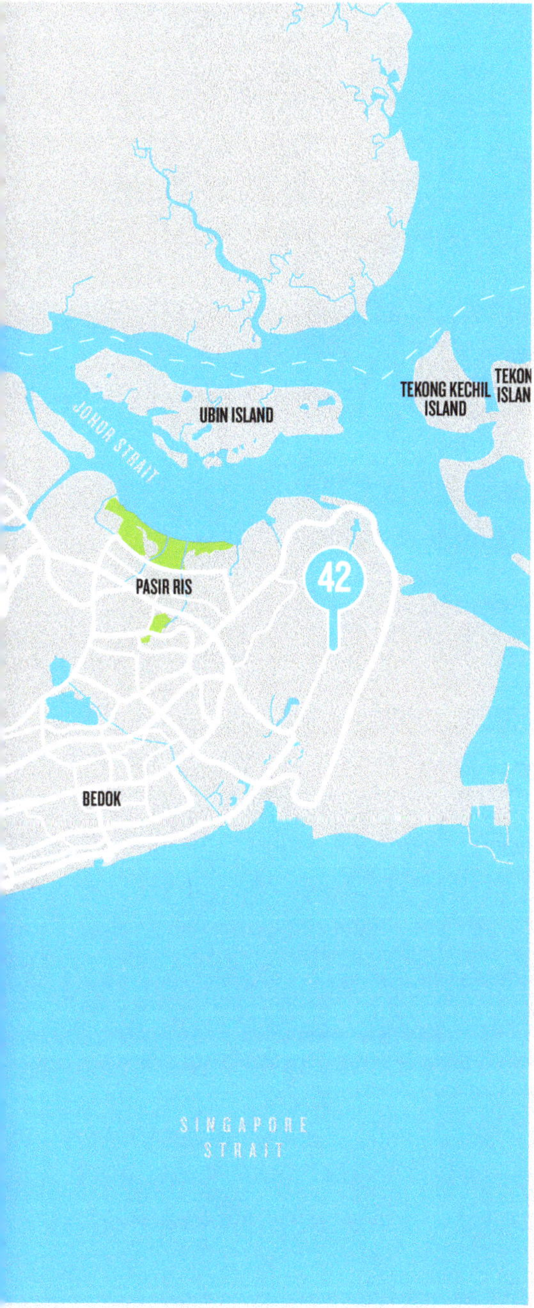

36.
HERE (2009)
View Road Hospital
page 102

37.
RED DRAGONFLIES (2010)
Tunnel along the Jurong Line, KTM Railway
page 104

38.
SANDCASTLE (2010)
Chung Cheng High School, 40–56 Goodman Road
page 106

39.
IT'S A GREAT, GREAT WORLD (2011)
Former Great World Amusement Park (now Great World City), 1 Kim Seng Promenade
page 108

40.
ALL THE LINES FLOW OUT (2011)
Cashin family's house (aka the Pier), off Lim Chu Kang Lane 9
page 110

41.
MY LUCKY STAR / FEICHANG XINGYUN (2013)
Marina Bay Sands Hotel
page 112

42.
ILO ILO (2013)
Changi Airport Terminal 2
page 114

HERE (2009)

LOCATION *View Road Hospital*

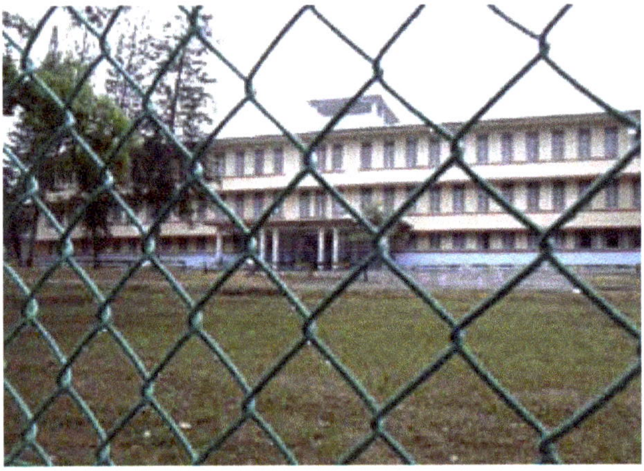

HERE WAS SHOT in a secluded compound surrounded by greenery, located at the end of a stray road close to the edge of Singapore in the Woodlands District. Back in the 1960s and 1970s, the building was once a barrack for a contingent of the Gurkhas from the naval base. In the mid-1970s, the building was handed over to the Ministry of Health which proceeded to convert it into a secondary facility for the then overcrowded Woodbridge Hospital, Singapore's sole mental institution. View Road Hospital introduced alternative rehabilitative programmes for its patients, making full use of the repose granted by its wide naturalistic surroundings. *Here* poses an interesting mirror to its location's historical past as it weaves in an impressionistic portrait of a community of mental patients in the process of rehabilitation. The film is bookended by shots of a car journey towards and away from the hospital that highlights the noise and movement of the city. In stark contrast, the scenes in the hospital are affected by a lethargic slowness that conjures a looming silence. While the characters speak in disembodied tones, devoid of overt gestural and expressive emotions, the location itself brings forth a dramatic vitality. While the hospital serves as a contemplative space, *Here* finds its force in the exterior of the compound, through sudden focuses on foliage seen through a window, and when the patients transverse through greenery on their afternoon walks. In a particular scene, the camera pans slowly through the surroundings of the hospital before coming to a halt at a frame of foliage. The non-diegetic sound of two patients singing the Christian hymn 'Amazing Grace' is introduced, and the foliage is gently manipulated in minute detail to illustrate the ebbs and flows of the atmosphere. View Road Hospital ceased operations in 2001. It was used as a foreign worker dormitory for a short period of time before falling back into misuse in the present, where it's heavily fenced and guarded by CCTVs. ***Low Zu Boon***

Photo © Low Zu Boon

Directed by Ho Tzu Nyen
Scene description: Foliage around View Road Hospital
Timecode for scene: 0:14:57 – 0:17:40

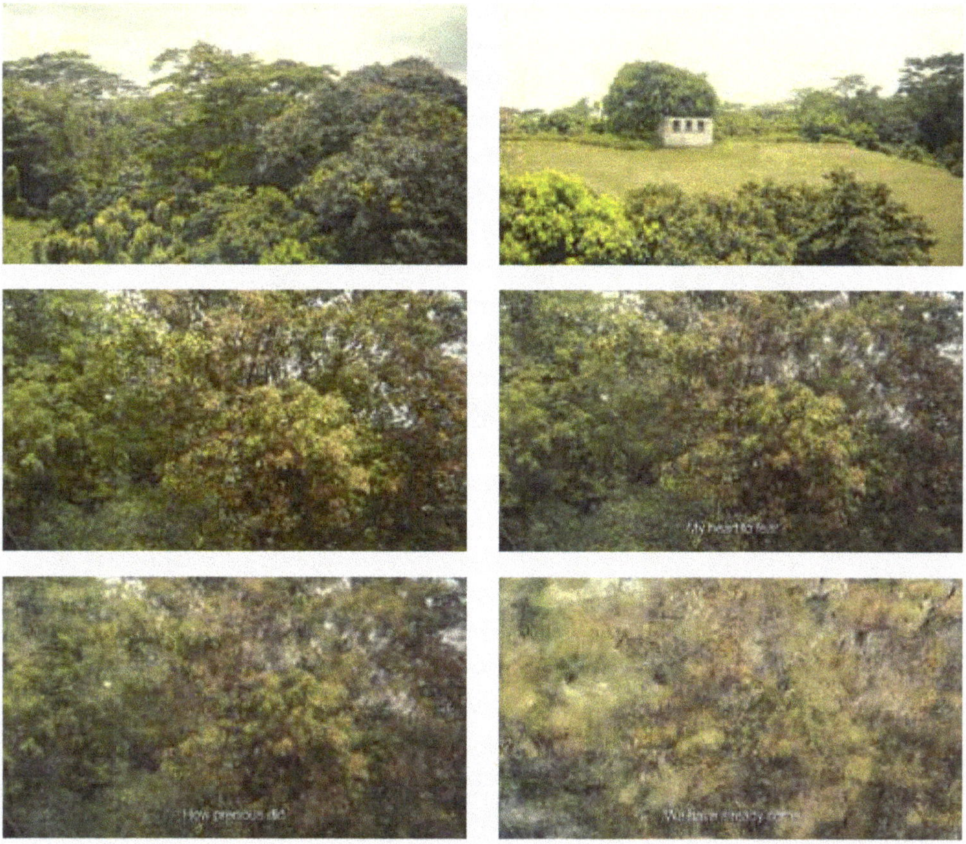

RED DRAGONFLIES (2010)

LOCATION *Tunnel along the Jurong Line, KTM Railway*

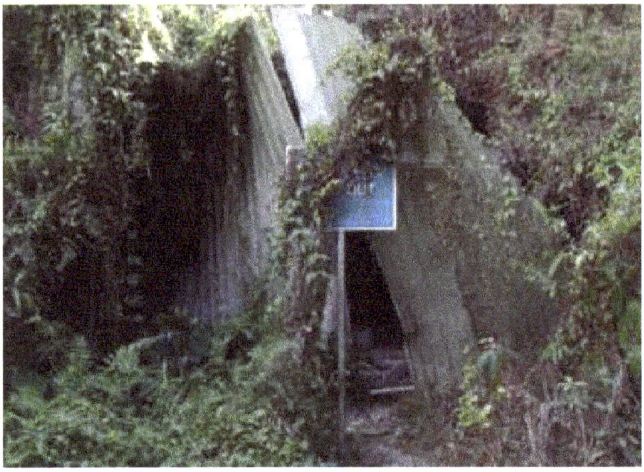

THE MAIN PROTAGONIST in *Red Dragonflies* is imagined as a symbolic space. Yet it's not exactly space in the traditional sense but a pathway that finds meaning through its illustration of time, a pathway where memories that spectrally permeate and linger in the present are linked with a premonition of future events. The pathway in the film is the KTM railway line, a main transportation link between Singapore and Malaysia from 1923 till 2011, when the last train ran its course. In recent decades, the line existed quietly, losing its currency to new modes of transport. *Red Dragonflies* was in production when there was a resurgence of public interest in the railway due to the announcement of its inevitable cessation. The film exhumes the fragility of a forgotten space stuck in time that once facilitated movement. In what is presented as a fragment of childhood, a scene follows Junjie, Rachel and Tienwei as they explore the Jurong Line, an abandoned segment of the railway tracks which cuts through a dense forest. Tienwei and Rachel impatiently trudge into a railway tunnel as Junjie trails behind. He seems to be consumed by an internal weight as he wearily yet introspectively observes his surroundings. As he enters the tunnel, he finds himself engulfed by overwhelming darkness which evaporates the perception of time into nothingness. Environmental sounds are reduced into near silence in perhaps the quietest passage in the film. Junjie's melancholic perceptivity of his surroundings heightens the fragile nature of time and the futility of remembrance, and this is further accentuated by the faint glimmer of light at the end of the tunnel casting shifting silhouettes of the three students. Yet it is also darkness itself that becomes a canvas that facilitates the virtual movement of time. In this sense, the tunnel can be seen as a symbolic anchor that informs the fluid and diagonal movement through different time periods in *Red Dragonflies*. **→ *Low Zu Boon***

Photo © Low Zu Boon

Directed by Liao Jiekai
Scene description: Junjie, Rachel and Tienwei enter a railway tunnel
Timecode for scene: 0:16:23 – 0:18:49

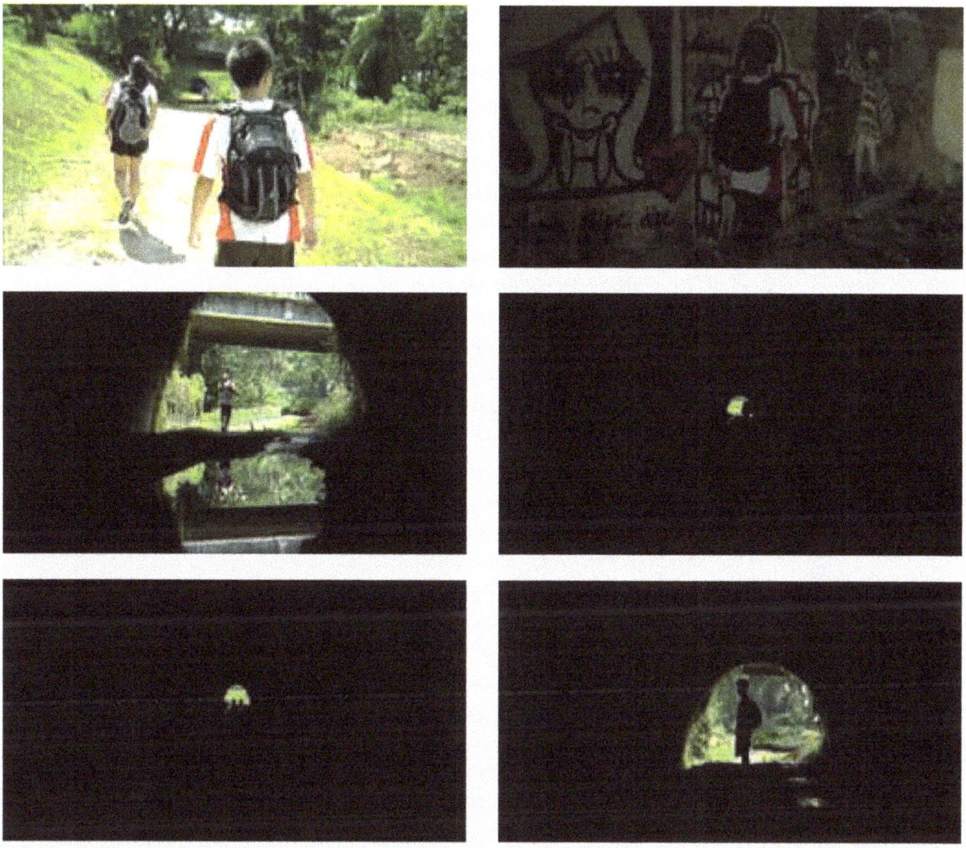

SANDCASTLE (2010)

LOCATION

Chung Cheng High School, 40–56 Goodman Road

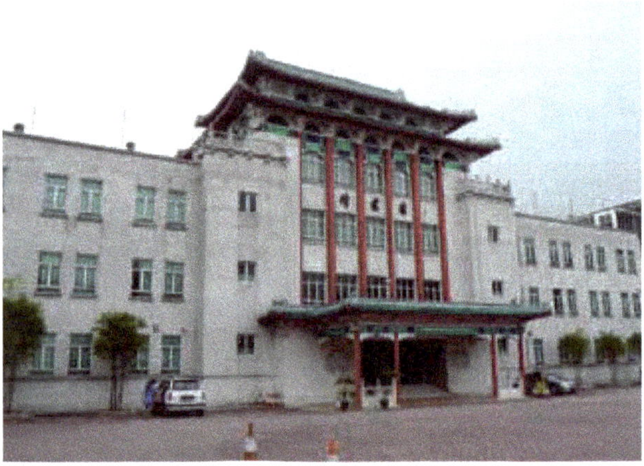

IN *SANDCASTLE*, Boo Junfeng reveals the dysfunction that the youths of today face when they strive to forge an identity amidst the ahistorical environment of contemporary society. He does so through En, a teenager on the threshold of adulthood, awaiting his conscription to the army for National Service. He is uncomfortable with the Christian and nationalistic values harboured by his mother and stepfather. However, he finds solace with his ailing grandparents, from whom he discovers a collection of photographs and letters which reveal his mother and deceased father's veiled past as student activists during the anti-colonialist and class-conscious struggles of the late 1950s. In one scene, a friend reads to him a letter written by his father in exile. In the letter, he asks En's mother if she remembers a play they wrote together about a man who spent his life searching for a Utopia under the sea, whether she thinks this world still exists, and if he gives up the search now, would he have lived in vain? The contents of the letter are read as a voice-over, as we see En visiting Chung Cheng High School, where in 1956 his father participated in a series of student demonstrations in retaliation of the government's ban on the Singapore Chinese Middle School Students' Union for alleged 'communist' activities. Knowing that En's father's detention and exile spanned a total of 27 years when the letter was written imbues this passage with a strong sense of melancholy, of a forced disavowal of one's ideology, which seems strikingly authentic in the light of the belief systems circulating amongst En in the present. In *Sandcastle*, the significance of Chung Cheng High School as a site where politics was once physically practised by students, and its aftermath which signals the gradual demise of political agency in Singapore, is resurrected as spectres permeating the emptiness and silence of the space. As En explores the school, we sense his desire to understand his father, his passage to maturity and perhaps, the potential for a political awakening. **⇢Low Zu Boon**

Photo © Toh Hun Ping

Directed by Boo Junfeng
Scene description: En visits Chung Cheng High School
Timecode for scene: 1:07:14 – 1:08:16

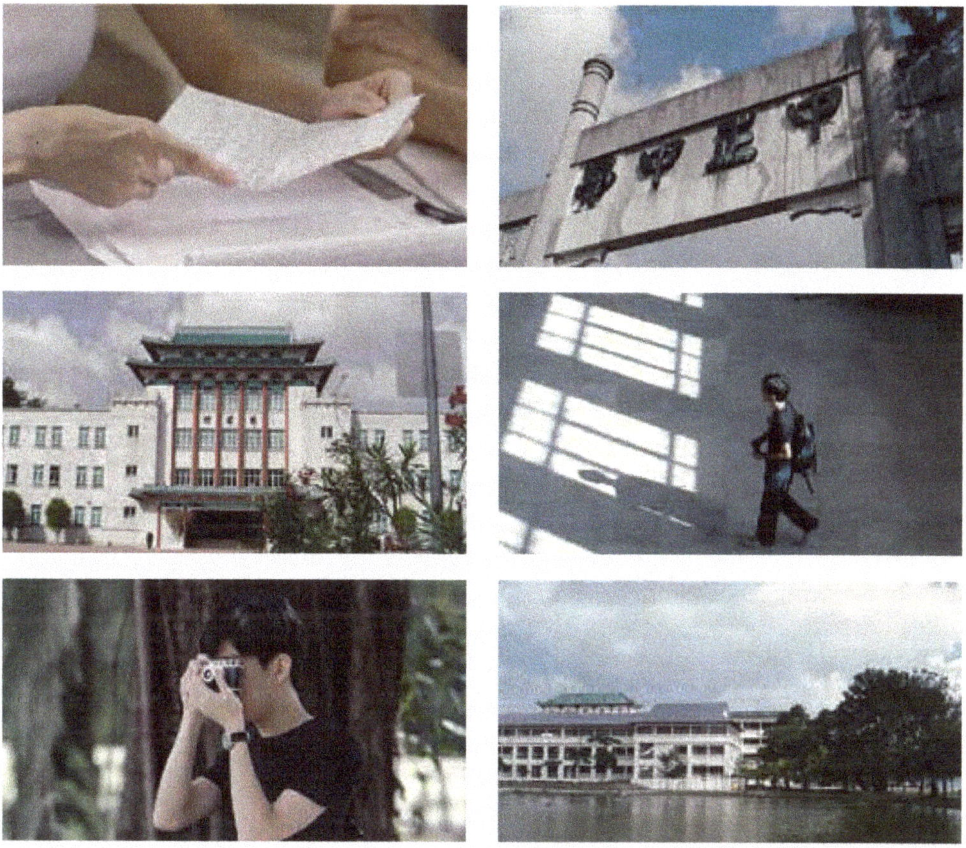

IT'S A GREAT, GREAT WORLD (2011)

LOCATION

Former Great World Amusement Park (now Great World City), 1 Kim Seng Promenade

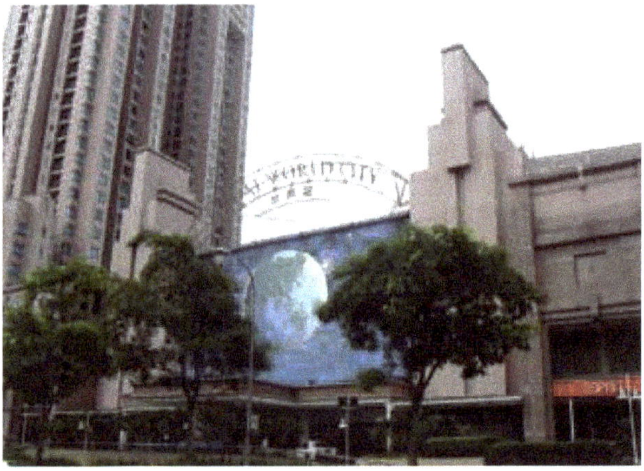

KELVIN TONG, a great film critic and movie buff, devotes a nostalgic paean to a once popular amusement park. The park depicted in the film was not the original one (it closed in 1978), but was instead a film set constructed in a former army camp. Using old photographs and anecdotes from folks who used to frequent the park as reference, this imitation of the hugely popular 'Great World' Amusement Park (better known as 'Tua Seh Kai' in Hokkien) was designed with faithful recreations of the park's icons: the distinctive main entrance to the park; the renowned 'Sky Theatre' where the Singapore premiere of *Around the World in 80 Days* (Michael Anderson, 1956) was graced by Elizabeth Taylor; the 'Ghost Train' ride; the 'Flamingo' nightclub; 'Wing Choon Yuen' Cantonese restaurant; and stalls of 'tikam-tikam' (games of chance, from a Malay phrase which means 'to choose randomly'). 'Reminiscence' and 'Legacy' are major themes in the film, which revolves around a young photographer visiting an old-timer of the park. He recalls the good ol' days as he pores over photographs of personalities associated with the park's heydays from the 1940s to the 1970s. However, the 'legacies' that the amusement park and its filmic re-creation leave behind are but mere vestiges of an era/place that are today evoked mostly for nostalgia; for purposes that are none-too-critical. No physical traces remain of the old amusement park. Where it once stood is now a nondescript shopping complex with a contrived name – 'Great World City'. ➾ ***Lorenzo Codelli and Toh Hun Ping***

Photo © Sengkang (wikimedia commons)

Directed by Kelvin Tong
Scene description: The premiere of 'Around the World in 80 Days'
Timecode for scene: 0:17:55 – 0:19:16

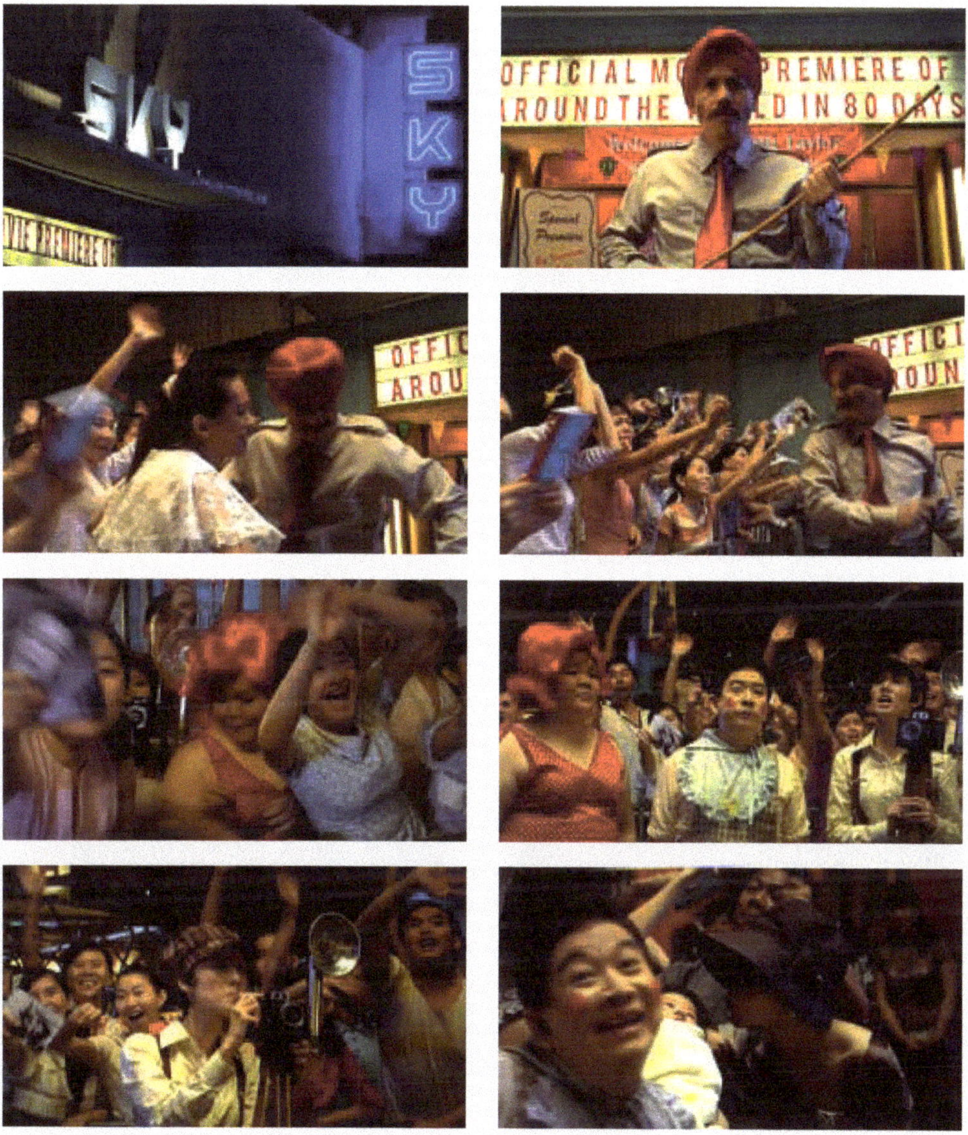

Images © 2011 Boku Films, Raintree Pictures

ALL THE LINES FLOW OUT (2011)

LOCATION *Cashin family's house (aka the Pier), off Lim Chu Kang Lane 9*

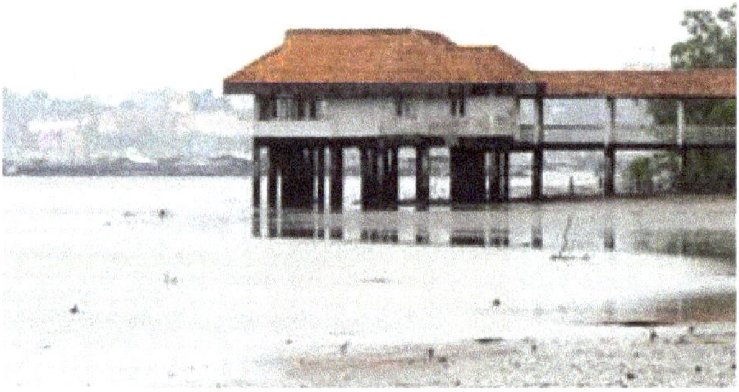

A TABLEAU OF human figures clad in what seems like laboratory coats are dispersed along a stretch of a water canal. They move slowly through the space surveying the environment. The camera zooms into one of their perspectives, revealing a micro ecosystem of fishes and plants existing amidst the derelict confines of the canal. A white-coloured chemical is released into the water and it diffuses down the canal like a fog. What follows in *All the Lines Flow Out* is a point-of-view journey through the water canals of Singapore, passing through housing and industrial estates, until architecture gives way to a vastness of raw concrete, green spaces and eventually the edge of Singapore island opening up to the sea. As a former sailor, Charles Lim's artistic *oeuvre* is concerned with the maritime geography and history of Singapore. In *All the Lines Flow Out*, Charles explores the stratification of the island by revealing the waterways of Singapore. Some previously existed as natural flowing rivers which have been canalized and fitted into the network of drainage systems throughout the island. As the film reaches the boundary between land and sea, Charles chooses to film a seafront house built in the 1910s at the end of a pier in Lim Chu Kang. It was owned by the Cashin family until the Japanese occupation, when it was used as a recreational facility for Japanese troops. After the war, it was reacquired and refurbished by the Cashins who named it 'The Pier'. In 2009 it was handed to the Singapore Land Authority who are now looking to utilize it as gateway to the neighbouring Sungei Buloh Nature Reserve. As land reclamation activities and the tightening of national boundaries have resulted in the removal of many piers which used to exist along shoreline, the Pier remains a striking visible reminder of Singapore's past, an existing boundary marker and gateway to the archipelago. Charles's camera moves into the house, comes to a stop at a shot of the sea, then abruptly cuts to a shot of a body plunging into the sea and its frantic pulsations. ➾ ***Low Zu Boon***

Photo © Toh Hun Ping

Directed by Charles Lim
Scene description: The Cashin family's house as a gateway to the sea
Timecode for scene: 0:19:33 – 0:21:11

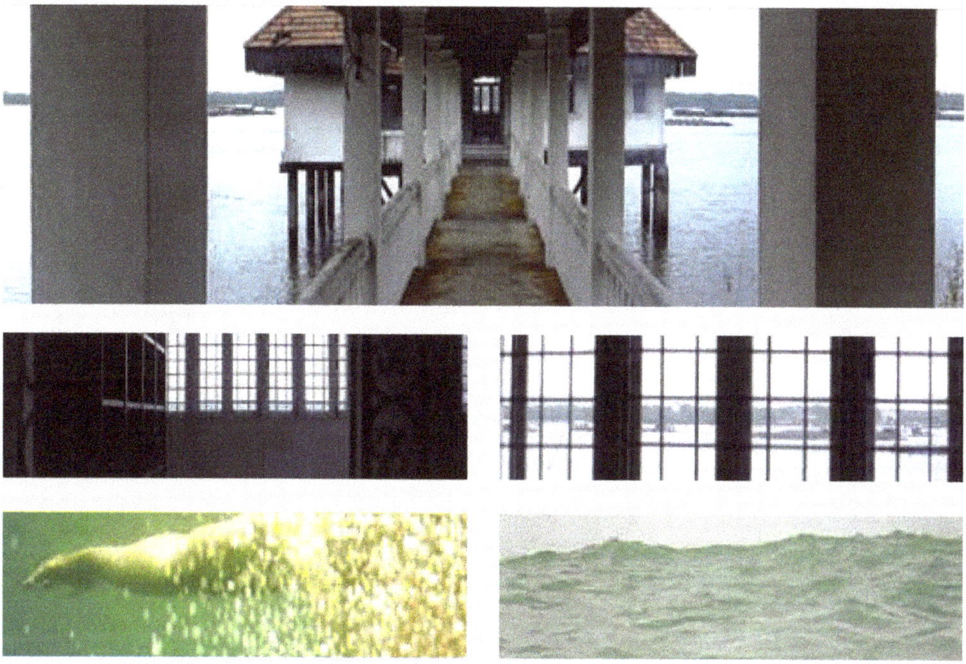

MY LUCKY STAR / FEICHANG XINGYUN (2013)

LOCATION

Marina Bay Sands Hotel

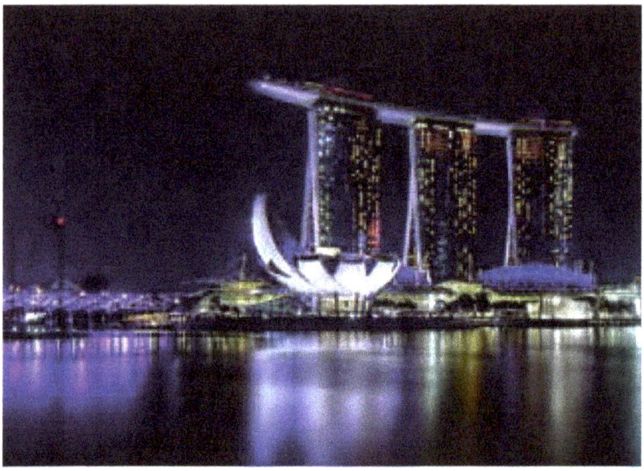

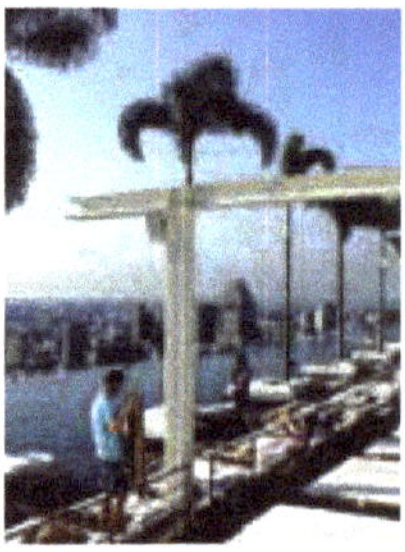

CHINESE MEGASTAR Zhang Ziyi, doubling as executive producer and lead actress, gets a dream holiday in the upper levels of paradisiac Marina Bay Sands Hotel. From its Sky Park located on the 56th floor overlooking the sea waves, the ArtScience Museum, Gardens by the Bay, shipyards, golf courses, the Business District, the mythical Merlion, the Esplanade theatres, and the whole town's faraway hills and neighbourhoods, heroine Zhang Ziyi 'can see forever' – like Barbra Streisand did in her musical hit *On a Clear Day* (1970). American TV director Dennie Gordon might not display Vincente Minnelli's utopian flair; she is anyway quite able to blend the more blatant product placements and tourist ads within a romantic fairy tale spiced with some light James Bond's touches. The breathtaking night skydiving over Marina Bay Sands of weightless Zhang, embraced to her athletic beau Wang Leehom, reveals the three reclining towers as giant plastic menhirs, digital SFX on an unthinkable scale. ➾***Lorenzo Codelli***

Directed by Dennie Gordon

Scene description: Two secret agents are watching over an underworld dealer

Timecode for scene: 0:18:11 – 0:19:27

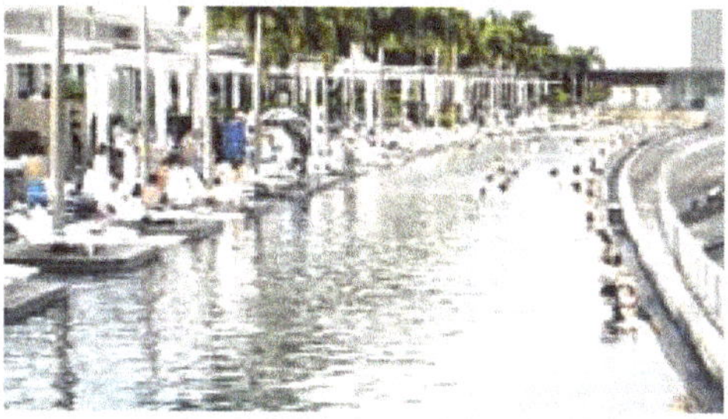

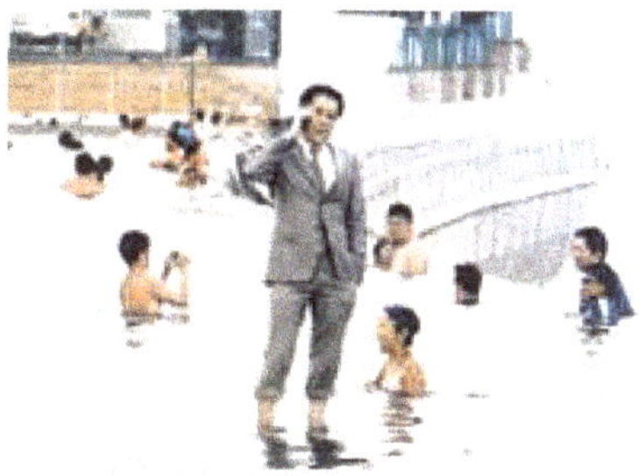

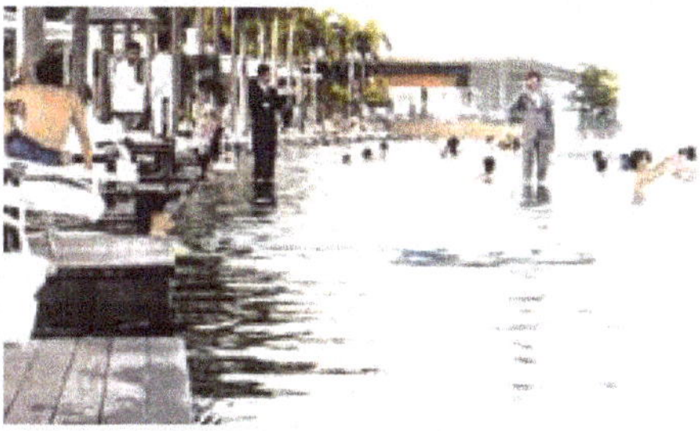

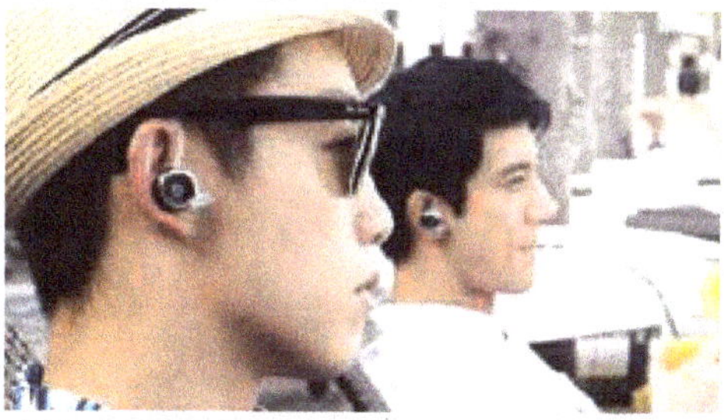

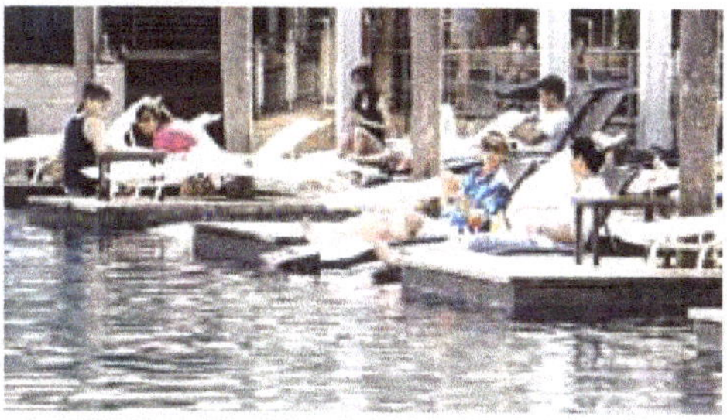

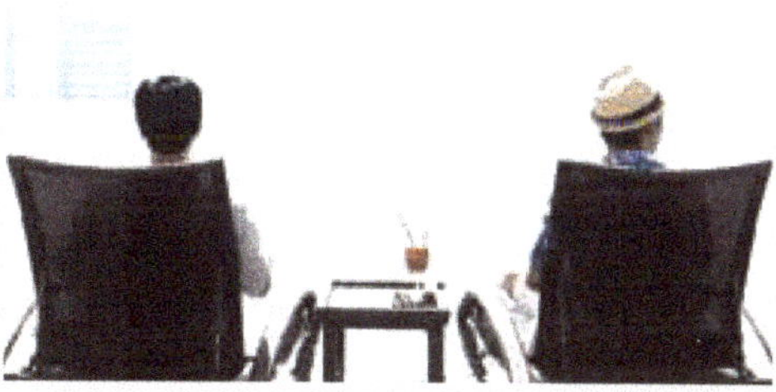

ILO ILO (2013)

LOCATION *Changi Airport Terminal 2*

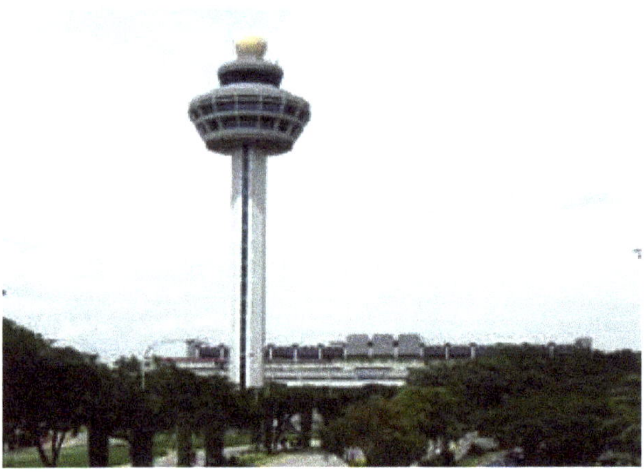

THE RELATIONSHIP between foreign maids and their employers, Singaporeans, is an obsession recurring in films such as Kelvin Tong's chilling horror *The Maid* (2005) and Eric Khoo's social miniature *No Day Off* (2006). Debutant Anthony Chen reconstructs some memories of his own childhood in 1997 telling about a middle-class family suddenly hit by the Asian financial crisis, and 'saved' day by day, in various ways, by a Filipino maid. The angelic woman sweetly played by Angeli Bayani has left her family in Iloilo province, and is trying to adapt to a harsh environment, which includes an imperious pregnant mom (Yeo Yann Yann, who is really expecting), an unlucky and frustrated dad (Chen Tianwen) and one of the most unbearable *enfants terribles* ever put on-screen (Koh Jia Ler). Inspired by Jean Renoir's humanistic spirit, Anthony Chen acknowledges that every single character has his/her own reasons. Chen's chronicle of a near past is exquisitely detailed and balanced between realism and idealism, tragedy and comedy. The whole audience at Cannes's Directors' Fortnight premiere was crying at the end, as is the kid saying farewell to his once despised maid, and cutting off a lock of her once smelly hair. The universality of this parable about *interdependence* was rewarded with Caméra d'Or as best first work at Cannes, four Golden Horse Awards at Taipei and a worldwide distribution.
➾Lorenzo Codelli

Directed by Anthony Chen
Scene description: The maid says farewell to the kid in a taxi
Timecode for scene: 1:32:16 – 1:33:55

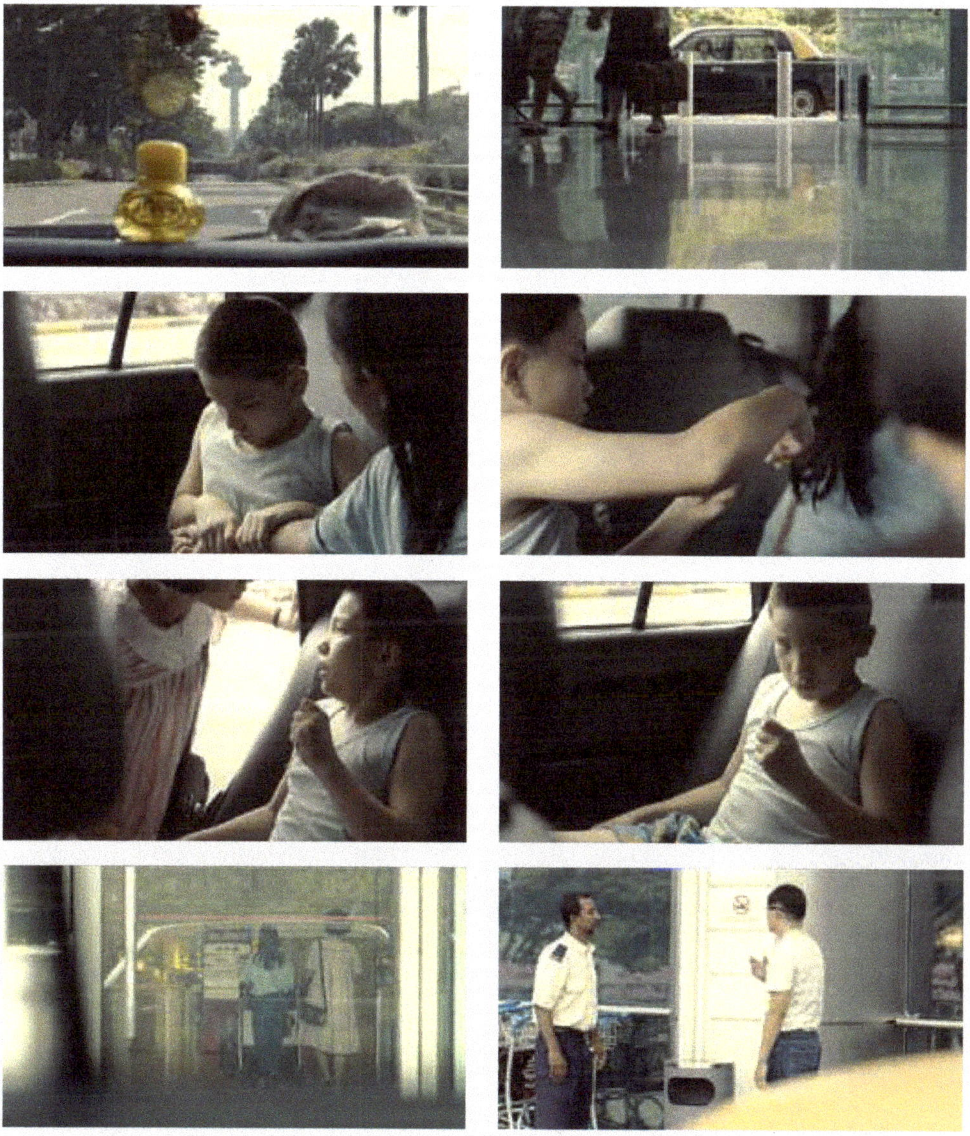

GO FURTHER

Recommended reading, useful websites and film availability

BOOKS

On Issues of the Malayanization of Chinese-language Cinema
by Yi Shui
(Nanyang Yin Shua She, 1959)

Cathay: 55 Years of Cinema
by Meileen Choo, Lim Kai Tong and Yiu Tiong Chai
(Landmark Books, 1991)

Catalogue Pathé des années 1896 à 1914
by Henri Bousquet
(Plein Chant, 1993–2004)

Kaca Permata: Memoir Seorang Pengarah/ Glass Jewel: Memoir of a Director
by Jamil Sulong
(Dewan Bahasa dan Pustaka, 1993)

Memoir Hamzah Hussin: Dari Keris Film ke Studio Merdeka/A Memoir of Hamzah Hussin: From Keris Film to Studio Merdeka
by Hamzah Hussin
(University Kebangsaan Malaysia, 1997)

Layar Perak dan Sejarahnya/The Silver Screen and Its History
by Wahba and M.Amin
(Fajar Bakti, 1998)

Shohei Imamura: Entretiens et témoignages
by Hubert Niogret
(Dreamland, 2002)

The Shaw Story: A Preliminary Study
ed. by Wong Ain-ling
(Hong Kong Film Archive, 2003)

The Imperial Screen: Japanese Film Culture in the Fifteen Years' War, 1931–1945
by Peter B. High
(University of Wisconsin Press, 2003)

Le Cinéma de Singapour: Paradis perdu, doute existentiel, crise identitaire et mélancolie contemporaine
by Raphaël Millet
(L'Harmattan, 2003)

Kinda Hot: The Making of Saint Jack in Singapore
by Ben Slater
(Marshall Cavendish, 2006)

Singapore Cinema
by Raphaël Millet
(Editions Didier Millet, 2006)

The Glorious Modernity of Kong Ngee
ed. by Wong Ain-ling
(Hong Kong Film Archive, 2006)

Dictionnaire du cinéma asiatique
ed. by Adrien Gombeaud
(Nouveau Monde Editions, 2008)

China Forever: The Shaw Brothers and Diasporic Cinema
ed. by Poshek Fu
(University of Illinois, 2008)

The Cathay Story – Revised Edition
ed. by Wong Ain-ling
(Hong Kong Film Archive, 2009)

120 Malay Movies
by Amir Muhammad
(Matahari Books, 2010)

Latent Images: Film in Singapore – Second Edition
by Jan Uhde and Yvonne Ng Uhde
(National University of Singapore, 2010)

BOOKS (CONTINUED)

Asian Film Journeys: Selections from Cinemaya
ed. by Rashmi Doraiswamy and Latika Padgaonkar
(NETPAC/Wisdom Tree, 2010)

Asian Women in Film
ed. by Meileen Choo and Zhang Zhen
(Cathay Organisation, 2011)

P Ramlee: Erti yang sakti/P Ramlee: The Bright Star
by James Harding and Ahmad Sarji
(MPH Group, 2011)

Filem Melayu dari Jalan Ampas ke Ulu Klang/Malay Fim from Jalan Ampas to Ulu Klang
by Salleh Ghani
(Perbadanan Kemajuan Filem Nasional Malaysia, 2011)

Behind the Camera: Personal Recollections of Contemporary Singapore Cinema
ed. by Yuni Hadi
(Objectifs, 2013)

Cinémathèque Quarterly
ed. by Vinita Ramani Mohan, Ben Slater
(National Museum of Singapore, 2011-2013)

ONLINE

The Hunter: Location scouting in Singapore's filmic history
http://sgfilmhunter.wordpress.com

Singapore Film Locations Archive
www.sgfilmlocations.com

The Moving Visuals Co.
www.tmvc.sg

"Clearly you've never been..."
http://sporeana.blogspot.sg

Objectifs
www.objectifsfilms.sg

Singapore Film Society
http://sfs.org.sg/

Media Development Authority Singapore
www.mda.gov.sg

Photo and Film Library
http://www.folcoquilici.com/en/archiviocine_b.html

Singapore Infopedia
http://infopedia.nl.sg

Newspaper SG
http://newspapers.nl.sg/

→

CONTRIBUTORS

Editor and contributing writer biographies

EDITOR

Lorenzo Codelli is a film journalist, historian and archivist, a Cannes Festival adviser, contributor to *Positif, Urania* and other publications. Author of books about Italian and international filmmakers, and editor of festival catalogues.

CONTRIBUTORS

Philip Cheah is a film critic and the editor of *BigO*, Singapore's only independent pop culture publication. He is Vice President of Network for the Promotion of Asian Cinema (NETPAC), and is currently programme consultant for *Asian Film Online*, the Jogja-NETPAC Asian Film Festival, the Tripoli International Film Festival of Resistance, Shanghai International Film Festival and the Dubai International Film Festival. He co-founded the South-east Asian Film Festival and is Advisor to the Hanoi International Film Festival.

Adrien Gombeaud is a writer, journalist and film critic. He contributes to magazines such as *Les Echos* and *Positif*.. He is the editor of *Dictionnaire du cinéma asiatique* (Nouveau Monde, 2008) and author of essays and novels.

Wahyuni A. Hadi is an arts curator specializing in film and media projects. As a partner of Objectifs Centre for Photography and Film, Yuni co-founded the distribution label Objectifs Films. She authored and edited the book *Behind the Lens* (Objectifs, 2012). She is the Executive Director of the 25th Singapore International Film Festival 2014.

Daniel Hui is a film-maker and writer. A graduate of the film programme in California Institute of the Arts, his films have been screened at film festivals in Rotterdam, Hawaii, Manila, Seoul, Bangkok and Vladivostok. His writings have been published in prominent cinema journals, including the *Cinematheque Quarterly* of the National Museum Singapore. He won the Pixel Bunker Award for International New Talent at the Doclisboa International Film Festival for his debut feature film *Eclipses* (2013).

Low Zu Boon studied screen and cultural studies and currently works as a film programmer.

Carlo Montanaro, university professor, film historian, exhibition curator and festival organizer based in Venice, Italy, is one of the founders of the Pordenone Silent Film Festival, and chairperson of the Italian Film Historians Association as well as author of film history books.

Hubert Niogret is a film producer of short films, features and documentaries, including several about cinema; documentary maker; member of the Editorial Committee of the French monthly movie magazine, *Positif*; author of books about Akira Kurosawa, Julien Duvivier, Shohei Imamura, etc.

Warren Sin is a film programmer at the National Museum of Singapore Cinémathèque. Since 2009, he has been involved in several film retrospectives dedicated to Federico Fellini, Satyajit Ray, Edward Yang, the films of the Kong Ngee Motion Picture Production Company, as well as thematic retrospectives such as 'Once Upon a Time in the Orient,' and 'Visions of the East: Asia Through French Eyes.'

Ben Slater is a writer, film critic and lecturer based in Singapore since 2002. His writings on film have appeared internationally, in such publications as *Cahiers du Cinéma*, *Vertigo* and *Screen International* and he's the author of

Kinda Hot: The Making of Saint Jack in Singapore (Marshall Cavendish, 2006). He's edited issues of *Vertigo*, the South East Asian web journal *Criticine*, and the *Cinémathèque Quarterly* (published by the National Museum of Singapore). He's a lecturer at Nanyang Technological University and has a blog, *sporeana.blogspot.com*.

Stephen Teo is Associate Professor in film studies at the Wee Kim Wee School of Communication and Information, Nanyang Technological University. He specializes in Asian cinemas, with a focus on Hong Kong cinema and other Chinese-language films. He is the author of *Hong Kong Cinema: The Extra Dimensions* (BFI, 1997), *Wong Kar-wai* (BFI, 2005), *King Hu's A Touch of Zen* (Hong Kong University Press, 2007), *Director in Action: Johnnie To and the Hong Kong Action Film* (Hong Kong University Press, 2007), *Chinese Martial Arts Cinema: The Wuxia Tradition* (Edinburgh University Press, 2009) and *The Asian Cinema Experience: Styles, Spaces, Theory* (Routledge, 2013).

Toh Hun Ping is a video artist, writer and former art lecturer. His video works have screened at international experimental film festivals (Paris Festival of Different and Experimental Cinema) and were presented in art venues both as video installations and live-performance projections (Sculpture Square and Substation, Singapore). In preparation for his next video work, he is researching into the history of film production in early-mid-twentieth-century Singapore. He also finds time to blog at *sgfilmhunter.wordpress.com*, a website about film locations in Singapore.

Jan Uhde, Professor Emeritus, taught Film Studies (1970–12) at the University of Waterloo, Ontario, Canada. MA, Masaryk University, Brno, Czech Republic; PhD, University of Waterloo. His publications include *Latent Images: Film in Singapore – Second Edition*, with Yvonne Ng Uhde (Ridge Books, National University of Singapore Press, 2010); *Latent Images: Film in Singapore*, with Yvonne Ng Uhde (Oxford University Press, 2000); *Vision and Persistence: Twenty Years of the Ontario Film Institute* (University of Waterloo Press, 1990). He has published in Canada, the US, Germany, the Netherlands, Czech Republic, Singapore and Italy. His other research interests focus on the identification and distancing mechanisms of film viewing; the non-authored modifications and manipulation of films; and the Czech animator Jan Švankmajer. He founded the journal *KINEMA* in 1993.

Yvonne Ng Uhde is the co-author of *Latent Images: Film in Singapore – Second Edition* (Ridge Books, National University of Singapore Press, 2010); *Latent Images: Film in Singapore* (Oxford University Press, 2000. She has written on Singapore and Asian cinema in Canada, Singapore, the US, the UK and Italy.

Silvia Wong is a journalist with several years of experience. She was a magazine editor before joining *Screen International* as its South East Asia correspondent and is currently contributing editor of *Film Business Asia*. She has also moved behind the camera as a film producer and screenwriter.

RECOMMENDED BY THE WORLD'S LEADING FILM CRITICS...

Praise for World Film Locations: New York
'An elegant tribute to the films and locations that have given New York its private real estate in our minds. The contributors are so immediately readable and movie-savvy.' – **Roger Ebert**

Praise for World Film Locations: London
'A superb book, indispensable for any cinephile interested in London's psychogeography. I could pore over it for hours.' – **Peter Bradshaw**

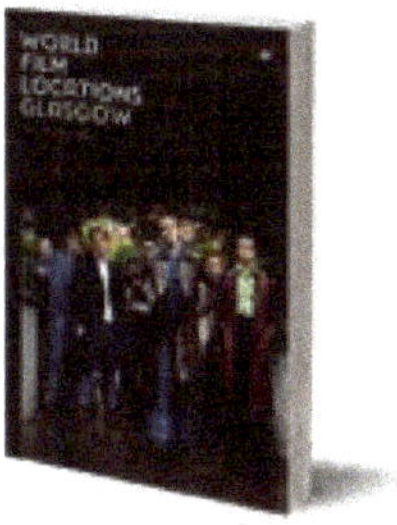

GLASGOW

Edited by
Nicola Balkind
ISBN 9781841507194
PB £15.50 / $22

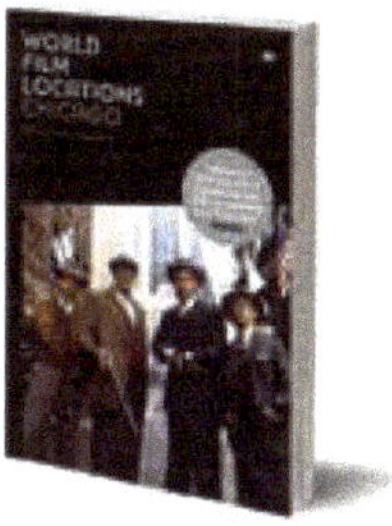

CHICAGO

Edited by
Scott Jordan Harris
ISBN 9781841507187
PB £15.50 / $22

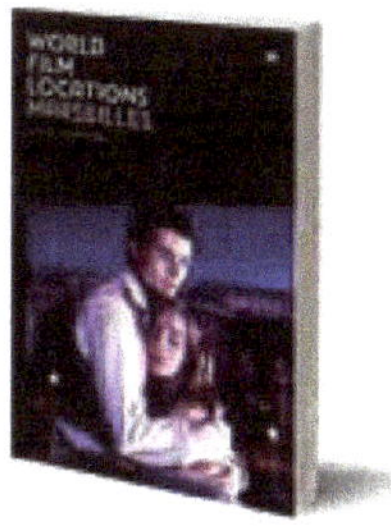

MARSEILLES

Edited by
Marcelline Block
ISBN 9781841507231
PB £15.50 / $22

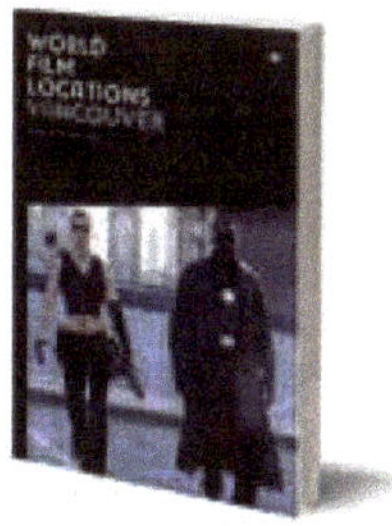

VANCOUVER

Edited by
Rachel Walls
ISBN 9781841507217
PB £15.50 / $22

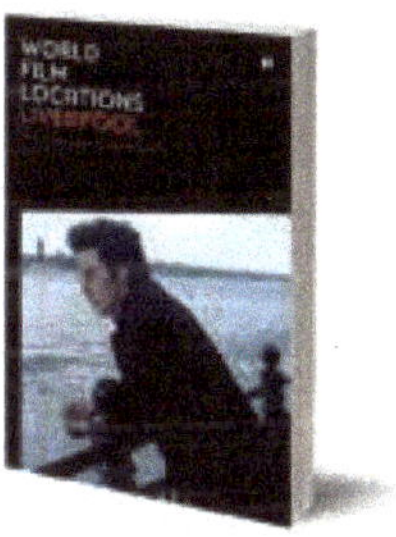

LIVERPOOL

Edited by
Jez Conolly and Caroline Whelan
ISBN 9781783200269
PB £15.50 / $22

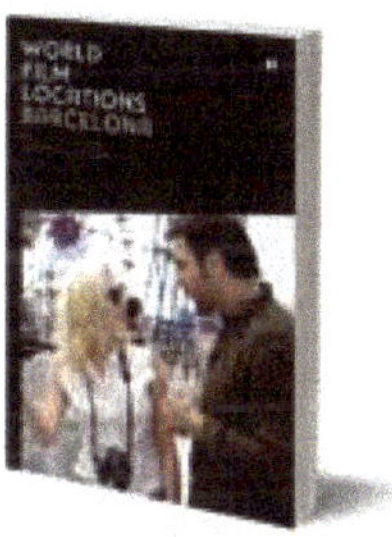

BARCELONA

Edited by
Helio San Miguel and Lorenzo Torres J. Hortelano
ISBN 9781783200252
PB £15.50 / $22

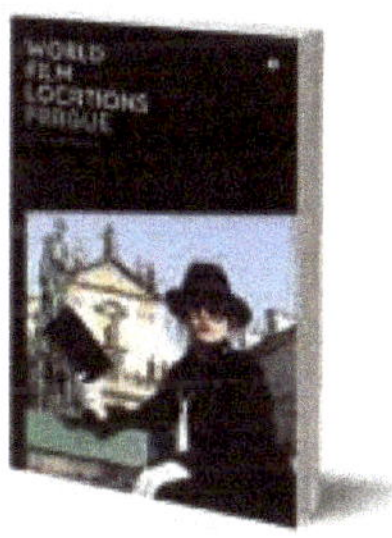

PRAGUE

Edited by
Marcelline Block
ISBN 9781783200276
PB £15.50 / $22

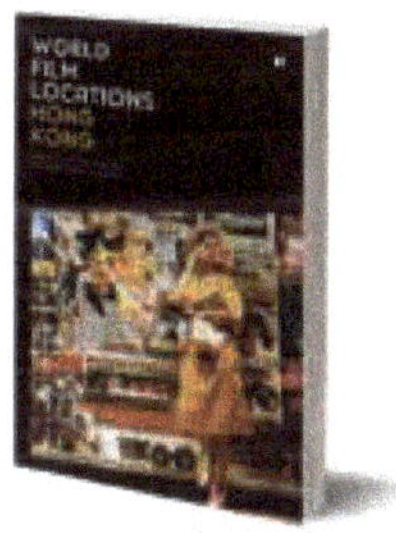

HONG KONG

Edited by
Linda C. Lai and Kimburley Choi
ISBN 9781783200214
PB £15.50 / $22

'AN ELEGANT TRIBUTE TO THE FILMS AND LOCATIONS THAT HAVE GIVEN NEW YORK ITS PRIVATE REAL ESTATE IN OUR MINDS. THE CONTRIBUTORS ARE SO IMMEDIATELY READABLE AND MOVIE-SAVVY.' – ROGER EBERT

Find us on Facebook For further information and to order books visit: **www.intellectbooks.com**

FILMOGRAPHY

All films mentioned or featured in this book

12 Storeys (1997) 44, 81, 99
15 (2003) 44, 84
15 (The Short Film [2002]) 78
25 Million Pounds (1996) 74
Ah Boys to Men (2012-13) 81
Ah Long Pte Ltd (2007) 80
Allen Ginsberg Gives Good Head (2007) 44
All the Lines Flow Out (2011) 101, 110
Apocalypse Now (1979) 32
Around the World in 80 Days (1956) 108, 109
Asthenic Syndrome, The (1989) 45
Be with Me (2005) 83, 88
Best Bet, The (2004) 80
Between Two Classes / Antara Dua Darjat (1960) 34
Bionic Boy (1977) 56
Black Magic 2 (1976) 47, 54
Blonde from Singapore, The (1931) 26
Boccaccio 70 / Le tentazioni del dottor Antonio / The Temptations of Doctor Antonio (1962) 84
Bring 'Em Back Alive (1932) 26
Broken Heart / Patah Hati (1952) 11, 18
Bugis Street (1995) 48
Casablanca (1942) 16
Charlie's Angels (1976-81) 56
Coconut Plantation / À travers une plantation de cocotiers à Singapour (1910) 11, 12
Curse of Pontianak / Sumpah Pontianak (1958) 11, 24
Cut (2004) 83, 84
Devil's Mask / Toping Saitan (1940-41) 6
Divorce Madness / Gila Talak (1963) 29
Dreams from the Thirld World (2008) 83, 94
Eating Air (1999) 65, 72, 99
European Nights / Europa di notte (1959) 32
Five Ashore in Singapore aka Cinq gars pour Singapour aka Cinque marines per Singapore (1966) 29, 42
Flooding in the Time of Drought (2009) 99
Forever Fever aka That's the Way I Like It (1998) 2, 65, 70
Fulltime Killer / Chuen Jik Sat Sau (2001) 65, 76
Gardens by the Bay (2013) 5
G.I. Executioner / Wit's End (1975) 52
Goldsnake: Anonima Killers (1966) 28
Gone Shopping (2007) 83, 92
Hawaii 5-0 (1978) 29
Here (2009) 98, 101, 102
History of Postwar Japan as Told by a Bar Hostess (1970) 50
Homerun (2003) 80
I Not Stupid (2002) 80
In Search of the Unreturned Soldiers in Malaysia / Mikikanhei o otte (1971) 47, 50
In the Realm of the Senses (1976) 45
Intimate Confessions of a Chinese Courtesan (1972) 45
Invisible City (2007) 96
Ilo Ilo (2013) 5, 80, 99, 101, 114
It's a Great, Great World (2012) 101, 108
Jiran Sekanpong (1965) 98
Krrish (2006) 83, 90
Last Blood, The (1990) 47, 60
Leila Majnun (1934) 6
Lion City (1960) 98
Lost Images: Films from the Ivan Polunin Archive (2009) 83, 96
Maid, The (2005) 114
Malaya War Record: A Record of the March Onward / Mare senki: shingeki no kiroku (1942) 11, 14
Mat 3/4 / Mat Tiga Suku (1964) 29
Mee Pok Man (1995) 65, 66, 123
Mephisto (1981) 45
Mister John (1979) 27
Mondo Cane (1962) 29, 32
Money No Enough (1998) 80, 81
Moon over Malaya (1957) 11, 22
Mouldy Bachelors, The / Bujang Lapok (1957) 11, 20
My Lucky Star / Feichang Xingyun (2013) 101, 112
My Mother-in-Law / Ibu Mertuaku (1962) 29, 34
Nanyang Trilogy (1957) 22
New Immigrant, The (1927) 6
Night Cargo (1936) 26
Nitwit Movie Stars, The (1961) 7
No Day Off (2006) 114
On a Clear Day (1970) 112
On to Delhi / On tsu Delhi (1943) 14
Pain (1994) 44
Passion Flower (1986) 27
Pearl / Mutjara (1940-41) 6
Pirates of the Carribean: At World's End (2007) 27
Poisonous Blowpipe / Sumpitan Racun (1961) 29, 30
Poligamy / Bermadu (1940-41) 6
Pontianak (1957) 24
Pontianak's Revenge / Dendam Pontianak (1957) 24
Pretty Polly (1967) 28, 47, 48
Profound Desire of thr Gods, The (1968) 50
Rich and Strange (1931) 26
Red Dragonflies (2010) 98, 101, 104
Road Less Travelled, The (1997) 65, 68
Rogue Trader (1999) 27, 65, 74
Sandcastle (2010) 101, 106
Sandokan, Pirate of Malaysia (1964) 26
Saint Jack (1979) 2, 26, 29, 47, 48, 58
Satay (1958) 98
Shark Woman / Samarang (1933) 26
Singapore (1947) 11, 16, 26
Singapore (1960) 90
Singapore Gaga (2005) 83, 86
Singapore Rebel (2005) 45
Singapore's Vegas (2012) 5
So Darling, So Deadly aka Agente Joe Walker operazione Far East aka Kommissar X: In den Klauen des goldenen Drachen (1966) 26, 29
Stand up Virgin Soldiers (1977) 27
Straik / Mogok (1957) 7
Tanamera: Lion of Singapore (1989) 27
They Call Her... Cleopatra Wong (1978) 47, 56
Three Wives / Madu Tiga (1964) 9
Tiong Bahru (2012) 27
To Singapore, with Love (2014) 5
Trilogy of Life (1971-74) 45
Trishaw Puller / Penarik Beca (1955) 9, 32
Vengeance Is Mine (1969) 50
Vertigo (1958) 30
Victim of Slander / Korban Fitnah (1959) 8, 9
Virgin Soldiers, The (1969) 27, 28
Vision of Persistence, A (2001) 44
Wit's End (1975) 47, 52, 94
Young Ones, The / Muda Mudi (1965) 6, 7

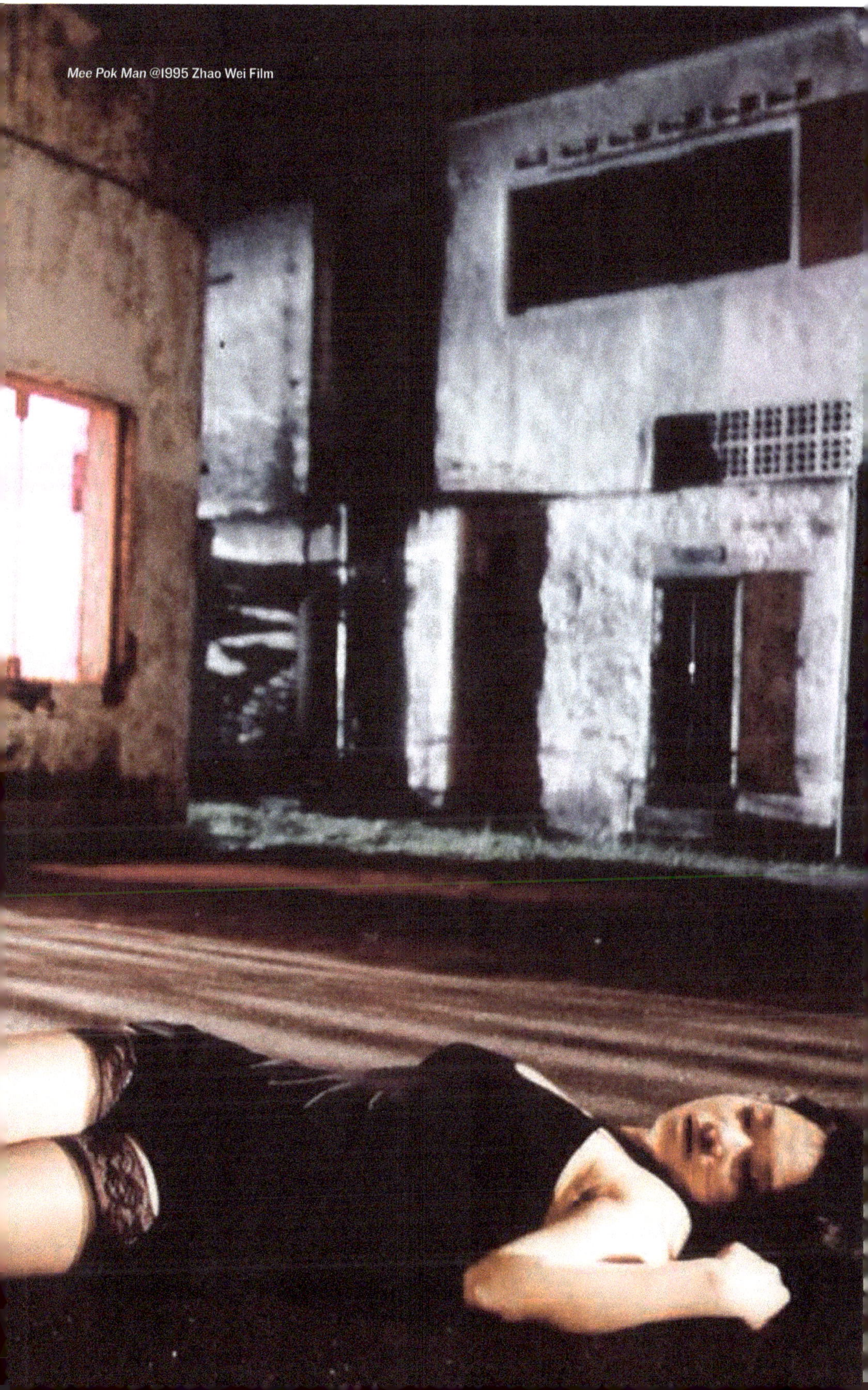

Mee Pok Man ©1995 Zhao Wei Film

WORLD
FILM
LOCATIONS
EXPLORING
THE CITY
ONSCREEN

www.intellectbooks.com